The Smart Aleck's Guide
to American History

WHATEVER

The Smart Aleck's Guide to American History

BY **ADAM SELZER**

DELACORTE PRESS

Library of Congress Cataloging-in-Publication Data
Selzer, Adam.
The smart aleck's guide to American history / Adam Selzer. – 1st ed.
p. cm.
ISBN 978-0-385-73650-3 (trade)–ISBN 978-0-385-90613-5 (lib. bdg.)–
ISBN 978-0-375-89593-7 (e-book)
1. United States–History–Miscellanea–Juvenile literature.
I. Title.
E178.3.S457 2010
973–dc22
2009003897

The text of this book is set in 10-point Baskerville Book.

Book design by Marci Senders

Printed in the United States of America

10 9 8 7 6 5 4 3 2 1

First Edition

For Grandpa Carl
(who won World War II)
and the rest of my awesome family

Thanks to the whole Smart Aleck staff (even the interns) and all the people who helped make this project work, including (but not limited to) Eli Selzer; Nadia Cornier; Jonathan Spring; Ronica Selzer; Aidan Davis (thanks for playing quietly!); Kathleen Cromie; Carol White; Sherman Dorn; Marc Federman at Joelsongs; Stephanie Elliott, Colleen Fellingham, Marci Senders, and everyone at Delacorte Press; Troy Taylor; Ken Melvoin-Berg; Hector Reyes; Willie Williams; Lindsey Harper; Michael G. Smith; Mike Falkstrom; Jennifer Laughran; Daniel Pinkwater (and everyone else at the speakeasy); Peter Stone Brown; Robert Zalas; and, of course, lonely ol' Charles Carroll. We still remember you, Chuck!

And a big thanks to Davy Crockett, Andrew Jackson, Martin Frobisher, Ulysses S. Grant, and Bjarni Herjólfsson—even though you're dead, I'm sure you guys can still kick my butt any time you like. So no hard feelings, okay? Give Preston Brooks a big slap for me. I also wish to apologize to the many people who had to be left out of this book because they weren't funny enough. Try growing some comical facial hair next time, geniuses!

CONTENTS

INTRODUCTION

Let's get the main question out of the way: why do you need to know this stuff? Teachers may hate us for saying this, but frankly, you kinda don't. Oh, sure, we could throw in some line about "those who don't remember the past are doomed to repeat it," but, in reality, you'll probably just have to repeat History 101.

Most people know next to nothing about history—and even what they *think* they know is mostly wrong. Indeed, most people don't know George Washington from a washing machine, but they seem to get along reasonably well in the world anyway.

There are a lot of things out there that you don't *really* need to know. For instance, unless you live in Vermont and plan to run for state government, we can't think of a single good reason why you'd need to know that the capital of Vermont is Montpelier.

Here's the thing, though: **just because you won't be able to use this stuff to get a job doesn't mean you shouldn't know it.** Knowing history will, quite simply, make you a smarter and more well-rounded person. You might find a section here that's so interesting you want to go learn more about it from

more reputable historians. In fact, we hope you do. Knowing the basics of history—and knowing that some of the bits of trivia people like to bring up all the time aren't really true at all—will give you one major advantage over people who don't: you'll be better than they are.

We also think that you should understand that nobody really *knows* all that much about history. When your teacher tells you about some battle or another, it may be that the only accurate thing in the story is the date.[1] What we know of history is often just what the winners of the battle described, and they weren't always telling the truth. Many famous stories were written down hundreds of years after they happened by people who based what they wrote on rumors and hearsay. There's a lot left to find out and a lot left to argue about; for instance, people still get into fights over what the Civil War was all about, and

---

[1] Actually, we're focused on the big picture, so we're leaving out as many specific dates as possible. You'll never remember them anyway, and on the off chance that you ever *do* need to know the exact date of the Battle of Tinkledribble, we figure you can look it up without too much trouble. You're welcome.

no one really has a clue what Christopher Columbus looked like (though we're betting he was one ugly fellow).

Yes, your teacher is probably wrong about lots of stuff. Being a smart aleck in history class is easy if you know how.

We're the Smart Aleck staff. We're here to help.

MEET YOUR SMART ALECK STAFF!

They say that "history is written by the winners," which makes the Smart Aleck staff winners (even if we are the back-row hooligans of the textbook industry)! Our motto: a smart aleck who coasts may get a passing grade, but one who reads ahead may take over the entire class.

ADAM SELZER is the author of a handful of subversive young adult and

middle-grade novels that get banned occasionally. He snuck into being a historian through the back door, initially by becoming a professional ghost in-

vestigator and tour guide in Chicago and then by organizing the Smart Aleck staff to sort out this American history business once and for all. He is the boss around the Smart Aleck headquarters and enjoys making other people bring him coffee.

ELI SELZER is a big Billy Joel fan. Dr. Joel once asked, in song form,

"Should I try to be a straight-A student?" Using an obscure algebraic formula, he determined that "if you are, then you think too much." Eli was a straight-A student, but he sure didn't think too much. He lives in Los Angeles now, and got a job on the Smart Aleck staff by being the boss's brother.

PROFESSOR WILLIAM ROSEMONT, ESQ., our resident conspiracy theorist (historians have to deal with a *lot* of these), spent most of his time at headquarters shouting that everything we say about the South in the Civil War chapter is a "dirty Yankee lie" (so, yes, we've already heard it). He has PhDs in history, Aztec anthropology, engineering, and Lithuanian literature, but we really just keep him around to fix the pinball machines.

BRIAN EDDLEBECK is the guy who wrote all the jokes in this book about things that smell bad. Blame him. All references to nudity that didn't get cut by the good folks in the standards and practices department are his, too.

KENSINGTON ANN CHELSEA is an ex-con (and is still wanted in six states) but showed up (uninvited) at the office one day to teach us a song about how to build an Anderson shelter (see Chapter 9). Hiring her for the staff got us a wicked tax break, and the shelter came in surprisingly handy.

NOT PICTURED:
Fifty interns not important enough to name!

CHAPTER

THE EARLIEST AMERICAN SETTLERS:
BRAVE, BOLD, AND RICH IN MINERALS

> "For the execution of the voyage to the Indies, I did not make use of intelligence, mathematics or maps."—Christopher Columbus, who wasn't kidding about the intelligence part

INTRODUCTION

Imagine that it's about 1493. You were born a manure shoveler in some rural European village, and odds are pretty good that you'll die with manure on your boots, if you can afford boots in the first place. If you can't afford boots, you'll die with crap between your toes. Either way, your life will be hard, smelly, and unpleasant. There's no chance you'll ever work your way up to being head manure engineer or anything; that just isn't the way it works. If you were born poor, you're almost certainly going to die poor.

Then, one day, you get word that a whole new world has been discovered, and that it's full of wonders and treasures that are yours for the taking if only you'll go on a voyage to explore it and cram your religion down the locals' throats. If you survive the voyage, you can trade in your manure shovel for a life of endless riches and adventure.

How could anyone have turned that chance down?

The earliest European explorers and settlers had absolutely no idea what they might find in the Americas. This is difficult to imagine today, when we have a general idea of what exists in the world—we can even be pretty sure that we won't run into a two-headed monster or a city made out of gold even if we ever go to Mars. But in those days, they had no idea what might be hiding behind the trees on the new continent on the other side of the ocean. At no point since have people been confronted with anything quite so big and mysterious as the New World must have looked to those sailors.

Of course, very few of the early explorers and settlers actually ended up getting as rich as they planned to. Most of them probably got plenty of

Are these guys saying "There goes the neighborhood" or "Boy, I hope those guys are bringing us beads and trinkets"? Incidentally, the story that Manhattan Island was purchased from Native Americans for twenty bucks' worth of beads and trinkets is one of those "fascinating facts" that doesn't happen to be true.

adventure, but settling a new world was dangerous work, so much so that explorer and settler are probably right at the top of the list of Jobs in Which You're Most Likely to End Up Being Eaten. But working in manure piles wasn't exactly safe, either, and there was no chance that they'd ever name a new country after you because of something you did at *that* job.

And so, all across Europe, adventurous people threw down their shovels and sailed across the sea.

WHO WAS HERE FIRST?

So who discovered America? Any idiot will tell you it was Christopher

> "Man must have held his breath . . . face to face for the last time in history with something commensurate to his capacity for wonder."—F. Scott Fitzgerald, a direct descendant of Francis Scott Key, author of "The Star-Spangled Banner," on what the discovery of the New World must have been like

Columbus, but that's just proof that he or she is an idiot, or uninformed, anyway. Most modern historians are of the opinion that Columbus couldn't

Costumed guys "make history come alive" for tourists by reenacting a Viking battle. Witnessing a real one would scar most people for life. For the record, the guys with cameras are not authentic.

No one knows what Christopher Columbus looked like. The guy in this famous painting, known as the Piombo portrait, is probably just some random jerk from Bologna, not Columbus himself. In fact, many famous pictures of historical figures from precamera days are unlikely to be even remotely accurate. ✗

navigate his way out of an outhouse if you gave him a compass and a map. He *did* bump into a new continent that none of his contemporaries knew was there, though, and kick-started a whole new era of exploration, which probably ought to count for something, but he wasn't the first guy, or even the first European, to get there. He also never set foot on what is now the United States—or, for that matter, on the North American continent. On his famous voyage in 1492, with his fleet the *Niña,* the *Pinta,* and the *Santa Maria,* the first land they came to was what we now call San Salvador, an island near the Central American isthmus.[2] The

sailors, many of whom had been stuck on a boat with Columbus for months, rejoiced—Columbus was not the most popular guy in town. Some say that the Spanish queen only funded his voyage because it would get him out of her hair for a while.

Columbus hung around the Canary Islands for about a month, explored Cuba for a bit, and eventually headed home in 1493. He made two return voyages to explore more of Central America and the nearby islands, but he had no idea what sort of discovery he'd made—he insisted to the last day he was alive that he had been in Asia, which is what he'd been looking for in the first

---

2 An isthmus is a small piece of land connecting two big ones. The Central American one is formed of the countries Belize, Honduras, Guatemala, El Salvador, Costa Rica, Nicaragua, and Panama. An easy way to remember this is B.H.G.E.S.C.R.N.P.—Big Honkin' Gorillas Eat Sexy Canadian Realtors, Not Pickles.

place. He also went to great lengths to make sure his crew told people he'd been in Asia—he threatened to cut out their tongues if they said otherwise. The crew, who enjoyed having their tongues for both talking and tasting things, kept their mouths shut.

The first European thought to have sighted mainland North America was a Norwegian Viking by the name of (get this) Bjarni Herjólfsson. He first spotted land in 986, 506 years before Columbus and his band of hooligans arrived, but he never stopped—he was lost at sea at the time, trying to find Iceland.

Later, another bunch of hoodlums would follow Bjarni's route. They were led by Leif Eriksson, a Viking who bought a boat from Bjarni. Eriksson and his men became the first Europeans known to have set foot in North America around the year 1000; while no one has proven that they ever made it as far as the modern-day United States, there's some evidence suggesting that Vikings were in Minnesota in 1030. They would have felt right at

"HOW'D THEY GET HERE?"

For years, we called the people who were already here when the European explorers arrived Indians, since Columbus thought he was in India. Now, they're usually called Native Americans (or First Nations, if you're in Canada). But that's probably not much more accurate than calling them Indians, since *their* ancestors probably migrated to North America, too. So, how did they get here in the first place? Some of the theories include:

THE BERING STRAIT LAND BRIDGE: The most popular theory has long been that a small group of people walked over from Siberia between nine and twenty thousand years ago, back when there was a land bridge connecting the two continents.

ABORIGINAL THEORY: Some say that Australian aborigines could have sailed here more than twenty thousand years ago.

NORTH ATLANTIC THEORY: Ancient Europeans may have traveled over by boat, following ice routes from Greenland, to the East Coast.

THE TOURIST THEORY: This theory holds that there were actually ancient tourists who got lost trying to find the Grand Canyon gift shop. Scientists reject this theory and call us mean things for suggesting it.

John Cabot (real name Giovanni Caboto), explorer and snappy dresser, was an early explorer of North America who ended up being written out of history for the most part just because he was working for the British. Here, he points at something gross on the ground and says, "Okay, guys, who did that?" ✷

✷ ✷

MYTHS OF HISTORY

Stories that Columbus had trouble getting funding because of a belief that the Earth was flat were supposedly made up by Washington Irving, who is best known today for writing "The Legend of Sleepy Hollow." That the Earth was a sphere had been well known since the days of the ancient Greeks, though you could still sometimes get in trouble for saying it out loud in front of big shots from the local church. ✷

home in the cold there, and everyone knows that Vikings loved lutefisk.[3]

Of course, there's no way to tell if Leif and Bjarni were *really* the first Europeans to arrive; even the Vikings themselves didn't think they were. Early Viking explorers said they were attacked by groups of white people as

---

[3] Lutefisk is a gelatinous fish dish. See *The Smart Aleck's Guide to Weird Things Minnesotans Sometimes Eat.*

STUPID HATS OF HISTORY:
THE CONQUISTADOR HELMET

Francisco Pizarro, who conquered the Inca empire, shows off his conquistador helmet. Like most conquistadores, he stuck a feather in his helmet—and called it macaroni! [4]

✻ ✻ ✻ ✻ ✻ ✻ ✻ ✻ ✻ ✻

soon as they landed, and the natives told them there were other pale people nearby who worshipped a wooden cross that they carried around—which was a pretty darned European thing to do in those days. That the natives were able to communicate with the Vikings at all is a pretty good indication that fishermen from Europe had been there be-

fore; in fact, there are also some records that were discovered a few years back that pretty much prove it. However, we'll never know who these fishermen who discovered the New World were. Having found a good fishing spot, they apparently kept it a secret.

Some say that all this evidence that white people who worshipped crosses showed up before Columbus supports the theory that St. Brendan, an Irish explorer, had been to North America as early as the sixth century. According to the stories, he and sixty pilgrims sailed across the Atlantic in search of the Garden of Eden. They ended up on a "blessed isle" that may or may not have been North America. But there's no solid proof that Brendan actually existed, let alone sailed across the ocean. The stories about him were written down centuries after his death.

So how did we come to get a day off on Columbus Day but not on Bjarni Day? In the 1700s, few people in America had ever heard of Columbus, and wouldn't have cared about him if they had. In those days, credit for "discovering" America was usually given to John Cabot, an Italian guy who explored Canada (while working for the British) in 1497 and 1498. Nobody mentioned Columbus until America started to become a nation of its own. When the United States started up, people

---

[4] These are the jokes, folks. Try the buffet.

✻ 10 ✻

needed to have some new national heroes to admire, and they wanted some that weren't associated with the British. Someone suggested Columbus, and people started naming everything in sight after him. He went from a historical footnote[5] to a national hero very quickly, and stayed a national hero for a good couple of hundred years before people went back to thinking he was a jerk.

PONCE DE LEÓN: HOW GULLIBLE WAS HE?

Ponce de León founded the first colony in Puerto Rico in 1508. He and his sailors brought diseases that killed the natives in great numbers, but he ended up pretty rich himself. In 1513, he started to explore the area north of Cuba—now Florida—making him the first European who we absolutely *know* set foot on the land that would become the United States. But others had probably been there before; he's said to have run into at least one Native American who spoke Spanish.

According to legend, de León went to Florida to search for the fountain of youth, a pool of magical waters that would keep people young forever. In reality, he was probably not *that* gullible.

The first known story of his looking

Juan Ponce de León, keepin' his fingers crossed that he won't get eaten by cannibals.

for such a thing came in a history book written in 1535—years after de León died—which stated that de León went to Florida looking for the waters of Bimini, which, he had been told, would cure his impotence. By 1615, the story had turned into de León looking for a pool that would grant eternal youth. Neither of these bodies of water actually existed, though both would explain why so many old people go to Florida nowadays.

EL DORADO: FOR THE EVEN MORE GULLIBLE

You have to remember that no one had any idea what this new world might contain; at a time when many people never got more than a few miles from their homes, tales of things that

---

5 Like this one!

sound downright ridiculous to us nowadays seemed perfectly plausible. Even if de León wasn't looking for the fountain of youth, it was probably only because he hadn't heard about it.

One legend that got around quite a bit was that somewhere in the New World was a city containing fabulous riches—or even a whole city—or *seven* cities—made entirely out of gold. The most famous of these legends today is the legend of El Dorado, the city of gold.

The original story of El Dorado, the one that sent explorers packing, was not of a *city* of gold, it was a story of a golden *king*. According to legend, every so often the king of a South American tribe called the Muisca would cover himself in gold dust and jump into a lake, carrying with him a whole bunch of jewels and gold nuggets as offerings to the gods. This may in fact have been true—conquistadores, Spanish explorers, heard about this firsthand from some of the Muisca. But they didn't have any gold cities, or even very much gold. Still, the legend persisted, and several expeditions were launched to find the place. They even tried to drain Lake Guatavita, which is in Colombia, a couple of times to see if there were any jewels in it (and supposedly found some, though they never quite drained the lake completely).

Somewhere along the line, the leg-

Amerigo Vespucci worked as a navigator on several voyages to the New World. A couple of letters recounting his voyage greatly exaggerated his role. Some historians say he was talking a big game, and others say that he didn't really even write the letters at all. But they were popular reading, and in 1507, people started naming the American continents after him (unless you're one of the people who believe they were naming it after Richard Amerike, a guy who funded some of the pre-Columbus fishermen's expeditions). That's life for you—daring explorers who get eaten by cannibals are lucky to get a toll road from Scranton to Schenectady named after them, but some navigator gets two whole continents!

end of the golden king morphed into legends of a golden city. Stories of cities of gold were nothing new by 1492; rumors that there was a golden city someplace in the world had gone around since the Middle Ages, when even what was going on in the next country over was a big mystery to most people. But since hundreds of years of

SOME EARLY SPANISH COLONIAL FAILURES

SAN MIGUEL DE GUADALUPE (1526): This settlement fell apart so quickly and completely that we don't even know if it was in present-day Georgia or South Carolina. Served 'em right, in a way: these settlers were the first to use African slave labor in America.

THE NARVÁEZ EXPEDITION (1527): A crew of six hundred set out to install Panfilo de Narváez as governor of the Gulf Coast. All but five of them died.

PENSACOLA (1559): The original settlement was destroyed by a hurricane after about a month. The survivors tried to build it again but gave up in 1561. Eventually, it was rebuilt, and today it is the Red Snapper Capital of the World. Inspiring, ain't it? ✗

explorers and armies tramping through Europe and the Middle East had failed to turn up any golden cities, news that there was a whole new continent out there to explore was all some treasure hunters needed to hear. Guys like Francisco Coronado and García López de Cárdenas mounted enormous, expensive expeditions to find the golden cities they had heard about all their lives. They both came up empty-handed, but in the process, López managed to discover the Grand Canyon. Later, of course, that canyon would be-

come a gold mine in terms of tourist dollars. If only he had thought to open a gift shop.

THE FIRST SETTLEMENTS

After Columbus's success at *not* starting any colonies, there were several failed attempts to settle the New World in the 1500s, mostly by the Spanish, in Florida and California. But historians generally agree that the Spanish really sucked at forming settlements in those days. They were pretty good at wiping out *other* civilizations, but not so great at starting new ones of their own.

Their first *successful* settlement was Saint Augustine, Florida, in 1565. Of course, the term "successful" is relative; Saint Augustine had a bit of bad luck early on. It was attacked and burned by the English, then again by pirates, who once showed up and killed just about everyone who lived there. But the settlement survived and remained under Spanish control for nearly two hundred years.

It wasn't until well after the founding of Saint Augustine that the British decided to get in on the act of colonizing the New World. In 1578 and 1583, Sir Humphrey Gilbert made unsuccessful attempts to set up a colony in America. After he died, Sir Walter Raleigh took over the job. He sent ships full of settlers over to North America,

"What dost thou make of this, Wayne?" "I haven't the foggiest notion, Vern." "It verily beateth the heck out of me, Jim." ✻

✻ ✻ ✻ ✻ ✻ ✻ ✻ ✻ ✻ ✻ ✻

commanding them to establish a colony and name the land Virginia, in honor of Queen Elizabeth, who was known as the Virgin Queen (though a lot of people think she and Walter were *awfully* close, if you get our drift).

✻ ✻ ✻ ✻ ✻ ✻ ✻ ✻ ✻ ✻ ✻

Sir Walter Raleigh models the latest bib. He wore this thing by the docks. Are *you* man enough to try that? No. No, you are not. ✻

We hate to break it to you, but your life will not be as interesting as Sir Walter Raleigh's. He hung out with kings and queens, explored new worlds, searched for El Dorado, and was in charge of the first English colony in the New World. Plus, he popularized tobacco among the English, and is credited with planting the first potato in Ireland. Tobacco turned out to be bad news, and the potato thing probably isn't true, but still—it's more than anybody is ever going to credit *you* with if you don't get your act together.

Raleigh personally supported the first colony in Roanoke, having told the potential settlers that they'd strike it rich by finding gold—possibly even El Dorado—in America. You might say that he started the tradition of telling European emigrants that the streets in America were paved with gold.

The people Raleigh talked into becoming settlers picked an island near present-day Virginia for their colony, and once they arrived, they busied themselves with attacking and burning native villages. Funnily enough, the natives were not very keen on this and started attacking back. Since the natives were fighting with them, not helping them find food (with which they needed all the help they could get), the settlers didn't end up having much to eat. When a ship came to check on

THE FIRST ENGLISH KID

A few weeks into the second colonization of Roanoke, a settler gave birth to a girl with the really cool name of Virginia Dare. Virginia was the first white Anglo-Saxon Protestant to be born in America. ✷

these colonists in 1586, everyone was hungry and wanted to go home, and all but fifteen returned to England. This is why, to this day, the Roanoke, Virginia, high school football team is called the Quitters.[6]

Undaunted, and still intent on impressing the queen and hooking a nation on tobacco, Raleigh sent another group across the Atlantic in 1587 to make another attempt at a colony. The island he sent them to was not so much an island as it was a swamp (today, realtors would call it a rustic fixer-upper in a historical neighborhood—steps to beach, free heat,[7] no pets), and the natives who lived nearby were not very

friendly. To survive, the colonists would be depending entirely on supplies sent from England now and then.

A supply ship was supposed to come to bring them some gear in 1588, but it didn't. That was the year that the Royal Navy launched an attack on the Spanish Armada, and with a war going on, everyone sort of forgot that there was a colony to take care of. No supply ship actually came until 1590, and by then, the colonists had vanished. All they left behind was the word "Croatoan" carved into one post, and "Cro" carved into another. Most people assumed that this meant that they had gone to Croatoan Island, but a massive storm kept anyone on that supply ship from being able to search for them.

No one ever found out for sure what had happened to these colonists. Some say they starved to death, others say they were killed by the natives, and still others say they moved north and settled among some peaceful natives (perhaps

---

[6] It isn't really. As we understand it, the main mascots of the Roanoke-area teams are the Patriots and the Colonels. See *The Smart Aleck's Guide to Coastal Virginian High School Mascots and Other Wastes of Papier-Mâché.*

[7] Note: In apartment listings, "free heat" usually means "there's no central heat, just a radiator."

While we're on the subject, if you're in Chicago, "garden level" means "basement." In New York, if the listing says "2-bedroom in Park Slope, $1200/month," the apartment will not be anywhere near Park Slope—there's nothing *that* cheap there. And if you're in Los Angeles, "Sherman Oaks-adjacent" probably means the apartment is in Mexico. These are valuable lessons, kids. You're welcome.

only to be slaughtered later by less peaceful ones). This is one of those mysteries that will probably never be solved. There are a lot of those in history.

Years after the colonies failed, in 1594, Raleigh himself explored South America in search of a golden city that was supposed to be at the head of the Caroní River. When he made it back to England, he claimed to have found it, but he was lying through his teeth. In reality, he hadn't even made it up the river.

Nearly twenty years later, he went back looking for El Dorado. During this expedition, he and his men sacked a Spanish outpost, and the Spanish ambassador demanded that King James have Raleigh executed. King James had never liked Raleigh anyway, and had him beheaded in public in 1618.

JAMESTOWN

The first English colony that *lasted* any length of time was Jamestown, which was founded in 1607 by the Virginia Company, a private company (as opposed to one sponsored by the government). They raised money from investors to set up the colony not in the name of the Crown, but in the name of the three "G's"—glory, God, and gold. Actually, it was mostly just gold, but throwing glory and God into the mix probably looked good on paper.

John Smith, the guy from the Disney movie about Pocahontas (which has very little basis in fact), was arrested for mutiny on the voyage over and spent about half of the trip incarcerated; the crew planned to hang him as soon as they hit land. However, upon getting off the ship, they opened sealed orders from the Virginia Company that

John Smith claimed that Pocahontas (above) risked her life to save his when he was about to be bludgeoned to death. Most people doubt his story these days; anything you hear about what really happened is in fact just a guess. Pocahontas and Smith were never romantically linked, but she *did* become friends with the colonists—and saved their butts by bringing them provisions every few days. After Smith went back to England, Pocahontas married an Englishman named John Rolfe, changed her name to Rebecca, and went to London, where she spent the last year of her life living as a celebrity. This engraving of her was made in 1616, which means it might actually be a realistic portrait. ✶

named Smith a member of the governing council, thereby saving his butt.

The colonists picked the site, on a peninsula in the James River, mainly because they thought it would be easy to defend from any invading armies, but also because there were no natives living there to kill them off. Unfortunately, the fact that they were wide open to both malaria and pirates went right over their heads.

Pretty soon, they realized *why* the natives weren't living there: the land was pretty much useless. The water was undrinkable, the land was unfarmable, mosquitoes were everywhere, and the nightlife was horribly dull. Still, rather than finding a better place, they stayed, and those who didn't die of dysentery or attack by the natives (who didn't live there but showed up within two weeks to attack them anyway) managed to build a fort.

The leader of the group, a guy called

WHAT HAPPENED TO THOSE CROATOAN GUYS?

So what happened to the lost colony? Historians have come up with a ton of theories over the years, such as:

1. THEY WENT TO CROATOAN ISLAND. Leaving this word carved into the post may have meant that they had moved to Croatoan Island nearby.

2. THEY DIED. Some believe that they starved to death due to a lack of supplies or were killed by natives, presumably of the Croatoan tribe (thus explaining the message). Given the way this chapter has gone so far, this seems reasonable enough, but if they were being attacked, they probably wouldn't have had much time to stand around carving things on posts.

3. THEY BECAME HOPI. Some say they were adopted into the Hopi tribe or some other nearby tribe. There were many vague reports of at least a handful of colonists surviving someplace in mainland Virginia over the years.

4. THEY BECAME CHESEPIAN. When Captain John Smith founded Jamestown in 1607, Chief Powhatan told him that the Roanoke settlers were living about fifty miles away with the Chesepian tribe. He also told Smith that he'd just finished killing them. He showed Smith some English tools as proof, but no bodies were found. However, this is probably when Smith decided to be reeeeeally nice to Powhatan.

Vasco Núñez de Balboa.

Christopher Newport, loaded up his boat with tons and tons of what he *thought* was gold, and sailed back to England ready to spend it, leaving about a hundred colonists behind. When he got to London, he found out that it wasn't gold at all—it was actually iron pyrite, aka fool's gold, which was

FATES OF THE EXPLORERS

Plenty of the early explorers of America came to bad ends. In fact, most of them ended up getting killed and/or eaten—not necessarily in that order.

VASCO NÚÑEZ DE BALBOA: Discovered the Pacific Ocean and was then betrayed by a rival, who had him beheaded.

JOHN CABOT: Vanished at sea.

MARTIN FROBISHER: Explored the colder parts of Canada (fun!) and ended up loading his boat with fifteen hundred tons of what he thought was gold. Like Christopher Newport, he learned the hard way that it was iron pyrite. Unlike Newport, he didn't learn his lesson. He went back to Canada and loaded up thirteen hundred tons of what turned out to be—once again—iron pyrite. He then became a pirate and was shot to death in 1594.

HUMPHREY GILBERT: Tried to found a colony in Newfoundland, failed, and died in a storm on the way home.

HENRY HUDSON: Annoyed his crew and was sent away in a little boat with a tiny crew, never to be seen again.

FRANCISCO PIZARRO: Conquered the Incas, then was stabbed to death by rivals.

JOHN RATCLIFFE: Became the second president of the Virginia colony, then was tortured to death by the women of Powhatan's tribe.

JUAN DÍAZ DE SOLÍS: Explored the southern part of the new continent. Also eaten by cannibals.

HERNANDO DE SOTO: Explored the Southeast for four years, then died of a fever.

GIOVANNI DA VERRAZZANO: Discovered that the new land was a "new world," not just a pretty big island. He was eaten by cannibals.

A Pilgrim prays for a safe, successful voyage. Unfortunately, this ship, the Speedwell, *sprang a leak, forcing them to turn around. We're guessing they had someone* else *do the praying before the next attempt.*

pretty much worthless. The quest for glory, God and gold wasn't exactly off to a rip-roaring start.

The investors from the Virginia Company were a bit miffed at ol' Christopher. They wrote a letter to the colonists demanding that they send over some money, a lump of gold, news that they'd found "the South Sea," and at least one colonist from the second Roanoke colony that had disappeared. John Smith sent a letter back telling the investors that if they wanted a successful colony, they should have sent better colonists. As it was, he said, the company shouldn't get their hopes up, as the colonists were too busy trying not to get themselves killed to be all that worried about finding gold for a bunch of jerks back in England.

In 1609, Smith went back to England and wrote a book about himself in which he referred to himself in the third person. He spent a good chunk of the book bragging about how great he was, and most people now assume that

Martin Frobisher. ✴

you shouldn't believe a word of it. Still, the fact is, Jamestown did reasonably well under his leadership, and tanked after he left. The years 1609 and 1610 are referred to as the Starving Time, when 80 percent of the colonists starved to death. Your teacher may not mention this, if he or she is one of those dainty types, but there's some evidence that they ended up eating each other when things got really lean. Those who were alive and uneaten were eventually shipped back to England.

But new settlers continued to be sent over, and by 1619, the colony was doing well enough to hold the first meeting of an elected government in the United States. However, the Crown didn't exactly think that a 20 percent survival rate could be considered "thriving," and in 1624, they revoked the Virginia Company's charter and officially made Virginia a royal colony instead of a private one. The Colonial period had officially begun.

Many school history books brush over all this stuff, because even most of the *less* dainty teachers don't much like to talk about people being slaughtered or eaten. Instead, they focus on the Pilgrims, who were just about the most boring human beings ever to walk the earth, but who at least didn't get eaten.

THE PILGRIMS

The Pilgrims were a group of religious separatists who got kicked out of England. They moved to Holland,

Myles Standish was hired to be the Plymouth colony's military commander, in case some army wanted to take it over. He became an unlikely romantic hero after Henry Wadsworth Longfellow wrote a poem about him, but by the time the poem was published, Standish had been dead entirely too long to reap the benefits. ✴

MAYFLOWER DESCENDANTS
Throughout your life, you will probably meet many, many people who claim that their ancestors came over on the *Mayflower*. Many of them think this makes them "true" Americans—more American than *you'll* ever be, anyway. Ignore them. It's cool to know your family history and all, but you can't really take credit for the good things your ancestors did unless you're also willing to take the blame for the bad things they did. ✴

Plymouth Rock as it appeared back in the 1920s. It's even *less* impressive-looking nowadays. ✻

where they could worship as they chose, but didn't like it there, and when one of them wrote mean things about the king of England, the king sent people to Holland to arrest him. So they decided to move to the New World, where there wouldn't be any kings or Dutch people to bother them.

The sailors on the *Mayflower* called the Pilgrims "glib-glabbety puke stockings." Yes, the word "puke," along with most of the swearwords people use today, had been in common use for centuries by then.

Of course, the New World had long since been colonized by then, so why do some people think of them as the first Americans? After all, coming over for religious reasons isn't really that much more "American" than coming over to get rich (less so, if we're being totally honest). But while most earlier settlers came to get rich and ended up getting eaten, the Pilgrims came looking for freedom—and against all odds, they found it.

The Pilgrims initially set forth for America on two ships, the famous *Mayflower* and another, smaller ship called the *Speedwell*. But the *Speedwell* soon sprang a leak, forcing them to turn back. It was later said that the leak had

The first Thanksgiving: a veritable treasure trove of stupid hat jokes.

been sprung deliberately by the crew, who resorted to sabotage to avoid spending several weeks holed up on a ship with the boring ol' Pilgrims. Eventually, they all piled onto the *Mayflower* and made the journey on a single ship.

The *Mayflower* had been built for cargo—it normally held wine, not people. And the Pilgrims were the sort who got seasick easily.

Over the course of the trip, many fell ill with tuberculosis or scurvy (everyone's favorite sea disease). They arrived in November after a two-month voyage and spent the next few months living aboard the ship, since they were in no way capable of building a shelter good enough to survive the winter on land. By the end of the winter, when they were ready to go ashore, just over half of the Pilgrims and about half of the crew had already died.

THE PLYMOUTH COLONY

There are some landmarks that just aren't worth the trip, and one of these is Plymouth Rock, in Plymouth, Massachusetts. It sounds like a cool thing to see: the rock where the *Mayflower* came to rest, beginning one of the first successful settlements of the new world. But in reality, it's just a rock. And it's not very big or impressive. And the Pilgrims probably never actually landed on it; the story that they did came from a ninety-three-year-old guy in the 1740s, over a century after the landing. And he'd just heard it from his father, who had heard a rumor about it years before. In those days, the first rule of history was apparently to believe whatever old people said. Actually, it still pretty much is.

The American soil was far, far better for farming than anything the Pilgrims had ever seen before, and there were more animals to kill and eat than they'd probably ever dreamed of. But they were afraid to eat anything they didn't recognize, and lived mostly on the salted meat and biscuits they'd brought with them. By the end of their first winter, nearly half of them were dead, and most of the rest weren't doing so well, either. At one point, only six or seven people were well enough to do any farming or hunting.

It's almost certain that they all would

PURITAN NAMES

There was a brief craze among Puritans for giving their kids really long names, like The Lord Is My Shepherd I Shall Not Want Jones, or Fight the Good Fight of Faith Johnson. Just another reason to be glad you weren't born until much later. ✸

have died if they hadn't met Tisquantum, a Native American who spoke English. He had been kidnapped and brought to England in 1605, then returned to America with John Smith in 1614 or 1615. He was promptly kidnapped by a guy who attempted to sell him into slavery, and he ended up in England again in 1618. He arrived back in America the next year, only to find that his entire village had been wiped out by a plague.

Even more miraculous than the fact that he spoke English was the fact that

Tisquantum is more commonly known as Squanto. No one is sure *why* he's usually called that today, but some believe that history books started calling him that in the 1870s because it was easier for kids to remember. Kids in the 1870s must have been pret-ty dumb.

STUPID HATS OF HISTORY: THE CAPOTAIN

The capotain (now called the Pilgrim hat) was like a top hat that just wasn't trying very hard. ✸

he didn't hold a grudge. Having been kidnapped and sold into slavery more than once, and having had his whole village wiped out by a disease that had surely been brought by Europeans, he could hardly have been blamed if he'd kept his distance from the Pilgrims. But instead, he taught them how to farm and quite simply saved their butts. He also negotiated a peace between the Pilgrims and the local tribes that lasted for fifty years.

THE FIRST THANKSGIVING

When people talk about the first Thanksgiving, they usually say that the Pilgrims had a big feast to thank Tisquantum and the nearby tribes for helping them not to starve to death. But the first Thanksgiving was really just a traditional harvest feast. Both the English and the Native Americans traditionally held big celebrations around harvest time.

The Pilgrims invited about ninety of the natives for a feast that went on for about three days. We're not entirely sure what they ate, but it probably included geese, swans, deer, and ducks. Turkey and pumpkin were probably present. Green bean casserole and sweet potatoes with marshmallow topping were probably not.

There were also some games played—obviously, they couldn't just eat for three days straight without a break. One of the Pilgrims who was present wrote, "Among other recreations, we exercised our arms." Did these guys know how to party or what?

THE PURITANS: BORING GUYS WITH EXCITING SEX LIVES

In England around this time, the Puritans, a group who wanted to radically reshape the government and the Church of England (rather than just setting up their *own* ultrareligious colony, like the "separatist" Pilgrims), came to power in England and began to send colonists over to the New World to reshape that, too.

Today, when we call people Puritans, we usually mean that they're boring prudes who don't drink, smoke, have

"Exercised our arms" doesn't mean they had arm-wrestling matches, it means they had target practice with their muskets. Shooting stuff is still a Thanksgiving tradition in Texas.

sex, or read books with wizards in them. In fact, though, the Puritans were very much into sex—they practiced a thing called bundling in which single male visitors to the house would be invited to spend the night in the same bed as any single girl of marrying age to see how they got on. In theory, the two were just supposed to cuddle, not have sex, and there was supposed to be a board between them. In practice, this wasn't always the case. The Puritans actually don't seem to have thought of premarital sex as a particularly big deal (though they were certainly against *extra*marital sex), but if the bundling led to a pregnancy (as it often did), the couple were married at once, whether they actually liked each other or not.

THE SALEM WITCH TRIALS

After the Pilgrims, history books usually come to a long, long gap. Apparently, outside of Puritans impregnating other Puritans, nothing

If you were raised by Puritans, you'd probably end up acting like this, too.

INTERROGATING WITCHES

One of the most famous methods of interrogating witches in Europe was dunking, or holding them underwater to see if they'd use their magic powers to escape. Puritans never used dunking in Salem. They *did*, however, apparently try to root out witches in Salem by making "witch cake." This cake was made from rye and the pee of afflicted children and fed to a dog. The idea was that if the children were really bewitched, the dog would also act bewitched after eating the cake. Dogs were widely believed to be witches' "familiars." Once again, be glad you're not a Puritan. Or a Puritan's dog. ✶

interesting happened from about 1620 up until the 1690s. That's when Puritan colonists living in Salem, Massachusetts, decided to start accusing each other of witchcraft. Accusing people of witchcraft and then torturing them to death was nothing new—it had been going on in Europe since the Middle Ages—but this was the first major outbreak in America.

The Puritans were terrified of the largely unexplored continent where they were living, and we think we can call them superstitious without offending too many people. Since most of the unexplored continent hadn't been settled by Christians, like most of Europe had by then, they truly believed that they were living in the devil's country and that the devil would surely fight back against their invasion of his turf. They tended to think devils, demons,

and witches were lurking behind every tree in the forest. The writings of Cotton Mather, a Boston minister, assured them that this was the case.

The minister in Salem at the time was a fellow named Samuel Parris. He decided that in addition to getting his salary, he should also own the

Cotton Mather, a Puritan minister, wrote very influential books that convinced people to be on the lookout for witches. He was brought into Salem to try to help the afflicted girls, and some blame the whole ugly affair on him and his ability to whip people into an antiwitch frenzy. Don't read Harry Potter books in front of Cotton Mather. ✶

parsonage. Several locals got upset and decided to stop paying him.

Shortly after that, his nine-year-old daughter and her eleven-year-old cousin began suffering from violent fits, during which they screamed, bit people, and threw things around the room. When the adults determined that the fits weren't because of epilepsy, they jumped to the next logical conclusion: the girls had been possessed by the devil.

Exactly what was really wrong with the girls will probably never be known. Some say they might have been hallucinating as a result of eating some sort of mold; others say they were suffering from a nerve disease now known as Huntington's chorea. It's also possible that they simply made the whole thing up to get attention.

Giles Corey gets railroaded in court. ✴

But people back then believed that they had been possessed by the devil, who, they assumed, was working with Tituba, a slave in the Parris household whom the girls named as a witch. Their word was good enough for the locals to assume Tituba was guilty; after all, the girls were white, and Tituba wasn't.

When pressed to name other witches, the girls named Sarah Good, a poor woman who would curse under her breath at people if they didn't give her free food, and Sarah Osborne, an old woman who, in addition to being downright annoying, had committed the sin of marrying her indentured servant. Neither Good nor Osborne attended church, which made them easy targets as witches.

Soon, several others were accused of being witches, too. It's important to note that none of these women were actually witches or even pagans—they were mostly just people who didn't fit in. Some may have been lesbians, and some may have had Down syndrome or some misunderstood physical ailment. Others were just plain unpopular.

And once people started accusing each other of witchcraft, things got ugly quickly. The town lapsed into witch-hunt mania, and soon, as many as two hundred people had been imprisoned. By the time the mania ended, twenty of them had been executed, and five more had died in jail.

None of them were burned at the stake or thrown off a cliff, like some accused witches in Europe had been. The method of execution was hanging, except in the case of eighty-year-old Giles Corey, who was pressed: when he refused to enter a plea in court on the grounds that the whole witch hunt was ridiculous, the magistrates interrogated him by piling heavy stones on top of him—a method that, unbeknownst to them, had been illegal for twenty years. Even as the stones got heavier and heavier on top of him, he refused to enter a plea. His last words before he was finally crushed to death were said to be "more weight." Truly, this man had stones.[8]

The witch trials were apparently enough excitement to last people a long time. History books often don't mention a thing between about 1692 and the 1770s. We'll follow suit.

SOME OF THE STUFF WE MISSED

Since no historians can cram everything important into one book, we'll try to briefly touch on some of the stuff we've skipped over at the end of every chapter, so you can go look 'em up for yourself.

Some of the stuff we missed from the days of the Vikings up to 1770 or so:

The French and Indian War: A war from 1754 to 1763, mainly involving the French, who were also setting up colonies, and the Iroquois confederacy, who sided with the French, against the British. The British won, but many American colonists were rather annoyed that their sons were killed to protect British interests. This was actually the fourth war between the British and the French and Indian groups in America, the previous three being King William's War (1689 to 1697), Queen Anne's War (1702 to 1713), and King George's War (1744 to 1748). This was George II, not the guy colonists rebelled against later, for the record. That was George III.

The Royal Proclamation of 1763: A proclamation that prohibited settlers from going west of the Appalachian Mountains. It was widely unpopular with colonists and was never enforced.

Town crier: The guy often seen in colonial reenactments ringing a bell and shouting "Hear ye!" before reading the news. Really more of a European thing than an American thing; London still has one.

Quilting bees: How people amused themselves in those days.

Jonathan Edwards: A preacher who scared the crap out of people. His

William Penn: *The founder of the Pennsylvania colony and an early champion of democracy and freedom. Your teacher might tell you he's the guy on the Quaker Oats box, but the Quaker Oats company says this isn't true (though the resemblance is striking).*

sermon "Sinners in the Hands of an Angry God" is one of fairly few "literary" works from this period that is still kinda famous. Not recommended for bedtime reading.

Anne Bradstreet: A Puritan poet who was really something of a free thinker (especially as Puritans go).

END-OF-CHAPTER QUESTIONS

MULTIPLE CHOICE

1. Why don't you ever see guys named Panfilo anymore?

    a. It sounds too much like some kind of fancy bread.

    b. Naming a kid Panfilo has been globally outlawed since 1987.

    c. My grandfather is named Panfilo! How dare you insult my heritage?

    d. Who cares? I'm naming *my* kid Bjarni.

(ANSWER: LET'S GO WITH A, BUT WE CHALLENGE YOU, THE NEXT GENERATION, TO MAKE IT D.)

2. Why did so many colonists die?

    a. They were quitters who did not give 110 percent.

    b. A meteor struck the area.

    c. They couldn't get enough of the sweet, crunchity taste of their shipmates.

    d. Benjamin Franklin had not yet invented the Franklin Stove.

    e. None of the above.

(ANSWER: D, OF COURSE.)

3. What would you do if you found yourself transported back in time to Salem in the 1690s?

    a. Shake hands with Giles Corey.

    b. Use modern science to check people for Huntington's chorea.

    c. Ask for some cake.

    d. Run like a nerd out of gym class.

(ANSWER: D, IF YOU HAVE ANY SENSE, BUT YOU MIGHT WANT TO DO A FIRST, JUST FOR BRAGGING RIGHTS.)

4. Are you going to eat that pickle?
   a. Yes.
   b. No.
   c. Hang on, I'll see how hungry I am after I finish my burger.
   d. I just licked it, still want it?
   e. That's no pickle, that's my wife!

(ANSWER: A. EAT YOUR PICKLES, KIDS. AND DRINK YOUR ORANGE JUICE, OR YOU'LL GET SCURVY!)

ESSAY

1. When all those manure shovelers left to explore new lands, what happened to the manure?

2. What do *you* think happened to those Croatoan guys—and what gave you *that* idea?

3. Didn't anything *besides* the witch trials happen between about 1692 and 1770? Can your teacher name *one* major event from that era in American history? Were people so busy keeping from starving and holding quilting bees that they didn't have time to do anything noteworthy?

RESEARCH ASSIGNMENT

Find out what a quilting bee is—and what in the world is fun about it, if anything.

WORD SEARCH! TO HELP YOU LEARN...

See if you can find the words "Viking," "Bjarni," "Raleigh," "Panfilo," "Croatoan," and "Native American" in the following block of random text:

YOUDOREALIZEOFCOURSETHATWORDFINDS
DON'TACTUALLYHELPYOULEARNANYTHING
ABOUTVIKINGSORBJARNIHERJOLFFSENOR
SIRWALTERRALEIGHTHEYAREINFACTJUST
POINTLESSBUSYWORKTOKEEPKIDSQUIET
SOTHETEACHERCANHAVEFIVEMINUTESTO
GRADEYOURESSAYSABOUTWHATHAPPENED
TOTHECROATOANGUYSORWHATSPICESMIGHT
HAVEMADEPANFILOTASTIERTOCANNIBALS
BUTWEWILLTAKETHISMOMENTTOPOINTOUT
THATNOTALLNATIVEAMERICANSWERE
CANNIBALSANDTHATNONEOFTHEMHAVEBEEN
FORSEVERALCENTURIESNOWOFCOURSE

CHAPTER

THE COLONISTS ARE REVOLTING

In the 1770s, colonists rebelled against British rule. Here, General George Washington bravely rebels against the basic rules of boat safety.

> "[My troops] are an exceedingly dirty and nasty people."
> —George Washington

INTRODUCTION

In the 1770s, British subjects living in the American colonies decided that they didn't care much for being ruled by a guy who was born into his job, got to keep it for life, and was widely believed to be insane (which he was). Any time he felt like it, King George III could march into their houses and act like he owned them, and he was only about a six-week boat ride away when the weather was good. The colonists also weren't terribly thrilled that King George III's army was going around burning buildings that they'd worked really hard on. "Well, shucks," they said. "We should at least be allowed to elect a guy before he takes advantage of us like that."

So they had a revolution and turned the colonies into their own darned country. A country in which all men (not to be confused with slaves, women, Native Americans, etc.) were created equal. A country in which nobody had to worry about midnight visits from a crazy monarch (except for maybe the staff at the White House after it was built). A country in which they wouldn't have to worry about having to sit through the Teapot Dome Scandal for nearly a century and a half.

Before the Revolution, the colonies were pretty much allowed to govern themselves. They could elect their own local representatives and only paid about a shilling[9] a year in taxes. People who lived in England paid about twenty times that, and if King George wanted to shove *them* around, he could be at their door by morning. The colonists didn't have any representatives in Parliament, but neither did most people in England, and *they* didn't complain much.

In fact, it didn't occur to anybody to declare independence at first, even when the regulars (British soldiers) started burning things. The colonies were actually more or less free to start with, and some polls indicated that only 13 percent of colonists supported independence in 1775 (though poll data back then was probably even less accurate than it is now, and the best researcher on staff can't figure out who took those polls).

So the war didn't start because the colonies declared independence—it actually started well before the idea to do so

---

[9] A shilling was one-twentieth of a pound. Economists don't really have an answer for how much a shilling in 1770 would be today, but it wasn't much. We figure it was about five bucks.

had even occurred to anybody, when the Crown decided to start messing around with (cue ominous theme music) . . .

. . . THE INTOLERABLE ACTS

The Stamp Act, instituted in 1765, meant that things like legal documents, newspapers, and playing cards had to be printed on specially stamped paper that proved a tax had been paid. The act came about because the British needed more money to pay for providing military defense to the colonies, which wasn't cheap. The British didn't think making the colonies chip in to

In 1770, a rowdy crowd of colonists got fired on by confused soldiers. The event became known as the Boston Massacre. It looked nothing like the engraving above, done by Paul Revere. For one thing, the people didn't *really* look like they'd been drawn by a caveman. The redcoats (British) thought they were being attacked, and were acting well within their rights (by 1770 standards). John Adams even defended them in court and saved them from being hanged. But the colonists were still a bit miffed.

help keep them from being invaded by France was unreasonable, but they were just starting to learn about how whiny Americans could be.

The colonists didn't like this act one bit, and decided that the best way to respond was mob violence: they broke into the houses of people in charge and burned them down. Once they'd been threatened with having all of their stuff burned, in addition to being tarred and feathered, most tax collectors weren't willing to collect the money anyway. The act was repealed in less than six months, and only a few suckers had paid even a penny.

Two years later came the Townshend Acts. First, the British, who hadn't yet learned their lesson, put taxes on common household items that were imported into the colonies. The colonists, naturally, responded with mob violence, having learned by then that burning stuff would probably solve the problem pretty quickly.

In 1773, John Hancock, now famous mostly for his big signature, organized a nonviolent boycott of imported tea. The East India Company, which was British, went from selling hundreds of thousands of pounds of tea per year to selling practically nothing.

The British responded with the Tea Act, which gave the East India Company—the Walmart of the

IT'S ALL ABOUT THE BENJAMIN

Benjamin Franklin had only two years of formal education, yet he managed to become a noted inventor, scientist, publisher, philosopher, and statesman. He signed both the Constitution and the Declaration of Independence and convinced the French to join the Revolutionary War on the colonies' side.

He's probably the most quotable of the founding fathers; some of his quotes, like "God helps those who help themselves," are often mistakenly thought to be right out of the Bible.

He probably did not, however, actually ever give himself an electrical shock by flying a kite with a key attached to it during a storm—that would be an excellent way to get killed. Presumably, the kite was attached to the ground. The details, like many things in history, are a bit muddy. Franklin didn't tell anybody except his son about the experiment at first; he was afraid other people would make fun of him, which they most certainly would have.

At the time, his reputation was much greater in Europe than it was in America. A few of the founding fathers, such as John Adams, thought he was a kook, and others thought he was "too English," because he'd spent so much time hanging out there, working for the government. Many people at the signing of the Declaration of Independence were afraid he might be a spy.

But as busy as all of this must have kept him, he still found time to sleep with an awful lot of women. Some estimate that he had as many as fifty children. This despite the fact that he was no great looker! Perhaps he was helped by having invented a musical instrument, the glass armonica, which was a sensation in Europe until rumors went around that the sound it made was so pretty that it caused mental disorders some decades later. This slight exaggeration may have set the stage for the days when even the ugliest rock star never hurt for late-night company. One can only imagine how Franklin would have fared on the social scene in an age when he could say, "See that face on the hundred-dollar bill? That's me, baby."

Franklin was also known as a world-class joker and prankster; some say that the reason he was not asked to write the Declaration of Independence himself is that the others were afraid he'd sneak a joke in. Check out www.smartalecksguide.com to see his writings about the possibilities of using science to make farts smell better!

Tarring and feathering was the practice of stripping someone down, covering them with tar, and then tossing on some feathers. If feathers weren't handy, dung would do. It was designed to humiliate a person so much that they left town, but in many cases, it did a lot more than that. It wasn't *usually* fatal, but when the tar finally came off, which took several days, the skin could be covered with burns, and various organs, such as the genitals, could be useless for life. ✶

Residents of Washington, D.C., are still suffering from taxation without representation—they pay taxes, but since the District of Columbia is not a state, they have no representative in Congress. Some people there *are* pushing to make it a state.

eighteenth century—tax breaks, so that they could offer tea at prices so low the colonists couldn't say no. As the enormous company pushed smaller organizations out of business, Sam Adams—now famous mainly for his beer—rounded up a group of guys called the Sons of Liberty for the famous Boston Tea Party.

THE BOSTON TEA PARTY

Outraged that the government would help a company offer tea at lower prices than their competitors, Adams and his pals dressed up like Native Americans, boarded one of the East India Company's ships, and threw the

None of the founding fathers was without flaws. They *did* manage to create a new country against all odds, which is more than *you* did—but if you really want to make fun of them, here's some ammo:

- George Washington was well known for crying like a little girl in public.
- Ben Franklin used to take "air baths," which some say were just an excuse to wander around the house naked. John Adams wrote that Franklin spent most meetings of congress asleep in his chair.
- Thomas Jefferson spent thousands of dollars on wine while he was president. That's millions in today's money. For most of his life he was in debt up to his eyeballs, which may be why he was never able to free his slaves (one of whom he was almost certainly sleeping with).
- Sam Adams did in fact have a brewery, but it was a colossal failure, costing him most of his inheritance. ✶

modern equivalent of millions of dollars worth of tea into the water. This effectively showed the British what the colonists thought of the Tea Act, and was probably a lot of fun. After all, since Sam Adams was running things, it's a safe bet that they had a few drinks first. However, this escapade did not exactly make the British think that the colonies were mature enough to be left alone, and they were awfully upset to see that much tea go to waste.

The British responded with some of the least tolerable acts yet. One stripped the colonies of the right to govern themselves. Another made it mandatory for people in Boston to let British soldiers stay at their houses, no matter how smelly the soldiers were. Apparently, the Crown *still* hadn't figured out that the colonies tended to respond to "intolerable acts" with mob violence.

The Continental Congress declared that these acts were illegal and suggested that people start up militias to fight back. Pretty soon, there were little local armies all over the place, ready to fight anyone from England who tried to push them around. Gradually, resistance to England turned from drunken mobs to organized military movements. These first soldiers were called the Minutemen, since they could be ready for battle in a minute (though it could just as well have been because a minute was about how

Hot-tempered though they were, the Boston Tea Partiers were still fairly polite, as mobs go. After throwing the tea overboard, they thoughtfully swept the decks. Ben Franklin, who wasn't present, insisted that the tea should be paid for, and offered to do so out of his own pocket.

King George III: a man who just didn't know when to quit. Plenty of people think the ruler of their country is insane, but in the case of King George III, they were right. Researchers today believe his insanity stemmed from a blood disorder called porphyria.

Paul Revere, apparently contemplating the important question of whether to knock the artist over the head with a teapot or brain him with a chisel. ✗

long they were expected to last against the British army).

Rather than conceding, the British ordered their troops to stamp out the militias, arrest revolutionaries, and engage in . . .

. . . A WHOLE BUNCH OF BATTLES

The first real battle of the Revolution was the Battle of Lexington and Concord in April of 1775. This fight wasn't for control of Lexington—nobody liked Lexington *that* much—the British merely planned to sneak in and confiscate the weapons the militias had stored there. The first shot to be fired in the battle becames known as "the shot heard round the world"; your teacher will probably want you to underline that, because it's pretty important. No

✗

one knows who—or even which side—fired that first shot, but it was fired in Lexington, officially beginning a war that would drag on for years.

The colonists were ready for the British to show up, thanks to guys like Paul Revere, who had warned them. Revere was a silversmith, and is known today as the guy who had his friend hang one lantern in the Old North Church if the British came by land, and two lanterns if they came by sea. Either way, he'd see them from his window and ride around to tell everybody to get ready to fight. This, of course, left the colonies woefully unprepared if the British launched themselves across the sea by catapult or tunneled in from underground, but fortunately enough, neither of those methods would have worked, anyway. Catapults were considered useless as modes of transportation in those days.

One night, two lanterns were hung,

and Revere jumped out of bed and got on his horse. He did not, however, shout "The British are coming." In 1775, most colonists still considered *themselves* British. Shouting "The British are coming" in the colonies would have been about the same thing as riding through Paris and shouting "Here come ze French!" People would have thought he was crazy.

What he shouted was "The regulars are out," which people knew meant they were about to be attacked by British soldiers—or possibly by guys who ate a lot of fiber. Either way, they knew to get ready for something messy. You'll notice that Revere wasn't saying a word about whether they were coming by land or sea, which seems odd, given all the trouble he'd gone to, to find out.

Revere didn't do all the warning by himself—there were actually three riders in his group, the other two being guys named William Dawes and Samuel Prescott. Nobody really thought of Paul Revere as a war hero—or thought of him at all, for that matter—until 1860, when Henry Wadsworth Longfellow wrote "Paul Revere's Ride," the poem that students were ever afterward forced to memorize. The poem is largely fictitious, and it can be argued that the reason Revere became famous while the other riders did not is that his name rhymed with "shall hear."

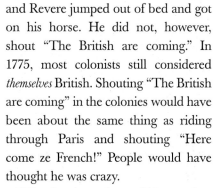

EXPERIMENTS TO TRY AT HOME!

Find a big merchant company that uses tax breaks to lower its prices and squeeze smaller companies out of business (there's probably one in your town!). Dress up in war paint and a Mohawk and start throwing their crap out of the store and into the street—see if the manager (and the police) understand that you're doing your patriotic duty!

The riders gave the militias enough of a warning that they were able to hold the British back. Without this warning, the British would have confiscated the weapons stored in Lexington, and it might have ended up being a very, very short war. But the British regulars didn't get a single musket.

The first real American attack on the British was the Battle of Fort Ticonderoga, where the British were storing one of their best cannons. The Green Mountain Boys, a group of soldiers who were not *exactly* a drunken mob, though they came pretty close, stormed the fort with help from Benedict Arnold, who had been sent to lead them in the charge. It turned out to be an easy battle; the British had left the front door unlocked, and only managed to fire one shot (some say not even that) before giving up and giving the Green Mountain Boys the cannon.

A short time later came the Battle of Bunker Hill, in which General Israel Putnam (or possibly Colonel William Prescott, no one really knows) said, "Don't shoot until you see the whites of their eyes." This was a reasonable order: muskets were terrible guns. If you saw the army advancing, it would take just about until you could see the whites of their eyes to get your gun loaded in the first place.

Putnam's (or Prescott's) advice didn't actually work out that well—the battle was a decisive victory for the British. But by waiting until the regulars were in range, the colonists managed to shoot over a thousand redcoats, and an awful lot of them were officers. The British knew that if they won three more battles like that, they wouldn't have much of an army left for the fourth battle.

Around this time came the Siege of Boston, the first great staring contest in American military history. The Continental army surrounded Boston, which was then occupied by the British soldiers, to keep them from moving out of the city. British attacks on these soldiers were unsuccessful. For months, the armies stayed put, waiting for the other army to make a move.

In July of 1775, General George Washington arrived to take control of the army and quickly sent some of them back to Bunker Hill, which they took back without any fight at all.

SMALLPOX

The British didn't leave Boston just because of the military. They were also afraid of—and probably grossed out by—the smallpox epidemic in Boston. Vaccination was still a fairly new idea then, and, since syringes hadn't been invented, people used quills. To most, the idea of being injected with the disease seemed remarkably stupid. But having troops vaccinated may have been Washington's most brilliant move.

HIT SONGS OF 1775

Both armies sang "Yankee Doodle" incessantly, but the song was originally meant to make fun of the Americans. It's full of insulting slang, and was sung in an exaggerated "American" accent. "Doodle" was a word for an idiot, riding into town on a pony was thought to be a very sissy thing to do, and a "macaroni" was a slang term for a fop (i.e., "fancy boy"). So in the first verse of the song, the Yankee Doodle prances into town on his pony, sticks a feather in his hat, and says, "Look at me! I'm *fab*-u-lous!" Even the word "Yankee" was slang for a hick, but the colonists started to use the word proudly, similar to the way people now call themselves rednecks as though it's something to be proud of.

There were actually dozens of verses, few of which are ever sung today. Several of them are on our Web page. Check out the verse the British troops made up in 1775 about Dr. Joseph Warren. Your teacher will hate us for suggesting it! Historians assume that there were probably *much* dirtier verses that no one wrote down at the time—soldiers make up dirty parodies of popular songs in just about every war. ✦

Those who remained spent several months waiting around outside of Boston. The staring contest ended in March of 1776, when the British blinked first. They sailed away, letting the colonists have Boston back.

In 1775, the Continental Congress offered the British a deal: they'd stop using mob violence and militias and stay a part of the British empire, at least on paper, if the Crown would stop letting Parliament have any authority over the colonies. King George III refused.

Still, the colonists thought that getting Boston back meant that the war was pretty much over. Congress was ready to write up . . .

THE DECLARATION OF INDEPENDENCE

Not every colonist was in favor of independence; a great many were still loyal to the Crown. In fact, right up until 1776, most of the colonists—even those who enjoyed mob violence—were proud to be British. But after the redcoats abandoned Boston, the revolutionaries were in charge of pretty much the entire country, and the loyalists didn't have a leg to stand on.[10]

By summer, all the colonies had overthrown their old governments and set up their own constitutions, making them states, not colonies, and the Second Continental Congress met in Philadelphia.

The Second Continental Congress was made up of a bunch of guys now known as the founding fathers, but they weren't the "band of brothers" we sometimes think of them as today. People are always trying to tell you what the founding fathers would think about some new law or another, but it's useless to try to guess what they would have thought about any modern issue.

---

10 For that matter, neither did delegate Gouverneur Morris (see page 59).

According to the back of the two-dollar bill, the founding fathers wore striped spandex pants to the signing of the Declaration.✗

In reality, they rarely agreed on anything, and anyway, no one can say if they would have the same opinions now as they held then, given the extent to which society has changed. Most of them seem to have thought most of the others were idiots. From the very beginning, Congress existed to fight.

After much debate, Congress decided to write up a declaration saying that the colonies were now free and independent states, and that all men (except for slaves, of course, and certainly not women) were created equal.

Thomas Jefferson was picked to write up the draft. Independence was actually declared on July 2, and the declaration was formally ratified on July 4.[11] Since it took a long time for letters to get to England, no one was able to tell King George about this right away. Supposedly, his diary entry on July 4 read "Nothing important happened today."[12]

It's important to remember that this was treason; the colonists weren't really

---

[11] We don't know what happened to this original copy. Thomas Jefferson said there was a copy of the Declaration in the room that day, and that John Hancock might have signed it (or something like it) to make it legal, but that copy has disappeared and was probably destroyed in the printing process. The famous copy dated July 4, 1776, that's on display in the National Archives was actually written later that summer.

[12] If it's true, he was right—the first paragraph of the Declaration was approved, separating America from England, on July 2, and John Adams, at least, assumed that July 2 would be the day people celebrated. The stuff on July 4 was really just a formality.

THE DECLARATION OF INDEPENDENCE

Plenty of people read the Declaration, which stated that "all men are created equal," and wondered what the heck Jefferson meant. Did this mean people were created the same size, or what? Others pointed out that it was a weird thing to hear from a "country" where slavery was so important to the economy.

In fact, Jefferson originally included a line attacking the slave trade, but a few states refused to ratify the Declaration unless the line was removed. The antislavery delegates had to decide that a declaration that didn't criticize slavery specifically was better than no declaration at all. ✗

Is this *really* what Washington looked like? We don't know for sure; most pictures of him were painted by one guy, who might not have been all that accurate. We can assume, however, that Washington didn't always look like he needed to pee, as he does here. ✗

free of English rule until King George said they were, and the risks were high. As Ben Franklin said, "We must all hang together, or we will most assuredly hang separately." If they were captured, the punishment for treason involved being hanged, cut down while still alive, and disemboweled; having your organs burned in front of you; and then being decapitated. These executions were a popular spectacle, though one can imagine that snack sales were slow.[13]

But the British Empire struck back.[14] Once news got back to England that the colonies thought they were independent, King George responded by sending in a *lot* more troops. They seized New York City and nearly captured George Washington in the process. They also took over New Jersey, even though it probably smelled funny even then. Soon, they were in firm control of most of New England.

---

[13] Well, you'd think so—but, in fact, vendors at public executions were said to do a pretty brisk business.

[14] For more on empires who strike back, see *The Smart Aleck's Guide to Why Star Wars Is Awesome*, Volume 16.

HENRY "HARRY" KNOX

You can't tell from the famous painting at the beginning of the chapter, but Washington *did* have boat safety in mind during the famous crossing. Several soldiers later reported that General Washington helped break the nervous tension on the boat by turning to Henry "Harry" Knox (above), a rather chunky officer who went on to be the first secretary of war, and saying, "Shift your fat butt, Harry, or you'll swamp the darned boat!" Only he didn't say "butt" or "darned." He said words that we're not supposed to print. This got quite a laugh out of the soldiers, and helped lift their spirits enough for them to take over Trenton armed mostly with muskets, which were useless in the damp weather. ✯

✯ ✯ ✯ ✯ ✯ ✯ ✯ ✯ ✯ ✯

WASHINGTON CROSSES THE DELAWARE: THE SIEGE OF TRENTON

A lot of Americans were ready to give up at that point, but George Washington planned a sneak attack. On Christmas Day, Washington and his troops very quietly snuck across the Delaware River and attacked the British. The British weren't expecting this; they were busy drinking to celebrate Christmas (which was pretty much the extent of Christmas celebrations at that time), and assumed that Washington and his men would be too busy dying of some dread disease or another to bother with attacking. With the British caught off guard, the colonists managed to take New Jersey back, which convinced a lot of them not to give up after all.

Of course, they might have thought differently if they'd known the war would last another seven years. The British were by no means losing at this point: they beat another part of Washington's army and took over Philadelphia, the capital of the new country-in-the-making. So the British were in control of Philadelphia and New York, while the colonists controlled only New Jersey.

The fighting looked like it could go on awhile, so the British finally decided that they'd take the deal Congress had offered earlier: Parliament would leave them alone if they just stayed a part of the empire on paper for economic reasons. But it was too late. Congress

The Continental army at Valley Forge, back before snow pants were invented. Scarves could be used to cover the neck, though one suspects they were also used to cover the nose.

effectively said, "You should have thought of that two years ago."

It might actually have been a smart move for Congress to take the deal at that point. Despite being in control of New Jersey, they were getting their butts kicked all over the Northeast, and there was no sign that they could win the war anytime soon. Plus, they still had to get through . . .

. . . THE WINTER AT VALLEY FORGE

Throughout history, many armies have been beaten more by the weather than by another army, and this was nearly the fate of Washington and his men. Washington had picked Valley Forge, a site not far from Philadelphia, as the place

for the army to camp for the winter; it was a good site, strategy-wise, but a little lacking in comfortable facilities.

When the army arrived, the snow was six inches deep, the winds were howling, and the soldiers were already worn out from marching. Their clothes were little more than rags, their boots were falling apart, and food wasn't delivered very often. Many soldiers had nothing to eat but "firecake," a mixture of flour, water, and sometimes salt that tasted about as good as it sounds. Soon, they began to get unpleasant diseases, like dysentery.

Living in cramped quarters with soldiers who had dysentery—which results in severe diarrhea—would have been dangerous (not to mention disgusting) in any weather. Around two thousand soldiers died, and another four thousand were declared unfit for duty. Many were probably thinking, "You know, I was ready to fight and die for independence, but

THOMAS PAINE: THE NUT WHO STARTED TWO REVOLUTIONS

Most colonists wouldn't have dreamed of separating from the Crown prior to 1776, and those who suggested as much were thought to be crazy. It never even occurred to most of the people who hated England to think about independence until Thomas Paine, a rude, crude man who bathed even less than other people of the day, talked them into it.

Paine wrote a pamphlet called "Common Sense," which argued not only that the king was a jerk, but also that a faraway island, such as England, could never keep up the task of ruling an entire continent. Nearly everybody in the colonies either read it or heard someone read it out loud. Soon, everyone was claiming they'd been for independence even back *before* it was cool.

It was a powerful pamphlet, outlining reasons to declare independence in plain language that even stupid people could understand. It was also a huge success: it sold more than a hundred thousand copies, making it the bestselling work of the day.

Since it was written anonymously, however, Paine never made a cent.

Having successfully talked the country into a revolution, he moved to France and wrote another pamphlet, "Rights of Man," which talked the French into revolting, too. The French revolutionaries ended up throwing Paine into jail for suggesting that they go easy on King Louis XVI, who had helped the Americans win the war. After getting out, Paine returned to America and spent most of his final years broke, lonely, and bearing what was described by friends as "the most disagreeable smell possible." Only six people attended his funeral.

GREAT MYTHS OF HISTORY

There is no solid evidence that . . .

- George Washington ever cut down his father's cherry tree. This came from a largely made-up biography in the mid-1800s.
- George Washington had wooden teeth. His false teeth were in fact mostly bone and "donated" teeth that may have been taken from dead soldiers. Reportedly, they hurt like crazy. Wooden ones would have been pretty unsanitary.
- The reason John Hancock signed his name in large letters was so the king could read it without his glasses.
- Betsy Ross ever sewed a flag in her life. No one is sure who sewed the first flag.
- Continental soldiers' ears hung so low that they could throw 'em over their shoulders.
- Patrick Henry actually made his "give me liberty or give me death" speech. It's a great speech, but if he really delivered it, nobody thought to write it down for more than forty years. This is the case with many, if not most, of the famous quotes of the day.

Washington: "Dear God, please let Ben Franklin invent some generic Pepto-Bismol." There is no evidence that this engraving depicts an actual event, which is why Valley Forge, Pennsylvania, won't put up a statue of it. ✴

nobody said anything about the trots!"

Meanwhile, those soldiers who were able to run across a field without requiring an outhouse at the other end spent the winter running drills and extensive training under the supervision of Baron Friedrich Wilhelm von Steuben, a former officer in the Prussian army, who turned them from a ragtag bunch of guys oozing gunk out of every orifice into an army that was ready to take on the British. At the end of the winter, just having survived was a huge morale booster, and they were

able to take Philadelphia back from the British, with the help of the French, who had decided to join in after . . .

. . . THE BATTLE OF SARATOGA: THE RISE AND FALL OF BENEDICT ARNOLD

The British planned to send in an army from Canada to capture the entire Hudson River Valley in 1777, sealing off New England from the rest of the country and most likely putting an end to the whole war. Knowing that this sort of

MAKE YOUR OWN FIRECAKE!

Mix flour and water (and salt, if possible) into a thick paste, and bake it on a cookie sheet until it's hard enough to break your teeth. Try it! We didn't, but you can. ✴

✴ 45 ✴

Benedict Arnold: A guy you won't be seeing on money anytime soon. Maybe they could put his right leg on the back of a quarter. ✻

✻ ✻ ✻ ✻ ✻ ✻ ✻ ✻ ✻ ✻

fight was coming, Washington sent Major General Benedict Arnold and his men up toward Canada to hold off the fight. A huge battle took place at Saratoga in which Arnold was shot just below the right buttock—the second time he'd been shot in his right leg. Even though Arnold pretty much single-handedly won this battle, most of the credit went to a guy named Horatio Gates. Still nursing his achy-breaky butt, Arnold became remarkably bitter.

Beating the British at Saratoga was the first event that made people throughout the world start to believe that the Americans could actually win the war. In particular, the French, who really hated the British and never missed a good chance to fight with them, started to think there was hope. Ben Franklin had been in Paris for some time, trying to talk them into joining the fight against the Crown (when he could tear himself away from flirting with women one-third his age, which, according to John Adams, is how he spent most of his time there). After they found out what Arnold and his men had done in Saratoga, they finally decided that it would be worth their while to help out. And the truth is, if it weren't for the French, the British probably would have won the war in the end, as ashamed as most Americans are to admit it.

Benedict Arnold, for one, wasn't wild about the arrival of French troops, having had his fill fighting against them in the French and Indian War. He was further upset that Congress wouldn't promote him to the rank of brigadier general or refund his wartime expenses. Having been shot twice in the same leg

EXPERIMENTS TO TRY AT HOME!

If they hanged a one-legged Benedict Arnold, would the awkward center of gravity cause the body to spin around and around? Find out! You'll need a saw, a length of rope, and a friend. For extra points, see if it would spin in the opposite direction south of the equator! ✻

Note: Don't really do this.

in service of the country, Arnold decided that he'd had just about enough. After being given control of West Point, he quietly offered to sell the fort to the British. Major John André of the British was captured with paperwork signed by Arnold and was promptly hanged as a spy by Americans who realized from the paperwork that Arnold had become a traitor. Knowing that he was sure to be caught, Arnold fled and joined the British army himself.

Arnold spent the rest of the war fighting for the British, though they never really trusted him. When he asked a captured American officer what would happen to him if *he* was ever captured—since he was, after all, still a hero of the Revolution—the officer said they'd bury his injured right leg with full military honors, then hang the rest of him. After the war, Arnold moved to England, where he tried to start up a shipping company. It failed, and he died pretty much forgotten, but with his leg still attached to his butt.

THE BRITISH START TO LOSE

Meanwhile, now that they were outnumbered in the Northeast, the British took over Savannah, Georgia, planning to move north. They assumed that plenty of the loyalist Americans would turn up to help them fight along the way, but not enough of them did. The two sides ended up engaging in one fight after another that didn't really have any strategic point, and the British began to get worn down.

As they marched north, the British figured that even if they didn't capture the South, they'd at least be rescued by the British fleet in Virginia. That fleet, however, was destroyed by the French, leaving the British army stranded in Yorktown.

In 1781, after several years of brutal fighting, General Lord Cornwallis finally surrendered the main British combat army to General Washington. By this time, Washington had actually lost more battles than he had won—in fact, no other modern general has lost as many battles as Washington did without losing the overall war. But the British army had grown heartily sick of the pointless battles and gross diseases. They were ready to give up.

Of course, there was still the tiny matter of King George's agreeing to recognize America as an independent nation. And King George, well known for being

Banastre Tarleton, a British officer, was commanding armies at the age of twenty-three. He became known as Bloody Ban after stories got around that his men had hacked to pieces soldiers who were trying to surrender. He later claimed the whole hacking business was an accident, but no one could quite imagine how anyone could "accidentally" hack someone to bits. ✱

✱ ✱ ✱ ✱ ✱ ✱ ✱ ✱ ✱ ✱

mentally ill, wanted to keep fighting, whether Cornwallis had surrendered or not. But his supporters had lost control

of Parliament, and in 1783, John Adams, John Jay, and Benjamin Franklin, always ready to show up with paperwork, negotiated a peace treaty (the Treaty of Paris) in which King George agreed to stop fighting and recognize that his former colonies were now independent.

America was officially a nation. A nation whose people could proudly say, "So . . . now what?"

A WHOLE NEW KING GEORGE?

So, America was a country. The problem was, it wasn't *much* of a country yet. It was a collection of thirteen states with no real common government—there was a national congress, but all it could do was suggest things to the states. It couldn't raise or collect taxes, which led to some problems. There was no constitution at the time, only the Articles of Confederation, a document that loosely

✱ ✱

THE NAME OF THE COUNTRY

Among his other accomplishments, Thomas Paine was the first to call our country the United States of America. But most people thought it was a lousy name. "What do we call ourselves, then?" they asked. "United Statesians?" Congress didn't much care for it either, and considered calling the new country Freedonia, Columbia, Alleghenia, or Appalachia. But no one could agree on one of these, so rather than have one more thing to fight about, they just stuck with the United States of America.

Was the Revolution a good idea? Canada took a different route: in 1867, it became a self-governing nation largely by asking nicely, dodging the two major wars it took America to become an independent, slave-free country. The Queen of England is still a figure in Canadian government, but try finding a Canadian who knows what the heck her job is.

tied the states together but didn't give the central government the power to do anything.

By the time the war ended, Congress was so strapped for cash that most of the soldiers hadn't been paid in years. Many were in terrible debt. The states had forced many farmers to borrow money and buy more land to grow food for the soldiers during the war; when the war ended and they couldn't pay off the debts, the states threw them into debtor's prison. People were starting to think that they'd fought to create

Cornwallis surrenders as the British army band, according to legend, plays "The World Turned Upside Down." After this, to show that there were no hard feelings, American and French officers threw lavish dinner parties for the British officers, except for Tarleton, who wasn't invited because no one could stand him. This sort of postwar party was standard army protocol in those days, but plenty of Americans were upset, wondering who the heck they'd have to surrender to in order to get food tastier than firecake.

Recent surveys show that most people think Benjamin Franklin was president at one point. By the time the country had a president, he was too old and feeble even for makin' time with the ladies, let alone running the country—plus, a lot of people thought he was crazy. He died about a year after Washington took office. ✱

✱ ✱

a new country but had created one big mess (along with several smaller ones back at Valley Forge).

People knew that using the military to start a republic had never really worked before (and it hasn't worked since, for that matter). Only a handful of republics had ever been formed, and in a couple of the best-known cases, the military leaders (Julius Caesar in Rome, for instance) had marched into town and declared themselves kings. Washington could very well have marched into Philadelphia, ordered Congress to disperse, and told people he was the king of America.

He wouldn't have met much resistance. Imagine the scene:

GEORGE: I'm here to tell you guys to go home. I'm running this joint now.

CONGRESS: Well, gee, George, nice to see you and all, but the thing is, well . . .

GEORGE: The thing is that I just kicked the crap out of the whole British

✱ ✱

THE FOUNDING FATHERS AND RELIGION

One can debate for hours whether most of the founding fathers were religious. Some were. Others weren't. Few, if any, actively spoke of setting up America as a Christian nation. Today, many people assume that in "the old days," everyone was either a devout Christian or the town atheist, but by some estimates, only about 7 percent of colonists belonged to a church at all in 1776! It's true that the Constitution never explicitly says that church and state are separate, but the document also never mentions God.

Many of the founding fathers may have been Deists, meaning they believed in God but also believed that he didn't interfere with the world, a popular theory at the time. Many were fairly religious, but probably not enough that they could carry the red states in an election today. Here are some quotes from the founding fathers:

- "Religion and government will both exist in greater purity, the less they are mixed together."–James Madison
- "The government of the United States is not, in any sense, founded on the Christian religion."–John Adams (or a document he approved, anyway)
- "Christian philosophy . . . [has become] the most perverted system that ever shone on man."–Thomas Jefferson
- "The way to see by faith is to shut the eye of reason."–Benjamin Franklin

Additionally, Thomas Paine had enough quotes against established religion that they could about fill a book by themselves.[15]

---

[15] For more information, see *The Smart Aleck's Guide to Thomas Paine's Views on Organized Religion.*

army, and I can certainly beat a room full of old men. Nice Independence Hall you have here. Shame if anything happened to it. That Liberty Bell looks especially breakable.

CONGRESS: All hail King Washington!

Washington's case would have been further strengthened by the fact that he would have been backed up by an army of angry men who enjoyed mob violence and blamed Congress for the fact that they were broke. Congress probably would have dispersed if Washington had told them to.

Believe it or not, a lot of people *wanted* Washington to break up Congress and be the new king–including most of his officers. Under the Articles of Confederation, the country was already falling apart, and installing Washington as king might well have put things on a more stable track.

The officers met in an auditorium to plan the details of taking over Congress, but Washington showed up to settle them down. To get their attention, he put on his glasses, which he'd never done in public before, to show that he'd lost a good deal of his eyesight in service to his country. Several officers sobbed at the sight of the general looking like a nerd; the glasses alone were enough to get them to listen to his orders to calm down. He barely even needed to make a speech. Historians generally ignore the theories that these were special eyeglasses with hypnotic powers, and stories that he then used them to make all of the officers do the hokey-pokey are considered apocryphal,[16] but it would have been pretty cool.

Meanwhile, back in merry old England, King George III said that if Washington didn't become king when the country was his for the taking, then he would be "the greatest man in the world." Normally, we make a big deal out of the fact that George III was out of his mind, but we choose to ignore that when he says nice things about Washington.

Washington then bade his officers farewell over drinks and obscene songs in a New York tavern, and attended a grand ball in his honor that Congress threw as a thank-you for not marching into town and shooting them. At the end of the ball, Washington formally resigned his job as general and walked out the door, where his horses were waiting for him, while the crowd gave him a standing ovation. Some said that it was the greatest exit in American history. Others pointed out that American history had really only started up a few

---

[16] In fact, we just made them up—see *The Smart Aleck's Guide to Lying*.

The Freemasons are a semisecret group who are, depending on who you ask, either a fraternity for adults or an ancient, mystic organization that secretly controls the whole world—like the Stonecutters on that episode of *The Simpsons*. Some people will tell you that everything in modern history has been a big conspiracy cooked up by the Masons. It's true that Washington and several other founding fathers were members— in the eighteenth century, pretty much everybody who was anybody joined the group sooner or later. But this doesn't mean the whole Revolution was a conspiracy . . . or does it?

weeks earlier, so there wasn't a lot of competition.

Whether Washington wanted to be king or not, everyone soon agreed that running the country as a confederacy wasn't working—though certain states never quite got the lesson through their heads. In 1787, Congress met in Philadelphia to revise the Articles of Confederation, but it soon became clear that just revising them wasn't going to be enough. A whole new constitution had to be written up, which is why they still call this convention . . .

...THE CONSTITUTIONAL CONVENTION

A lot of the old revolutionary heavyweights from the early days were present at the writing of the Constitution. Ben Franklin was well into his eighties by then, and in terrible shape. He was known as the convention's "sage," which meant that he was just there so they'd have a famous old smart guy there. He rarely did any debating, and most of his suggestions were shot down quickly. For example, he suggested that the meetings open with a prayer in the hopes that this would get the delegates to stop bickering. This was quickly shot down, and modern Congresses have proven that no amount of prayer will stop partisan fighting anyway.

He then suggested that government officials, including the delegates, not be paid a salary. The other delegates refrained from beating Franklin over the head with their canes (he *was* pretty frail, after all), but many started to wonder if Franklin had completely lost his mind.

Another of Franklin's ideas was that the president and other government types should only serve single-year terms, which would have meant that we'd have to sit through presidential campaigns every year, not just every four years. On the other end of the political spectrum, Alexander Hamilton suggested that elected officials serve for life, as long as they behaved. Imagine: Gerald Ford could have been in office for over thirty years!

One thing that Franklin did manage to push through was the nomination of George Washington as president of the convention. People *loved* George Washington. He had narrowly escaped capture and smallpox so many times that rumors were spreading that he could not be killed and was immune to all disease. After the Constitution was finally ratified, he would be elected the

nation's first president without really even bothering to run.

During the writing of the Constitution, slavery was one of the most heated issues, if not *the* most heated. Many delegates insisted that it be outlawed in the new country immediately, but one problem of having a democracy, not a monarchy, is that they couldn't just do away with it without enough people approving. Many of the delegates thought slavery was an abomination, but they also realized that the Southern states would never

Delegates crowd over to one side of the room so they can be in the painting of the signing of the Constitution— which wouldn't actually be painted for more than 150 years.

sign a constitution that outlawed it.

In the end, they reached a compromise: they refused to specifically *allow* slavery in the Constitution but put in a clause saying that Congress couldn't even talk about ending the slave trade for at least twenty years. Many assumed that it would be outlawed in all of the states by then anyway.

This didn't stop Franklin from pushing for an end to slavery only months later, though. He forced Congress to consider it again in 1790. After Southern delegates made long speeches saying they supported slavery because the Bible did, Franklin published a letter saying that their reasons were remarkably similar to the ones Algerian pirates used to justify enslaving Christians. It was his last published letter; he died a few weeks later.

It's ironic, considering that our country has always prided itself on being free, that America ended up being one of the last of the big, rich countries to abolish slavery; the practice was abolished in Britain (and its colonies) in 1833, a good thirty years before the Emancipation Proclamation was issued in America. Slavery remained a huge problem in America for the next seventy years after the Constitutional Convention, largely because even abolitionists knew there were not a lot of practical ways to end slavery in the South, where the economy depended on it. In hindsight, it's easy to say they should have just ignored the trouble and abolished slavery anyway. But before you say that, think about how your sneakers were probably made.

In the end, none of the delegates were convinced that the constitution they eventually agreed on was a particularly good plan of government. Everyone had to compromise, and nobody got exactly the setup they wanted. Under the circumstances, though, most of them figured they'd done about as good a job as they could, setting the standard for how effective Congress is to this day.

One thing, however, was still missing:

THE BILL OF RIGHTS

When the Constitution was first written, it didn't say a word about freedom of speech, religion, or any of that business. There wasn't even anything in it that said you didn't have to let soldiers stay in your house if they knocked on the door.

So Congress got together again and

YOUR LIFE, 1776

So, what would *you* have been doing in 1776? Well, if you had been born in the 1760s, odds are pretty good that by 1776, you would have been decomposing. Up to a third of all babies didn't live to their first birthday, and only about half of all people lived to age twenty in the colonies. Sanitation was pretty poor, healthy food was hard to come by, and disease was everywhere. In the mid-1770s, a smallpox epidemic killed well over a hundred thousand people. Life expectancy was only in the forties.

Even if you survived, life would have been rough. The good news is that you probably wouldn't have had to go to school, but the bad news is that if you were a boy, you would have been sent out to work at about the age of seven or eight to make money for your family. Boys were usually sent off to become apprentices, spending a few years being taught a trade by a "master." Girls were raised to be dependent on others—first their parents, then their husbands—for their entire lives. Their days were often spent on candlemaking, quilting, and other chores that some modern weirdos think are fun.

There was really no such thing as a teenager in America at the time. People reached their teen years, of course, but they were expected to act like adults by the time they were about seven. Young children were commonly dressed in robes that opened in the front, but as soon as they were old enough, they were dressed as miniature adults.

Contrary to what your teacher might have told you, you would probably not have been married with kids by the time you were sixteen. The average marrying age was twenty-two for women and twenty-seven for men—which is fairly surprising, considering that men that age could only expect to live for another fifteen to twenty years!

FACES ON MONEY

The best way to get your face on money is still to be president, but a few people got on by other means, such as:

ALEXANDER HAMILTON, $10 BILL: Hamilton wrote some of the Federalist Papers, served as the first secretary of the treasury, then was shot by Aaron Burr, the only sitting vice president ever to shoot anybody until Dick Cheney accidentally shot Harry M. Whittington in the face with bird shot in 2006. Whittington survived, but Hamilton didn't.

BENJAMIN FRANKLIN, $100 BILL: If the question is "How many people do you have to sleep with to get yourself on the hundred?" the answer is "lots and lots."

SALMON P. CHASE, $10,000 BILL: Chase was secretary of the treasury when Lincoln was president. We have no idea how he ended up on money; maybe his heirs bribed someone. This bill stopped being printed in the 1960s.

SACAJAWEA, $1 COIN: With this coin, Congress made up for the raw deal women *and* Native Americans have been getting in America for centuries![17]

We here at the Smart Aleck's Guide are in favor of getting politicians off money and putting on some *other* American icons. How about putting Miles Davis, Joe DiMaggio, or Frederick Douglass on some money? And we mean major currency, not those limited-edition coins that the mint prints up now and then to sell to coin collectors.

added ten amendments, which guaranteed such things as freedom of speech, freedom to join whatever crazy religion you like, freedom to keep your mouth shut, freedom from being tortured, freedom from being put on trial or arrested

---

[17] Yeah, right.

for no particular reason, and other useful things. The First Amendment alone grants the freedom of speech, religion, press, and assembly, and the right to petition the government to change the laws—though the government can still throw the petition right into Mr. Trash Can if they feel like it.

Two other amendments didn't make the cut. One regulated the number of representatives in the House and the number of constituents each respresentative could have (rejected, presumably, because it was boring), and one regulated how often Congress could give itself a pay raise. The latter was eventually ratified as the Twenty-seventh Amendment in 1992.

Having formed a new nation, Americans looked to the West, beyond the mountains, and softly said, "I'll bet some strip malls would look mighty good over there."

SOME OF THE STUFF WE MISSED

Here's a little bit about some of the things we left out. For more information, get off your lazy butt and research them yourself!

The Marquis de Lafayette: Commander of the French army; became a friend to George Washington and helped save America's butt.

The Federalist Papers: Essays by Alexander Hamilton, James Madison,

Francis Lightfoot Lee, thinking, "The sum of the squares of any two sides of an isosceles triangle is equal to the square root of the remaining side!"[18] ✯

and John Jay. Very important, but kinda boring. The ideas expressed in them influenced the formation of the American government.

Don't Tread on Me: The motto on a really cool flag with a snake on it that colonists used to wave to frighten the British (who apparently hated snakes). Officially known as the Gadsden flag.

Benjamin Rush: A founding father who was sort of a cynic. Called the state constitution of Pennsylvania "our state dung cart."

---

[18] Despite what the Scarecrow says in *The Wizard of Oz*, this is way off. See *The Smart Aleck's Guide to Incorrect Interpretations of the Pythagorean Theorem.*

AMENDMENTS

The Constitution can be changed, but it's a long process. Since the first ten amendments, out of more than eleven thousand that have been proposed, fewer than twenty more have been added, and most of those are about boring things like congressional protocol.

The Battle of Monmouth: The battle right after the winter at Valley Forge. It was sort of a tie, but no one expected the colonists to do anything but lose after that winter.

Molly Pitcher: A woman who heroically took her injured husband's place firing a cannon on the battlefield, making her one of the few female heroes of the Revolution.

Native Americans: We hardly mentioned them here, but they were around, of course. Suffice it to say that as usual, they got a raw deal.

John Paul Jones: This guy was sort of like a professional pirate, raiding British ships at sea and cutting off supplies to the British army, helping Washington immensely.

John Jay: A founding father who became the first chief justice of the Supreme Court.

The Hessians: German soldiers hired by the British. The headless horseman of Sleepy Hollow was one of these guys!

FORGOTTEN FOUNDING FATHERS

Here are a few founding fathers who never ended up on federal currency:

Button Gwinnett and Lyman Hall: Georgia delegates with funny names. Button ended up murdered in a bar fight (or a duel, depending on who you believe. The line between "bar fight" and "duel" is often blurry).

Charles Carroll: The only Roman Catholic signer of the Declaration of Independence, and the last signer to die (though he had pretty much been forgotten by then—see the next chapter).

Josiah Bartlett: The delegate from New Hampshire, ancestor of the fictional president on *The West Wing*.

John Lansing, Jr.: Refused to sign the Constitution, then mysteriously disappeared in New York several years later. He is thought to have drowned or been murdered; no one knows for sure. He's certainly dead by now, though . . . or is he?

Gouverneur Morris: One of the authors of the Constitution, though he is better remembered for having a peg leg and sleeping with other men's wives. Total party animal. Theodore Roosevelt wrote a whole book about him.

Francis Lightfoot Lee: A signer of the Declaration of Independence best known for being the brother of Richard Henry Lee, who first proposed the document. Also a relative (great-uncle, to be exact) of Confederate general Robert E. Lee.

END-OF-CHAPTER QUESTIONS

MULTIPLE CHOICE

1. Which of the following about George Washington is true:

  a. That whole business about the cherry tree.

  b. He could breathe fire, which scared the bejeezus out of the British, many of whom had relatives who had been eaten by dragons.

  c. He could throw a coin across the Potomac River.

  d. He was known as one heckuva dancer.

(ANSWER: D.)

2. Patrick Henry is known for saying:

  a. "If this be treason, then make the most of it."

  b. "Don't fire until you see the whites of their eyes."

  c. "Patriotism is the last refuge of a scoundrel."

  d. "Are you going to eat that pickle?"

(ANSWER: A, THOUGH HE PROBABLY NEVER SAID IT. THE ONLY RECORD WE HAVE OF THE NIGHT HE SUPPOSEDLY SAID IT INDICATES THAT HE SAID SOMETHING SORT OF ROWDY BUT THEN

IMMEDIATELY APOLOGIZED AND PLEDGED HIS
UNDYING LOYALTY TO THE CROWN.)

**3. True or False: Ben Franklin was
against drinking alcohol.**

(ANSWER: TRUE, BUT HE CHANGED HIS MIND.
TODAY, JUST ABOUT EVERY OTHER BAR PUTS
A QUOTE FROM HIM—"BEER IS PROOF THAT GOD
LOVES US AND WANTS US TO BE HAPPY"—ON
THE WALL.)

**4. The Boston Tea Party resulted
in:**

   a. King George granting colonists
independence before they
started fighting with solid food.

   b. A slight Earl Grey taste residents still detect in Boston
drinking water.

   c. A request from the fish to throw
in some sugar.

   d. The British sending in more
troops.

(ANSWER: D.)

**5. Tarring and feathering resulted
in:**

   a. Third-degree burns.

   b. People calling you "crazy
chicken man."

   c. Blistering.

   d. Unusable genitals.

   e. All of the above.

(ANSWER: E.)

6. Paul Revere was:

   a. A silversmith.

   b. A jockey.

   c. A prizefighter.

   d. A stuck-up, half-witted, scruffy-
lookin' Nerf herder.[19]

   e. A refrigerator repairman.

(ANSWER: A.)

**7. Founding father James Broom is
best known today for:**

   a. Signing the Constitution.

   b. Dying in 1810.

   c. Serving in the Delaware General
Assembly.

   d. Nothing, really.

(ANSWER: ALL ARE TRUE, BUT D IS CORRECT.)

SECRET ANSWER KEY TO YOUR TEACHER'S TEST ON THE REVOLUTION

A, D, C, B, A, A, B, D, C, A, D, B, FALSE, TRUE,
TRUE, FALSE, JOHN PAUL JONES. TRY IT!

ASSIGNMENT

   Write a rambling poem about
Prescott or Dawes.

---

[19] See *The Smart Aleck's Guide to Why
Star Wars Is Awesome, Volume 4.*

DISCUSSION

1. Lonely ol' Charles Carroll, a forgotten founding father. What do you suppose he's thinking here?
2. Who was better-looking, George Washington or Thomas Jefferson?
3. Assuming you didn't know what Valley Forge would be like ahead of time, would you have joined the army? What if you *had* known about it? If you said yes, are you some kind of sicko?
4. Which founding father do *you* think had the silliest name?

MNEMONICS!

Here are some rhymes to help you remember stuff from this chapter:

LAST NIGHT I WAS WATCHING
THE GREAT MUPPET CAPER
INSTEAD OF READING HAMILTON'S
FEDERALIST PAPERS.

LISTEN, MY CHILDREN,
AND YOU SHALL HEAR
ABOUT SAMUEL ADAMS—HE SURE LIKED
HIS BEER!

IT ISN'T SO NICE TO BE
PUNCHED IN THE GUT,
BUT BENEDICT ARNOLD WAS SHOT
IN THE BUTT.[20]

ROSES ARE RED, VIOLETS ARE BLUE,
BENJAMIN FRANKLIN
INVENTED THE STOVE.[21]

---

[20] Actually, it was just below the butt. See *The Smart Aleck's Guide to Traitors' Hindquarters.*

[21] If you want to get technical, it wasn't the stove, but *a* stove, called the Franklin stove. Also, we know this doesn't rhyme, but studies show that adding "roses are red, violets are blue" before a fact makes it 80 percent easier to remember. See *The Smart Aleck's Guide to Boy, Are You Gullible!*

CHAPTER

A NATION DECLINES TO BATHE

The spirit of Manifest Destiny saying, "Go west, young man, and stink up some other part of the country!"

"American gentleman . . . God forgive me for putting two such words together."
—Charles Dickens

INTRODUCTION

If Americans in the days just after the Revolution were known for one thing, it was a general lack of manners. British books describing how horribly Americans behaved were huge sellers in both England and America. Americans got a real kick out of books whose whole point was to tell them they talked funny, lived like pigs, and smelled like them, too.

Many of these books were just the work of English writers picking on their American cousins because they were still bitter about the whole Revolution thing, but they probably weren't far off when they pointed out just how bad your average American smelled. Bathing was considered strictly a novelty for the very rich, and most people in America were really quite poor. Even the richer people were pretty gross, especially by today's standards. When Louis Philippe, who would eventually become king of France, visited America, he was told at one place where he crashed for a while that there were no chamber pots (pee buckets) and that if he had to go, he should just open the window.

If there was a national pastime enjoyed by members of all classes in those days, it was spitting. Everybody was into spitting. People spit on the floors of their houses pretty openly, and though every member of Congress had his own spittoon in which to deposit

The nineteenth century was the age of the log cabin. It was also the era when a presidential candidate's drinking habits were viewed as a selling point. One of the few things anyone remembers about William Henry Harrison is that his campaign was based largely on the fact that he drank a lot of hard cider.

When Englishwoman Frances Trollope wrote a book about how dirty Americans were, outraged Americans responded in the most mature way possible: by drawing a picture that made her look like Jabba the Hutt.

✫ ✫ ✫ ✫ ✫ ✫ ✫ ✫ ✫ ✫ ✫

his chewed tobacco, most of them just spit on the carpet instead, which required less aim. Visitors to the Capitol

✫ ✫ ✫ ✫ ✫ ✫ ✫ ✫ ✫ ✫ ✫

Louis Philippe of France. Couldn't he just have used his hat?

remarked that you could barely tell which designs on the carpet were supposed to be there and which had been "added" by the congressmen.

Of course, this was the nineteenth century; the whole world was pretty nasty. Bathtubs and toilets weren't terribly popular in England, either. And in America, people were starting to move west. There were no rest stops or showers on the Oregon Trail, and Wet-Naps would not be invented for years. If people were hopelessly dirty and smelly, it wasn't like they could help it.

Still. Asking a future king to pee out the window? Early America was no place for the squeamish. Or for people who were in the habit of walking under Louis Philippe's window without an umbrella.

THE FIRST PRESIDENTIAL CAMPAIGNS

In 1796, George Washington decided that if he served more than two terms, he'd start to look like a monarch. So he stepped down as president, leading the country into the first real presidential election, which ended with John Adams as president and Thomas Jefferson as vice president.

Jefferson and Adams were actually members of different political parties: Adams was a Federalist, and Jefferson was a Democratic Republican. In those days, candidates didn't pick a running mate like they do now. The vice presidency went to whoever came in second in the election. This is an okay way to elect, say, a runner-up in case Miss America can't perform her duties, but for electing a vice president, it had its problems. Under this system, vice presidents spent all their time plotting revenge against the victorious president—after all, they didn't have much of anything better to do. The

Thomas Jefferson: style and a half*!*

DEAD POLITICAL PARTIES

- The Federalist Party wanted a rich nation with a strong military. Their favorite saying was "Those who own the country ought to govern it." Notable Federalists included John Adams and Alexander Hamilton.
- Democratic Republicans favored a strict interpretation of the Constitution. They ran the country for about twenty-five years, then gradually split into the two parties we know and complain about today.
- The Whig Party mostly existed to disagree with Andrew Jackson, but four members (William Henry Harrison, John Tyler, Zachary Taylor, and Millard Fillmore) became forgettable presidents. Abraham Lincoln was also a Whig when he was in Congress.
- The Know-Nothings, originally called the American Republican Party, then the Native American Party, this anti-immigrant party was so secretive that, when asked what they stood for, members were supposed to say "I know nothing." Most candidates today say pretty much the same thing when asked about their beliefs; they just take a lot longer to do it. ✯

vice president's job pretty much consisted of waiting around to cast tie-breaking votes in the Senate. They ended up with plenty of free time for things like dueling.

So the first bitter, nasty presidential campaign came in 1800, when Jefferson ran against Adams. Adams's supporters claimed that Jefferson was an atheist who would have all the churches in the country burned down and all the rich people killed (this sounds a little less extreme when you consider that people in France, where Jefferson had been hanging out, were doing exactly that at the time). Meanwhile, Jefferson's supporters portrayed Adams as a power-hungry maniac (in reality, he was just kind of a jerk). Today, a choice between these two founding fathers sounds like a great election, compared to the clowns people have had to pick between in most elections since, but in those days people saw it as a choice between a maniac and a heathen.

When the ballots were counted, Adams had been beaten by *two* Democratic Republicans. Jefferson and Aaron Burr received seventy-three electoral votes each, a perfect tie.

This meant that the House of Representatives had to decide which of the two would be president—and the Federalist-controlled Congress hated them both. After thirty-five rounds of voting, they still hadn't picked a winner, and the country very nearly slipped into civil war. Some of the Democratic Republican leaders were threatening to call their state militias to

Aaron Burr ran for governor of New York in 1804 rather than running for president again, and, in the process, got ticked off at Alexander Hamilton and challenged him to a duel. Burr won, became the first sitting vice president ever to shoot a guy, and was arrested for murder. He got off the hook, but his political career was over.

Tammany Hall was a political organization in New York that helped Jefferson win the election of 1800. These guys didn't just practice corruption, they positively rejoiced in it.

action to install Jefferson, who was actually a lot more popular with the voters than Burr, as president. Jefferson liked to call this the Revolution of 1800, largely because he liked calling things revolutions. In the end, they went with Jefferson rather than risk any fighting.

John Adams didn't forgive Jefferson for years. He retired to his estate to spend the rest of his years writing letters to colleagues, grooming his son to take over the family business, and doing the horizontal polka with his wife, Abigail, who had been such a trusted advisor during his presidency that some people consider them to have been copresidents.

THE WAR WITH THE BARBARY PIRATES

Most history books don't even bother to mention that from 1801 to 1805, the United States was at war with pirates—a rather glaring omission, we don't mind saying. The Barbary States, a group of loosely connected North African countries, expected foreign governments to pay money to ensure that these pirates wouldn't attack them. Explaining exactly how the power in North Africa was divided and what the pirates had to do with it would take a whole book by itself, so we'll spare you the details. Suffice it to say that the guys in charge had pirates working for them and expected governments to pay them in exchange for safety.

Back when the States were colonies, the British paid their ransom to the pirates for them, thereby protecting them from pirate attacks. After independence, however, it was up to the States to cover their own bills. Just about everybody felt that the United States should refuse to pay the pirates off, but there was an argument about whether such a decision was practical. Jefferson wanted to just stop paying altogether, and Adams wanted to wait until the new country could form a good enough navy to fight the pirates.

When Jefferson became president, the guy in charge of Tripoli, a North African country for which the pirates worked, demanded $225,000 from the United States—which was, at the time, a pretty sizable chunk of America's total revenue. Jefferson refused, so Tripoli declared war. Several other states from around Tripoli joined in,

Another Early Nineteenth Century Print Showing Decatur Leading His Men to Drive the Pirates Off the Captured "Philadelphia."

Lieutenant Stephen Decatur driving the pirates off the USS *Philadelphia*. The pirates had captured the ship, and Decatur and his men snuck back aboard and set fire to it so that the pirates couldn't use it. Decatur was made a captain soon after.

and the pirates began attacking U.S. ships, taking Americans hostage and treating them as slaves.

Congress never made a formal declaration of war, but Jefferson got permission to send what navy the United States had out to attack the pirates. The battles went on for four years before there was a peace treaty, and, even though it took a long time to come, America's victory did a lot for its reputation overseas: people around the world now knew that Americans might smell bad and talk funny, but they could stand up to pirates.

LEWIS AND CLARK:
UNEATEN EXPLORERS

In 1803, President Jefferson sent a couple of guys to Paris to offer to buy New Orleans from the French for ten million dollars. At the time, France had been taken over by a short weirdo named Napoléon Bonaparte, who had secret plans to set up an empire in North America. However, when the armies Napoléon stationed in America died of yellow fever, he gave up on the idea and surprised Jefferson's men by offering them the entire Louisiana Territory for fifteen million dollars, roughly three cents per acre. On July 4, 1803, Jefferson got to announce that the country had just doubled in size. Yellow fever germs came free with the purchase.

Even before he bought the Louisiana Territory, Jefferson sent out some

Lewis's and Clark's letters and diaries show us that they couldn't spell for beans (see our Web page!), but boy, could they dress!

explorers to look it over, get America into the fur trade, and collect scientific data. After he bought the land, the expedition became a much bigger deal—and legal. America suddenly had a huge new patch of land, and nobody really knew what it contained. There could have been elephants roaming around out there for all anyone knew—in fact, Jefferson fully expected it.

The explorers were led by Meriwether Lewis, a secretary with a taste for adventure, and William Clark, a veteran of the Revolution. Neither one of them knew the first thing about science or the wilderness, but they both had genuine guts. They were quite a ways into the expedition when they got word that most of the territory was now owned by America, so they weren't doing anything illegal. The fact that they were walking through their rightful territory, not sneaking around behind France's back, probably took some of the fun out of it, but they soon got far enough northwest to be out of the Louisiana Territory.

Legal or not, the whole journey was quite an adventure. The wilderness was still uncharted, and it was full of dangerous animals and Native American tribes who weren't always happy to see them. Once, the explorers were spared from being killed only when their guide, Sacajawea, recognized one

U.S. TERRITORIAL ACQUISITIONS

The Louisiana Territory is the white part. Cost of the average backyard: well under a penny.

of the attackers as her brother. But even Sacajawea couldn't have saved them from a bear attack; it's a miracle that no one got eaten. Only one member of the party died, and that was because his appendix ruptured.

Lewis and Clark were certainly not the first explorers to visit the uncharted areas. Trappers had been passing through occasionally for years. In the Northwest, the expedition met a group of Native Americans who already knew several English words, such as "musket," "powder," "dagger," and a handful of minor swearwords. Lewis and Clark told all the tribes they met

that they had a new "great father," President Jefferson, in the East, and that now that America, not the British, controlled the land, they could look forward to peace, health, and prosperity. Obviously, predicting the future was not Lewis and Clark's strong point. If the tribes they encountered had known what was really in store, they would have probably called the explorers something a lot harsher than the minor swearwords they'd picked up from trappers.

Both Lewis and Clark kept carefully detailed journals to record—with very poor spelling—everything that

couraging the Native Americans to get organized and fight the Americans, but others just plain didn't like the British and wanted to kick them out of North America once and for all, even if the United States had to invade Canada to get rid of the last of them.

At the time, America wasn't really set up for a war. The national army only had about twelve thousand soldiers, and was not well organized. But in July of 1812, a band of them invaded Canada, aiming to take it over. They got their butts kicked. There is nothing more embarrassing than losing a fight to Canada.[22]

And so the war began, but neither side really seemed that enthusiastic about it. England was too busy fighting against the French, as usual, to put much effort into a war with America, and America just didn't seem up to the challenge. Americans were also worried about the pirates of Barbary again, since they weren't following the terms of the treaty at *all* (something that the states probably should have guessed would happen when they made a deal with pirates). The United States only had a handful of major victories in the war: a few in naval battles that didn't really help much in the long run, and

Napoléon. Would you buy a used tract of land from this man?

happened, and they made note of every new plant and animal they came across. The journals coined more than a thousand new terms and set America up for the great taming of the wilderness and expansion of the country in the coming decades.

THE WAR OF 1812

Few people today know what the War of 1812—America's second war with the British—was all about. But few people knew in 1812, either. Some Americans were upset that the British had been en-

---

22 Except in hockey, of course. And curling. Those Canadians are fierce at curling.

one big one at the Battle of New Orleans in 1814, which took place two weeks after the treaty ending the war had been signed. Oops!

Today, there are exactly four reasons anybody ever talks about the War of 1812:

1. It's fun to make fun of the Battle of New Orleans.

2. During the war, shipments into Troy, New York, were labeled "U.S.," which people jokingly claimed meant that they were for Uncle Sam, after Samuel Wilson, an army inspector. The image of Uncle Sam caught on, and to this day you see a lot of people dressed up in a striped hat, blue jacket, and silly-looking beard making fools of themselves on the Fourth of July and in used-car commercials.[23]

3. The burning of the White House, which happened when the British managed to take over Washington for about a day in 1814. They burned most of the public buildings, but a hurricane forced them to leave the city before they even had time to paint mustaches on all of the portraits in the Capitol.

4. "The Star-Spangled Banner," America's more-or-less unsingable national anthem, was written during the

This painting of Commodore Oliver Hazard Perry's victory over the British fleet in the War of 1812 shows that Washington's revolution against boat safety rules had been entirely successful.

war. The author, Francis Scott Key, was observing the British naval bombardment of Fort McHenry and managed to see that the American flag was

Uncle Sam: "Pull my finger!" ✶

---

23 Well, this is one theory as to where the Uncle Sam thing started. There are many more.

William Hull, the general who invaded Canada. Only a presidential pardon saved him from being shot as a sentence for cowardice. He *does* sort of look like a wuss. ✷

✷ ✷ ✷ ✷ ✷ ✷ ✷ ✷ ✷ ✷

such popular songs of 1931 as "Smile, Darn Ya, Smile," "When Yuba Plays the Rhumba on the Tuba," and "Monkey Blues." We here at the Smart Aleck's Guide would really prefer to start our ball games with a rousing chorus of "Monkey Blues," but you can't have everything.

America didn't exactly lose the War of 1812, but nobody really won it. In December of 1814, a treaty was signed that ended the war without actually resolving any of the issues that started it. Both sides were just sick of the whole thing. This is actually how most wars, labor disputes, and marriages have been settled throughout history.

News of the treaty didn't reach New Orleans right away, though. Two weeks after the end of the war, the British attacked New Orleans. Even though they were hopelessly outnumbered, Americans decisively won the battle. Hundreds of British troops were killed or wounded, but America lost only a few dozen soldiers. Since the war was already over, it didn't really count for anything, but General Andrew Jackson, who commanded the army, became a national hero.

THE END OF AN ERA

Years after Jefferson left office, Jefferson and Adams made up and began a long series of letters in which they

still waving only because of the light from the rockets and bombs exploding near it. The next day, he wrote a poem about this on the back of a letter he had been carrying in his pocket. Key's brother-in-law noticed that you could sing the poem, with some difficulty, to the tune of a popular drinking song of the day called "To Anacreon in Heaven" and had some copies printed up with singing instructions. The song caught on, and years later, in 1931, President Herbert Hoover declared it the national anthem, choosing it over reflected on all they'd accomplished. The letters were carefully preserved, as both men knew that future American historians would see a final conversation between two men who had started the country as priceless. Historians agree that this was rather arrogant, but they're still glad to have the letters.

John Adams died on July 4, 1826, fifty years after July 4, 1776, which, by then, was known as Independence Day. History records his last words as "Thomas Jefferson survives," but, in reality, the last word was so slurred as to be impossible to understand. His actual last words were "Thomas Jefferson sssrmhrfffs." Given how wrinkled he must have been by then, we daresay that the whole scene was probably a lot like that scene where Yoda dies saying "There is . . . another . . . Sky . . . walk . . . er" in *Return of the Jedi.* Those who were present decided that he was going for "survives," but for all we know, he might have been saying "Thomas Jefferson smells" or even "Thomas Jefferson still owes me five bucks."

And what Adams didn't know, of course, was that Thomas Jefferson *didn't* survive—he had died that same day, just a couple of hours earlier!

And what neither of them knew, or probably cared about, was that one other signer of the Declaration was also

John Adams as he appeared when he got really old.

still alive. Lonely old Charles Carroll was alive and well at his house in Maryland, separated from his wife, and, judging by his picture, so, so

Lonely ol' Chuck Carroll

The Battle of New Orleans. How would you like to have been one of the two thousand British soldiers who were killed or wounded by guys who looked like pirates because no one told them the war was over?

alone. He wouldn't die for another six long, lonely years.

PRESIDENT JACKSON

Andrew Jackson first ran for president in 1824. He won more electoral votes than anyone else but didn't actually get more than half. Today, he would have been given the presidency, no questions asked.[24] But in those days, when no one got more than 50 percent of the votes, the House of Representatives got to pick the president. They picked John Quincy Adams, the son of John Adams.

The public, however, felt that Jackson had been robbed, and he started campaigning for the 1828 election before Adams was even inaugurated.

The three-year campaign was the bitterest presidential campaign yet. During the election, Adams's supporters claimed that Jackson's mother was a prostitute, that his wife had multiple

---

[24] Lots of guys who didn't quite make it to 50 percent of the popular vote have won elections. Lincoln won with only 40 percent in 1860. Hayes got 48 percent in 1876—his opponent actually got 51 percent and still lost! Grover Cleveland got 46 percent in 1892. Wilson got 42 percent in 1912 and 49 percent in 1916. Truman got 49 percent in 1948. Richard Nixon won with 43 percent in 1968, Bill Clinton got 43 percent in 1992 (and 49 percent in 1996), and George W. Bush got 48 percent in 2000. See The Smart Aleck's Guide to How Badly Andrew Jackson and Samuel Tilden Got Screwed.

Two photographs of Andrew Jackson from the mid-1840s, by which time he was old and in pretty bad shape. He doesn't look so tough to us, but we're betting that anyone who called him four-eyes or pumpkin face still got hurt. ✶

✶ ✶

husbands, and that he had hanged several soldiers under his command (the last part, at least, was true). Jackson's supporters, meanwhile, claimed that Adams had hired a prostitute to entertain the visiting Russian czar. People apparently thought hanging soldiers was much more acceptable than hiring prostitutes for visitors, because Jackson won in a landslide.

Jackson considered himself a man of

EXPERIMENTS TO TRY AT HOME!

John Quincy Adams liked corn. Can a full ear of corn be flushed down the Quincy (toilet)? How about two ears? How many ears' worth can be flushed if you remove the kernels from the cob first? Our record is four (with cob), and our plumbing bill is $357. See if you can get yours higher! But, as with all of these experiments, don't blame us if you get in trouble.

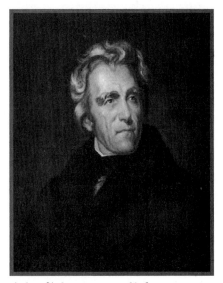

Andrew Jackson poses to get his face on money.

✶ 75 ✶

the people, and even invited the public to come have a meal at the White House now and then. He had the overwhelming approval of the rough-and-tumble frontiersmen, who saw Jackson as one of their fellow rednecks. After his inauguration, he invited his supporters into the White House for cake and ice cream, and the rowdy crowd trashed the place, turning chairs over, throwing food, and leaving mud everywhere. Even in the White House, American manners were nothing to

John Q. Adams: "Hurry up and take the stinkin' picture, cheese bag!" President John Quincy Adams was the first to install a toilet in the White House, which led to an all-too-brief craze for calling toilets Quincies. This 1848 photo was taken years after he left office, but makes him the earliest president to be photographed. ✗

brag about. No one and nothing was safe from flying poo.

Jackson was, in fact, just as rowdy as advertised. He was a big fan of dueling, fighting, and probably spitting. In 1835, he became the first president to survive an attempted assassination. Richard Lawrence, a mentally ill fellow who believed Jackson was keeping him from being king of England, among other things, walked right up to Jackson and attempted to fire two pistols at him. In what most people called a miracle, both pistols misfired, and Lawrence could only stand by, looking stupid, as Jackson's companions, including David "Davy" Crockett (who actually hated Jackson's guts but never turned down the chance to fight someone), grabbed him and held him down. Jackson reportedly turned around, picked up his cane, and proceeded to beat the crap out of Lawrence himself until his staff restrained him.

Today, Jackson is often considered one of our better presidents, but he's also remembered for being a serious jerk. All the rumors about his being a violent sort were true, and, as his supporters had expected, he gave many important jobs to people who weren't remotely qualified but happened to be his friends. This was nothing new, of course, but Jackson was a lot more open about it than most people had been. The unqualified friends Jackson relied on for advice became known as Jackson's Kitchen Cabinet, because, according to a popular joke, they had snuck into the White House through the kitchen door. In reality, Jackson would have happily let them in through the front door. As we've seen, he didn't even require hillbillies to scrape the crap off their shoes before coming in.

But the biggest smear on Jackson's record is his treatment of the Native Americans. He had been known as a particularly vicious Indian killer in his days as a general; his ruthlessness was legendary. Even when he wasn't fighting with them, he was known for kicking the natives off their land, then buying it himself at a bargain price.

As president, he took this practice a step further. By this time, most of the major tribes were living fairly peacefully, and Indian wars seemed like a thing of the past. Unfortunately for the tribes, they were living on valuable land, and Jackson apparently thought they had a lot of nerve to be living in spaces where white people could be growing cotton (with a little help from black slaves).

He called for five tribes to be removed from their land, and his supporters cheered his kind decision to simply kick them out of town instead

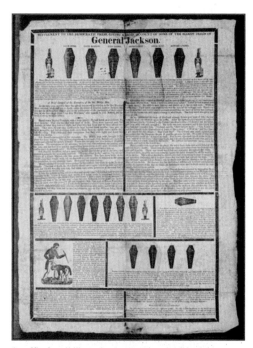

A coffin handbill, a sheet passed around by John Quincy Adams's supporters to make Jackson look like a murderous maniac. They didn't realize that many people wouldn't see this bloodlust as such a bad thing. See a bigger version on our Web page, www.smartalecksguide.com! ✻

of killing them. They delicately called the decision "removal." The Native Americans called it the Trail of Tears. In 1938, about fifteen thousand Cherokee Indians were removed from their land and forced to move to Indian Territory (which is now Oklahoma), and more than four thousand died on the way. Overall, about a hundred thousand Native Americans were forced to leave their land, and fifteen thousand died on the way west. Jackson never actually told anyone to remove the

DAVY CROCKETT

Born on a mountaintop in Tennessee, David Crockett actually claimed to have "kilt him a b'ar when he was only three." However, this claim was in an "autobiography" that he didn't write and that was almost certainly mostly nonsense.

After years as a trapper, soldier, and general roustabout, Crockett was elected to the House of Representatives in 1831. The Whig Party promptly began to promote him as their version of Andrew Jackson: a rough-and-ready guy who was just dumb enough to seem like a man of the people. There are a lot of differing stories about just how smart or dumb Crockett really was. Some say he was known as a quick wit and great speaker; others say that when he bragged about killing hundreds of bears, no one believed him. They believed he could kill bears, all right, but not that he could count up to the hundreds. To this day, no one seems to be sure whether Davy was a smart guy who pretended to be stupid because it was good for his image or was really just stupid. We here at the Smart Aleck's Guide lean toward "really just stupid."

The Whig Party hired a ghostwriter to write Crockett's autobiography, hoping to make him famous enough to run for president in 1836. Though the book did make Crockett famous, he failed to win reelection to Congress. According to his real auto-

biography, which he wrote (or at least approved) after the fake one came out, he finished his last speech before leaving Washington by saying, "You may all go to Hell, and I will go to Texas."[25] And that's what he did. In Texas, he and several others were offered a whopping 4,600 acres of land to help free Texas from Mexico, and, in short time, was killed at the Alamo. But legends about his life were so widespread that, more than one hundred years after his death, TV movies about him inspired millions of otherwise rational kids to go around wearing coonskin caps.

---

[25] Some say this was just what he *wished* he'd said. The story that he said it that night wasn't written down for thirty years, but he certainly said it over and over in the following months.

natives by force (he preferred forcing them to sign treaties), but he didn't seem to mind very much when some people removed them by force anyway.

Even back then, Americans were divided about this. The Indian Removal Act was rather popular with voters in the South but despised by voters in the North. The deepening tension between the North and South would soon reach the point of no return.

MANIFEST DESTINY

Even if President James K. Polk isn't remembered for anything other than his mullet, one of his favorite ideas, Manifest Destiny, gets a lot of space devoted to it in most American history books today. The basic concept of Manifest Destiny was that it was God's will that the United States expand all the way from the Atlantic to the Pacific and that anyone who wasn't white should get out of the way.

There were, however, those who believed that expanding westward was a bad idea, since it would mean incorporating Mexicans and other nonwhite people into the country. So the arguments for *and* against Manifest Destiny were both pretty much racist. In the end, the public was sold on the idea when they heard that California had gold in it.

Further stoking the people's passion for expansion was the Battle of the

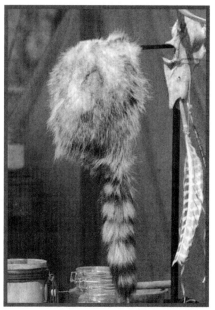

Hunters found these caps useful as camouflage, but nobody really thought they looked good. Davy Crockett only wore them as part of the image the Whig Party created for him, and Daniel Boone, the other guy known for wearing them, actually hated the things.

Alamo. In 1836, Texas was still a Mexican territory. Americans who had settled in Texas had already asked authorities in Mexico to let it become a U.S. territory, so that it could eventually become a state. There were many reasons for their wanting to be American, not Mexican, not the least of which was that the new Mexican constitution outlawed slavery, and many Texans wanted to keep it legal.

But Mexican president Antonio

López de Santa Anna refused to let Texas go, so the Americans there decided that Texas should secede from Mexico using force. An army of 187 men, including famed frontiersman Jim Bowie and former congressman and b'ar-killer Davy Crockett, tried for thirteen days to hold off an army of several thousand at the Alamo, a fort in San Antonio. It was a valiant effort, but in the end, all but three of the Americans were killed. To honor these brave fighters, Americans today have named a rental car company after the place of their slaughter. We bet they'd be thrilled!

Inspired by this story and shouting "Remember the Alamo," more armies of Texans managed to capture Santa Anna, who had left the presidency to lead the army, and send the Mexican armies into retreat. They then declared Texas to be a whole new republic and immediately applied for annexation into the United States.

Presidents Jackson and Martin Van Buren both declined to declare Texas part of America, fearing both war with Mexico and the kind of trouble that could result from adding another slave state to the country, which would have irritated the North. Tensions between the North and the South continued to grow.

THE MEXICAN–AMERICAN WAR

When President Polk proposed that Texas be made part of America, he claimed that he was not annexing Texas, but reannexing it, on the grounds that it had been a part of the Louisiana Purchase. The fact that it really wasn't didn't stop Congress from adopting his proposal. When guys with mullets, like Polk, spoke, Congress listened.

But declaring that the Republic of Texas was an American possession was essentially an act of war with Mexico (since Mexico still felt that Texas was theirs), and the Mexican-American War began right away. The U.S. government at the time didn't make any excuses for their attacks against Mexico; they didn't say they were fighting

James K. Polk: Business up front, party in the back, baby.

for Texan independence or oil or weapons of mass destruction or anything like that. They were pretty open about the fact that they were just fighting to take land away from Mexico.

The war was a short one, and was unpopular with a lot of people. Obscure figures like Abe Lincoln spoke out against it—like most Whigs (as he was then), he saw the war as nothing more than an attempt by the South to add more slave states to the Union, so that slave states would outnumber nonslave states. And Ulysses S. Grant, a soldier who would later become a Civil War hero and a forgettable president, called it "one of the most unjust (wars) ever waged by a stronger against a weaker nation." Henry David Thoreau, a noted philosopher of the day, went to jail after refusing to pay taxes that would have gone to support the war. That showed 'em.

The war lasted only two years, and America picked up a whole bunch more land—all of the Mexican possessions north of the Rio Grande, including California, Utah, and Nevada, as well as parts of several other present-day states. The government paid Mexico for the land, making it look like they'd bought it fair and square, but everyone knew they'd taken it by force.

Oregon Trail reenactors. Yep. They reenact this, too. Can't you just feel history coming alive?

THE OREGON TRAIL: AMERICA'S FAVORITE PLACE TO DIE OF DYSENTERY (EXCEPT FOR VALLEY FORGE, OF COURSE)

Now that America had enough land to stretch clear to the Pacific Ocean, people began to move west.

Actually, the great taming of the West had begun a few years earlier. In the mid-1840s, Oregon Fever broke out. This was the first, and last, recorded outbreak of this particular disease.

The government began to actively

Prospectors. There was gold in them thar hills, but, alas, not much soap. ✗

✗ ✗ ✗ ✗ ✗ ✗ ✗ ✗ ✗ ✗

encourage people to go west and begin to populate the vast stretches of available land, and thousands answered the call, as though they were setting off on a great adventure. Huge tracts of land were free for the taking on the frontier, and people who had never been able to improve their lot in life in the East were enchanted by the idea that all they had to do to become a rich landowner in the West was show up. Of course, they had to keep from dying of the trots first, but that seemed a small risk to take for all that free land.

Very few of those who traveled the trail were actually going to Oregon; some settled at various outposts along the way, and many others were going to California. The trail wasn't really a trail at all, in that there was no real path, road, or anything like that. It was really just a two-thousand-or-so-mile route that had been blazed by trappers in the preceding decades. People were constantly at risk of getting sick, running out of food, or being attacked by Native Americans who had already started populating the area long before.

But nothing—not adventure, or land, or Manifest Destiny, or the exciting chance to poop yourself to death—excited people like gold.

In 1848, gold was found at Sutter's Mill in California. Almost overnight, hundreds of thousands of settlers went to California, all hoping to strike it rich. San Francisco went from having a population of about a thousand in 1848 to twenty-five thousand in 1850.

By 1855, at which point most of the gold that you could get without enormous machinery to dig it up had already been found, something like three hundred thousand people had gone to California. Practically none of them got rich.

Other gold rushes brought settlers all over the West—most notably to Colorado and Nevada. Between 1845 and 1860, America added seven states.

As happy as this made the Manifest Destiny crowd, it also added fuel to the fire of the nation's most divisive issue—which, if you haven't figured it out already, was slavery. People were forced to decide whether these new states should allow slavery, and the old arguments started up all over again.

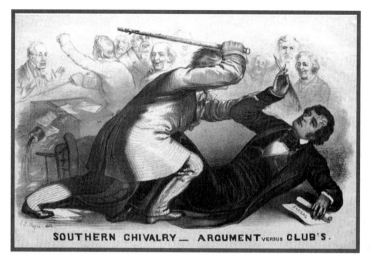

SOUTHERN CHIVALRY — ARGUMENT versus CLUB'S.

If Preston Brooks had had any class, he would have said "Sticks and stones may break my bones, but words will never hurt me" when Charles Sumner spoke out against slavery. Instead, he decided to demonstrate exactly what sticks and stones would do. Nice guy. Always had a smile for everyone.

SLAVERY

As more and more states joined the Union, and more and more senators became part of the government as a result, tension between the slaveholding Southern states and the nonslaveholding Northern states got worse and worse. Debates about whether slavery should expand into new territories went on endlessly.

It's only fair to note that these debates weren't just about the morality of slavery; in fact, they were more about economics. Northern businessmen had to compete with Southern businessmen, and slavery gave the Southern businessmen an advantage by providing them with free labor.

The debate raged throughout the nineteenth century, despite Congress's attempts to shove the issue aside. In 1817, when Missouri became a state, Congress agreed to the Missouri Compromise, which allowed slavery in Missouri but stipulated that it would be banned in any western territories north of the southern border of Missouri. This kept tension between slavery supporters and abolitionists from getting worse for the time being, but it also clearly defined the slavery issue as an issue of North versus South, and most people knew that it wouldn't solve the problem of slavery in America—it would only postpone it. It was like putting a Band-Aid on a bullet hole.

By the 1850s, the debate was getting violent. In 1856, a senator named

Harriet Beecher Stowe (above) wrote thirty books. She claimed that she didn't write the most famous one, *Uncle Tom's Cabin,* herself but that God wrote it through her. The novel, a tale of a runaway slave, opened people's eyes to just how bad slavery was, and deepened the division between the North and the South. When the war began, Lincoln is said to have called Stowe the "little woman who started this big war." She became one of the most successful writers of all time and spent her later years playing pranks on Mark Twain. Her favorite trick was to sneak up behind him and yell.

Charles Sumner made an antislavery speech before the Senate. Three days later, a South Carolina congressman named Preston Brooks considered challenging Sumner to a duel (which *always* solved every problem), then decided that it would be easier just to beat the crap out of Sumner with a cane. And that's what he did. While one of his friends held up a pistol to stop anyone from interfering, Brooks surprised Sumner by beating him so badly that it took him three years to recover. Brooks became a hero in the South. Some people today say that if every congressman were outfitted with a cane, C-SPAN would get a lot more exciting in a real hurry.

Further fanning the flames, Senator Stephen Douglas of Illinois introduced the Kansas-Nebraska Act in 1854. This repealed the Missouri Compromise and allowed new states to decide for themselves whether to allow slavery. Slaveholding states, which were determined to keep outnumbering nonslaveholding states so they could keep outvoting them, were not above sending militias to the new states to make sure they ended up allowing slavery.

The next president, James Buchanan, in part of the endless dance presidents in those days did trying to tiptoe around the issue, said that ending slavery was the Supreme Court's job. But in 1857, the Supreme Court handed down the Dred Scott decision, which stated that a man named Dred Scott was, as a slave, entitled to no more rights than a mule, or a horse, or any other piece of property. The ruling was terribly unpopular, at least in the North. Southerners seemed to think it was swell, and the tension between the regions got even worse.

In 1859, a man named John Brown decided that since the government had failed to solve the problem of slavery, he should do something about it himself. He was widely believed to have been completely insane, and the very fact that he thought he could end slavery with only an army of twenty-one people indicates that he must have been nuts at the very least.

In October of 1859, Brown and several of his followers—both white and black—made their first attack, a raid on Harpers Ferry, Virginia. They succeeded in taking over the federal arsenal there, but no slaves came forward to join them, and they were soon captured by the local militia, led by a young man named Robert E. Lee, who would soon be a Confederate general. Brown was quickly sentenced to hang.

Crazy though he may have been, Brown became a hero to abolitionists everywhere (who overlooked the fact that he had murdered several people) and a villain to the South, to whom he represented the North intruding on their way of life. His very existence made the tension between the North and the South even worse.

One of the spectators at Brown's execution was John Wilkes Booth, who later went on to be a famous actor, among other things. Also present was Thomas J. Jackson, later known as Stonewall Jackson, *another* future Confederate general, who brought a whole classroom full of military students to watch. This is the kind of field trip you probably couldn't get past the PTA

John Brown in 1856, before he really went off the deep end.

nowadays, but the symbolic significance of having Jackson, Lee, and Booth all present at the hanging of an abolitionist less than two years before the Civil War broke out is awfully tough to ignore. Of course, most of the people present thought that the conflict with Brown *was* the battle between the states that had been coming for years, and that his hanging would put an end to that whole business.

On the gallows, when he was about to be hanged, Brown said he was certain that slavery could "never be purged away but with blood," and that his own biggest mistake was to think it could be done with just a little bloodshed

85

John Brown in 1859. By this time, President Buchanan had put a price of $250 on John Brown's head. Brown responded by offering a reward of $2.50 for Buchanan's arrest. Where he got $2.50 to start with, Brown wouldn't say.

instead of an awful lot of it.

He may have been crazy, but he would soon be proven right.

A BATCH OF FORGETTABLE PRESIDENTS

You may never have heard of most of the presidents mentioned earlier in this chapter, and you can hardly be blamed for that. The nineteenth century was truly an era of forgettable presidents.

Martin Van Buren, who was made fun of for his sideburns back then, too.

There was hardly a memorable one (besides Lincoln) between Andrew Jackson and Theodore Roosevelt.

Andrew Jackson's successor, Martin Van Buren, is mostly remembered today for having really goofy sideburns. After Van Buren's first term, during which the economy nearly collapsed, the Whig Party, the Democratic Party's main rival in those days, nominated William Henry Harrison to run against him.

This campaign was the first that really resembled modern presidential campaigns, with big public rallies,

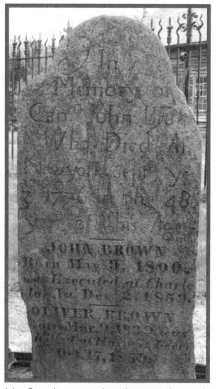

John Brown's grave, where he currently spends most of his time a-mouldering away.

songs, meetings, and slogans, which had been pretty much absent from earlier ones. In an attempt to cash in on Harrison's victory in a battle with an Indian confederacy at Tippecanoe, they made their slogan "Tippecanoe and Tyler, Too," which, oddly, didn't even mention Harrison's name, only the name of Tyler, the vice presidential candidate. Many people today recognize that slogan, but few know which president it refers to.[26]

In any case, the Whigs marketed Harrison as their version of Andrew Jackson, a rough-and-tumble man of the people. They claimed that Harrison had been born in a log cabin and was poorly educated, and that he enjoyed fighting and drinking hard cider (*just* the kind of background you

want in a president, right?). Meanwhile, they made Martin Van Buren out to be a wuss who perfumed his sideburns and rode around in fancy English carriages. We suspect that if he *did* perfume his enormous sideburns, people who had to stand near him probably thanked him for it. Bathing still hadn't really caught on as a national pastime.

Van Buren was actually not the

---

[26] And many only *think* they recognize it. They're thinking of *Winnie the Pooh and Tigger Too*, a 1974 Disney featurette.

William Henry Harrison, looking like he did on Day Thirty-two. ✪

wimp the Whigs made him out to be, though, and his slogan had more staying power: one of the clubs to promote him was called the Democratic O.K. Club, with O.K. standing first for Old Kinderhook (after his boyhood home in Kinderhook, New York). Then people started joking that it stood for "oll korrect." Van Buren got his butt kicked in the election, but the term "okay" survives.[27]

---

[27] This is one of the more common theories, anyway, though the term existed before then. The exact origin of the word "OK" is sort of a holy grail for linguists.

President John Tyler: Party machine! ✪

It certainly survived longer than William Henry Harrison. Harrison actually was a rich, well-educated guy— not the poor, rowdy simpleton his supporters had made him out to be— and decided to show people this side of himself by making a very brainy inaugural speech that went on for two hours. But to show people that, even at the age of sixty-seven, he was as strong and tough as ever, he refused to wear a coat while making the speech. He caught pneumonia and spent most of his presidency sick in bed, dying only thirty days into his term. Given just how forgettable presidents were in those days, you might say he was the only one smart enough to quit while he was ahead.

John Tyler, the vice president, took over, and proceeded to do very little that anyone remembers nowadays.

Millard Fillmore: In 1856, a few years after his short term as president, he ran and lost as the Know-Nothing Party's candidate. His great-grandfather was once kidnapped by pirates.

Zachary P. Taylor with his pants pulled *allll* the way up, like a big boy.

Next up was James K. Polk, who was widely unpopular, except that he worked like crazy and brought more land to the country than any other president—even Jefferson. Then came Zachary P. Taylor, who died about a year into his term, leading Millard Fillmore to take over until Franklin Pierce was elected a few years later. Few people today have ever heard of these guys unless there's a school or street named after them somewhere nearby.

Franklin Pierce is perhaps remembered for one thing today: being a lousy president. In fact, he's one of historians' favorite targets. Those of us who get sick of trying to find shocking things to say about Lincoln and Washington in order to make a buck sometimes start looking around for *truly* bad presidents to bad-mouth instead, and Franklin Pierce makes for a fine punching bag. A lifelong alcoholic who eventually sided with the Confederacy during the Civil War, Pierce seems to have been elected mainly because he was handsome and charming.

During the election, his party's motto was "We Polked You in 1844,

Voters were hypnotized by Pierce's amber waves of hair. ✗

Pierce's opponent in 1852, Winfield Scott, is possibly the only guy in history who looks even sadder than lonely ol' Charles Carroll in photos. He was nicknamed Old Fuss and Feathers. ✗

We'll Pierce You in 1852!"[28] Ew. We here at the Smart Aleck's Guide think that's probably the worst slogan ever. It must have worked, though, because Pierce won twenty-seven of the thirty-one states that were in the union at the time. By most accounts, Pierce was a decent guy once you got to know him, but that doesn't always translate to being a decent president.

At the time Pierce took office, things were fairly calm, slavery-wise; various compromises were keeping people from making too much noise about the issue. But with Pierce came the Kansas-Nebraska Act, and the fights started anew. His support for the act didn't make Pierce as popular as he'd hoped in the end, as the country was thrown headlong into new disagreements over slavery. Eventually, he became so unpopular that his own party decided not to nominate him for a second term, no matter how handsome he was.

Next in office was James Buchanan, who is at least moderately memorable for his cowardly (albeit politically shrewd) refusal to take a stance on

---

28 Everyone loves to complain about how campaigns rely on focus groups to pick their slogans these days, but at least they keep us from having to hear slogans this bad. See *The Smart Aleck's Guide to Sloganeering*.

As disappointed as historians are with Buchanan, he appears to have been just as disappointed in himself, judging by this dour portrait.

slavery. He is also remembered for being the only president never to marry, and, partly because of speculation as to *why* he never married, most articles about him today seem to focus not on his presidency (which is generally thought to be one of the two or three worst yet) but on the theory that he may have been gay. Certainly he was rumored to be at the time: he referred to his live-in companion, William Rufus King (Pierce's vice president), as his better half, and at least a couple of people referred to King as Mrs. Buchanan.

People will never agree on whether or not Buchanan was gay, of course, but they do generally agree that he was

one of the worst presidents, largely because he chose to ignore slavery at a time when arguments about the issue were getting more and more violent. But from another point of view, Buchanan's main job in office was the same as that of the last few presidents who had come before him: delaying the Civil War. He did a halfway decent job of it; states didn't begin to secede until the last months of his term, after his successor, Abe Lincoln, had been elected. That Buchanan couldn't talk these states out of leaving during his last months in office is probably his biggest failure.

SOME OF THE STUFF WE MISSED

James Madison (above): The principal author of the Constitution, later a forgettable president in the relatively slow era between Jefferson and Jackson.

Bleeding Kansas: A warm-up for the

Civil War in which pro- and anti-slavery forces fought to make Kansas a slave state.

The Creek War: A war with the Creek Nation (a Native American tribe) that was started in part over the symbolic significance of an earthquake.

Nat Turner: A slave who led a rebellion somewhat more successful than John Brown's.

Alexis de Tocqueville: A French traveler who wrote a book about Americans and their habits. His verdict: they stank.

The Great Triumvirate: Three senators (Henry Clay, James Calhoun, and Daniel Webster) who dominated the Senate in the 1830s and 1840s.

Fries's Rebellion: A revolt against taxes that involved farmers attacking tax collectors with hot water. John Fries was sentenced to hang for treason but was pardoned by John Adams.

The Era of Good Feelings: The period from 1815 to 1824, when the major political parties didn't fight much and when foreign affairs could be pretty well ignored since there were no wars.

The Monroe Doctrine: An 1823 doctrine that stated that Europe shouldn't colonize or interfere with newly independent nations in the Western Hemisphere and that the United States would put up a fight if they tried.

The Tariff of 1828: Raised the price of goods imported from Europe to help keep American products more affordable, and set off decades of boring tariff disputes.

END-OF-CHAPTER QUESTIONS

MULTIPLE CHOICE

1. Who was better-looking, Lewis or Clark?
   a. Lewis.
   b. Clark.
   c. Your mom.
(ANSWER: C.)

2. Who would you have voted for in 1800?
   a. Adams.
   b. Jefferson.
   c. Burr.
   d. William Henry Harrison.
(ANSWER: IF YOU SAID A, YOU'RE A FEDERALIST. YOU BELIEVE IN GOVERNMENT BY THE RICH (YA BIG JERK). IF YOU SAID B OR C, YOU'RE A DEMOCRATIC REPUBLICAN—YOU EXIST MAINLY TO OPPOSE THE FEDERALISTS. IF YOU SAID D, YOU DIDN'T READ THIS CHAPTER VERY CAREFULLY. EITHER THAT OR YOU LIKE YOUR POLITICIANS LIKE YOU LIKE YOUR GOLDFISH: DEAD AFTER ABOUT A MONTH.)

3. What was "54-40 or Fight"?
   a. A slogan popular with people who wanted to absorb Oregon into the United States.

b. A football play developed by Knute Rockne.

c. A popular tavern song about whoring and fighting.

d. Plan B for getting that stupid locker open.

(ANSWER: A. BUT WE DIDN'T COVER THAT. HAVE YOU BEEN READING OTHER HISTORY BOOKS BEHIND OUR BACK? 'CAUSE WE KNOW WHERE YOU LIVE!)

4. Which of the following presidents had the most impact on the future of America?

a. Harrison.

b. Tyler.

c. Fillmore.

d. Polk.

(ANSWER: OH, LET'S SAY . . . A. HIS WISDOM IS REFLECTED EVERY TIME SOMEONE SAYS, "PUT ON A COAT, OR YOU'LL CATCH YOUR DEATH!" ACTUALLY, THAT'S NOT HIS WISDOM, IT'S JUST WHAT WE LEARNED FROM HIS STUPIDITY.)

5. What was the cause of the War of 1812?

a. Boredom.

b. A need for a new catchy tune.

c. A pickle tariff.

d. That's no pickle tariff, that's my wife!

(ANSWER: A, FOR ALL PRACTICAL PURPOSES. PEOPLE WERE JUST KINDA SNIFFING AROUND FOR A GOOD FIGHT WITH THE BRITISH. WE DID GET A CATCHY TUNE OUT OF IT, THOUGH—"THE BATTLE OF NEW ORLEANS," WHICH WON JOHNNY HORTON, THE SINGIN' HISTORY TEACHER, A GRAMMY IN 1959. WE ALSO GOT "THE STAR-SPANGLED BANNER," OF COURSE, BUT WE HERE AT THE SMART ALECK'S GUIDE DON'T CONSIDER THAT VERY CATCHY.)

ESSAY

Today, there are people called isolationists who believe that America should leave the rest of the world alone, mind our own business, and not let anyone new into the country. Many of them favor building a wall to keep Mexicans out. But given that the Mexican-American War was about the *least* isolationist thing we've ever done, shouldn't they instead favor giving Texas back to Mexico? Why or why not? Note: "Because it's inconvenient" is not a very good answer.

MNEMONICS!

Need a way to remember that the post–Van Buren presidents were Harrison, Tyler, Polk, Taylor, Fillmore, Pierce, and Buchanan?

Just remember: H.T.P.T.F.P.B. To make it easier, you can come up with a sentence using words that start with those letters. A couple of examples:

HAVE THIS PICKLE,
THEN *FIVE* PICKLES, BUDDY!
OR
HAVE TO PUNCH THAT FANCY-PANTS
BUTLER!

(Note: As far as remembering that Tyler comes before Taylor, or Polk before Pierce, you're on your own, suckers.)

ASSIGNMENT ALERT!

Write a song about mouldering. We may post a few of them on www.smart alecksguide.com!

CHAPTER

THE CIVIL WAR:
AMERICA'S CHANGING BODY

> "When a stupid man is doing something he is ashamed of, he always declares it is his duty."
> —George Bernard Shaw

> "Duty is the sublimest word in the English language."
> —Robert E. Lee

> "The Civil War was like America's puberty. The country was growing rapidly, things were getting hairy down South, and blood was starting to flow down there."[29]—Brian Eddlebeck, a real historian

INTRODUCTION

You might not want to listen to anything your teacher—or anyone else—says about the Civil War. Historians don't agree on anything about it, and many of them get really upset if you don't agree with their take on the whole thing. In fact, you're about as likely to get in a fight *talking* about the Civil War as you would have been fighting in it. When we say the fundamental cause was slavery, some people are going to shout and call us revisionists, which is how historians insult each other. On the other hand, if we said it *wasn't* about slavery, historians who say it *was* would call us revisionists. See how this works?

History is usually written by the winners, but in the case of the Civil War, a lot of it has been written by the losers. These days, you hear people say that Robert E. Lee was the best general, or even the best human, who ever lived (he wasn't), and that Grant, the most famous Northern general, was a drunken jerk and a fan of slavery (he wasn't, though he didn't turn out to be much of a president). You might even hear that slavery was only a minor reason for the war, if it was a cause at all. In fact, it was absolutely the primary cause of the conflict.

However, there were many factors that combined to cause the Civil War. No war is caused by just one thing, and the North began fighting in the war to preserve the Union, not to end slavery. The South was worried that it no longer mattered in the country—the election of Lincoln showed that a person could become president without a single vote from the South, which had Southerners understandably worried about what would happen to the Southern states in the future.

---

[29] Come on. You didn't really think you were getting through a whole YA nonfiction book without something about "your changing body," did you?

All of this was made more complicated by the fact that many of the soldiers probably didn't know exactly what they were fighting for in the first place. Many, if not most, just joined whichever army was forming closest to their house. Different soldiers fought for different reasons—there were "good guys" and "bad guys" on both sides.

And the reasons for fighting continued to change over the course of the war. The Union didn't start out fighting to end slavery (at least not specifically), but it soon became an official goal of the war. And by the end of the whole thing, the Confederacy might have been willing to give up on slavery if it meant that they could be recognized as an independent country by England and France. It's hard to imagine now, but in those days the South was really desperate for approval from the French.

We can at least safely say that whatever reasons each soldier had for fighting, the result of the war was that slavery was abolished. After years and years during which presidents had to avoid the issue, lest they lose all support from Southern voters, all the tension between the two regions finally boiled over into a war that lasted four years, pitted brother against brother, and cost six hundred thousand lives. If the war hadn't happened, slavery would probably have stayed legal for

Can you figure out which Confederate soldier was fighting for slavery, and which was fighting for independence or states' rights? Before you answer, get ready to duck. No matter what you say, some historian is probably going to throw a folding chair at you.

decades; most of the presidents who came right after Lincoln were as forgettable as the ones who came right before him. It's doubtful that any of them would have had the stones to take on slavery.

ABRAHAM LINCOLN

Born to two uneducated farmers in a one-room log cabin, Abraham Lincoln

"Whenever I hear anyone arguing for slavery, I feel a strong impulse to see it tried on him personally."
—Abraham Lincoln

STUPID HATS OF HISTORY:
THE STOVEPIPE

Stovepipe hats, more refined, right-angled versions of the capotain, were useful if you needed to disguise yourself as a chimney, and doubled as a convenient place to hide stuff! ✶

grew up to be on the five-dollar bill *and* the penny. While some of the things he said about race would sound pretty backward and racist today, in his own day they were considered dangerously liberal.

Entering politics at the age of twenty-three, he served several terms in the Illinois state legislature. In the 1840s, he served in the House of Representatives as a member of the Whig Party, but his vocal opposition to the Mexican-American War (which was thought of as a really keen war by many people at the time) ruined his career. Then as now, speaking against *any* war could get you accused of being "unpatriotic." He ran for the Senate in 1858 against Stephen Douglas and lost, but the reputation he built in the process led him to win the Republican Party nomination and the presidency in 1860.

While he claimed to have no plans to end slavery (not because he liked it but because he didn't think he had the power to do so; it's not like the president could just snap his fingers and make slavery disappear), his personal antislavery sentiments were well known. This made him so hated in the South that he wasn't even on the ballot in most Southern states in the election, and won only two out of 996 counties in the Southern states in which he was on the ballot. Overall, he won only 40 percent of the popular vote—but he got a lot more votes than anyone else who ran that year.

Even before he was inaugurated, there

INTERESTING FACT

Not all Southerners favored secession; in fact, some historians hold that *most* Southern citizens didn't want their states to leave the Union or go to war. It was the politicians who made the decisions, and they never put it to a vote among the electorate.

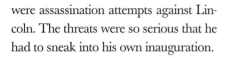

were assassination attempts against Lincoln. The threats were so serious that he had to sneak into his own inauguration.

THE STATES BEGIN TO SECEDE

Before all the westward expansion, there had been a decent balance between slave states and nonslave states. But as more nonslave states were admitted to the Union, slave states were worried about the future.

Furthermore, the arguments between pro- and antislavery forces had been getting more and more violent. In addition to the John Brown and Charles Sumner fiascos, when Kansas was admitted to the Union, proslavery militias stormed in to establish Kansas

THE CONFEDERATE CONSTITUTION

In early 1861, the Confederate government quickly drew up their own constitution. For the most part, they just used the same one as the Union, with only a few major changes. Funnily enough, given all the fuss you hear about states' rights, they didn't actually give the states more rights. Arguably, the states were even *less* powerful than they had been when they were in the United States.

They did include two things the writers of the U.S. Constitution didn't: they mentioned God (perhaps hoping to get on the big guy's good side) and included the following: "Article I, Section 9:4: No bill of attainder, ex post facto law, or law denying or impairing the right of property in negro slaves shall be passed."

The Confederate cabinet: they didn't last long as a country, but they knew a thing or two about lookin' good. There are plenty of stereotypes about hillbilly plantation owners, but most Southern landowners were actually refined and highly educated. After all, their light workload around the plantation left them plenty of time for studying.

as a slave state in battles that became sort of a warm-up for the war. People in the South were fearful that another guy like John Brown might have better luck in starting slave revolts, and state militias began forming to protect slaveholders from their slaves.

The election of Lincoln, who said the nation could not remain "half slave and half free," made the future seem even bleaker to the slave states. Lincoln didn't say he was going to end slavery, but his election made it look like abolition could be waiting around the corner and there wasn't much they could do to stop it. South Carolina announced that they were seceding from the Union only days after Lincoln was elected. Others followed close behind.

Supposedly, on his way out the door, President Buchanan shook hands with

Adam poses with Abraham Lincoln in 2007 after just three short classes in resurrecting the dead at the Shaker Heights Institute of Technology—don't delay, act now and call them toll-free for information that can start you on your way to an exciting new career in necromancy, auto mechanics, accounting, or restaurant management!

the newly inaugurated President Lincoln and said, "My dear sir, if you are as happy on entering the White House as I

No one died in the battle of Fort Sumter, but a cannon misfired during the surrender ceremony and ended up killing a Union soldier. Oops!

shall feel [on leaving it], you are a happy man indeed." But Lincoln wasn't a happy man, and the fact that several states responded to his election by dropping out of the country can't have been good for the poor guy's self-esteem.

While Lincoln had a reputation for partying (he enjoyed a good dirty joke), he suffered from crippling anxiety and depression. Some even say he was suicidal. This surely stemmed from a mental disorder, but you'd probably be depressed, too, if entire states hated you so much that they were willing to secede from the country to get away from you.

The eleven seceding states quickly formed their own country, the Confederate States of America. They picked Richmond, Virginia, as their capital, wrote up a constitution, and elected Jefferson Davis, who had most recently been a senator from Mississippi, as their first president.

One of the more popular ideas in the North at the time was to just let the Southern states go. If the South seceded today (and some people there still occasionally threaten to when they've had a few drinks), the war would probably be fought with lawyers, not soldiers.

It's possible that that's what might have happened then, too, if things had played out just a little bit differently.

Lincoln was determined not to attack the South unless they attacked first, and Jefferson Davis, the Confederate president, didn't want to attack first, either. But, very early on, the Confederacy decided to start taking over U.S. Army forts in the South by force, and Lincoln responded by fighting back.

ALEXANDER STEPHENS: CSA VICE PRESIDENT, RACIST

This is a dangerous chapter for us to write. Saying that the war was about slavery, even partially, is sort of sending a call to arms to Confederate supporters (and there are *lots* of them still around) to harass us and call us names. We're gonna get a lot of mail telling us that the war was really about tariff disputes, cultural differences, states' rights, or other such things. But we're pretty comfortable saying that the cause of the war all boiled down to slavery. Know how we know this? Because the Confederate states said so themselves! All four of the states that issued Articles of Secession (reasons they were leaving the Union) mentioned slavery early on—two mentioned it in the first sentence. Georgia's articles mentioned slavery more than thirty times! All of them made it abundantly clear that the reason they wanted to leave the Union was to protect the institution of slavery.

More quotes:

- "[Slavery] was the immediate cause . . . of our present revolution. Our new government is founded upon . . . the great truth that the negro is not equal to the white man."—Alexander Stephens, Confederate vice president (who was actually a bit progressive, in that he *did* think slave marriages should be recognized)

- "It is abolition doctrine . . . the very doctrine which the war was commenced to put down."—*The North Carolina Standard,* 1865, on the idea of allowing black soldiers to join the Confederate army
- "What did we go to war for, if not to protect our property?"—Robert Hunter, Virginia senator

See the Articles of Secession themselves on www.smartalecksguide.com if you don't believe us!

The Battle of Bull Run. Not pictured: picnickers.

The first battle of the war was over control of Fort Sumter, a Union fort in South Carolina. Davis had sent a few guys to D.C. to offer to pay for the fort so the army could take it peacefully, but the Confederates attacked before a deal could be made. The fort wasn't very well supplied, and it had been built to defend against attacks from the sea. The cannons faced the water and couldn't fire on invaders coming in from behind on land. After a thirty-four-hour battle, the fort's commander surrendered to the Confederacy.

One day later, Abraham Lincoln called for seventy-five thousand volunteers to form an army and put what he assumed would be a swift end to the rebellion.

Lincoln asked Robert E. Lee to command the Union forces. However, two days before, Lee's home state of Virginia had seceded from the Union. Lee was a loyal American who privately opposed slavery, but his real loyalty was to his home state of Virginia. Instead of taking over the Union army, he resigned and joined the Confederate forces.

Most people in the North expected that the war would be a short one; the volunteers Lincoln requested were only asked to serve for ninety days. Few believed that the Confederacy was capable of putting up much of a fight. After all, most of America's natural and manufactured resources were in the North—the value of all goods made in the South added up to about a quarter of the value of goods manufactured in New York alone. The North had a population of about 21 million, while the South had only 9 million—and 3.5 million of those were slaves, who weren't allowed to join the Confederate army. About the only thing the Confederacy had that the Union didn't was cotton, and you just can't beat an army by throwing cotton at it.

Still, the Confederacy took Lincoln by surprise. The first year was disastrous for the Union, and by the end of the whole thing, the Confederacy had managed to stay in the game for four years, which was a lot longer than anyone had expected. One of the great lessons of history is that sometimes a small, determined army can beat a

HELPFUL HINTS

If you ever get roped into being in one of those Civil War reenactments, try to get to play one of the picnickers. It may be the worst picnic you ever attend, but it'll beat being in the battle. And you'll still be "authentic"—probably more so than the battle reenactors, who tend to take so long to get shot that you'd think everyone on both sides had learned to shoot from the stormtroopers in *Star Wars*.

much larger one—like when America defeated England in the Revolution, just over four score years before.

THE BATTLE OF BULL RUN

The first *real* battle of the Civil War was the Battle of Bull Run, which was not far from Washington, D.C. Most people didn't think this would be the first *battle* of the war; they thought it would be the *whole war,* all by itself. Various well-to-do people from Washington came with picnic baskets in hand, intending to watch the short war while enjoying a sandwich. It turned out to be a pretty crappy picnic.

Union General Irvin McDowell didn't quite think his army was ready for a battle, but Lincoln had assured him that the Confederates weren't really ready, either, and encouraged him to attack them near Manassas, Virginia.

The battle was a disaster for the Union. Instead of wiping out the rebellion in one quick fight, the Union forces were sent fleeing in disarray. The picnickers raced back to their carriages and immediately created a traffic jam in the scramble to get back into Washington. Northern Virginia traffic hasn't improved for one minute since.

THE BATTLE OF SHILOH

Losing faith in General McDowell, Lincoln gave command of the Union

General McClellan doing what he did best: sitting on his butt.

army, the Army of the Potomac, to General George McClellan, who proceeded to sit on his butt for the better part of a year, afraid to do anything with the army. Some said he was just waiting around to run for president in 1864 and wanted to make sure Lincoln looked bad so he'd be easy to beat in an election. This was pretty much true: McClellan would go on to be the Democratic nominee. Lincoln kicked his butt, taking more than 55 percent of the vote and twenty-two out of twenty-five states.

Most of the next eight months after the Battle of Bull Run was very quiet. There were minor skirmishes here and there, but no major fighting. Lincoln, who wanted to get the whole thing over with, was furious.

But the tide began to turn. In February, Union forces under Ulysses S. Grant, who had just been made a general, captured Fort Henry and Fort Donelson, then took control of Nashville, Tennessee. These were the first major Confederate losses of the war.

In early April of that year, Confederate forces under General Albert Sidney Johnston launched an attack on Grant's army, with the intention of driving them away from the Tennessee River and into the swamp. The resulting battle, the Battle of Shiloh, became the bloodiest America had ever fought. More soldiers died in the two-day battle than had died in all previous American wars combined.

The night before the battle, as Grant's men camped out, General P.G.T. Beauregard warned General Johnston that attacking Grant's army was a bad idea. After all, though the Confederate army was about the same size as Grant's, they were equipped largely with antique muskets, and they had been acting about as sneaky as a marching band—they'd been test-firing the guns and making all the noises that armies tend to make for three days.

But it turned out that Grant's army had no idea that the Confederates were so close, and they were totally surprised to find themselves attacked at six o'clock in the morning. Early on, it looked as though the Confederate attackers might

😊

People who say the war *wasn't* about slavery have quotes of their own to throw at us, including the following, which shows up on dozens of Web pages and is repeated by countless history teachers and professors:

"If I thought this war was to abolish slavery, I would resign my commission and offer my sword to the other side."–Ulysses S. Grant

When you see a quote like this—from someone living or dead—on any Web page or book that doesn't cite its sources (like, say, this one), you should try to find a source for the quote before you go around repeating it. Grant never actually said anything like this; it was attributed to him later by people who made it up to make Grant look bad when he ran for president. The *New York Times* wrote a whole piece on the myth as early as 1872—see it on www.smartalecksguide.com!

camps could hear the screams of soldiers dying in the fields between the two armies. Then, just when many were probably wondering how things could get any worse, a thunderstorm rolled in.

In the midst of the rain, Sherman walked up to Grant and said, "Well, Grant, we've had the devil's own day, haven't we?" Grant looked up and casually said "Yes. Yes, we have. Lick 'em tomorrow, though." We're a little bit wary (for once) about saying anything smart-alecky about a bloody battle, so if you want a joke about the Union soldiers licking things, you'll have to make up your own.

actually defeat the Union troops.

Union Brigadier General William Tecumseh Sherman frantically tried to rally his troops. In the process, he himself was wounded twice and had three horses shot out from under him.

Meanwhile, General Johnston—who at the time was thought to be the best general the South had—was shot in the leg and quickly bled to death. Beauregard took over command of the army. By dusk, the Confederates were jubilant, feeling that they'd won the battle. The next morning, they planned to march in and finish Grant's army off.

It had been one heck of a rough day, and the night wasn't pleasant, either, even for the optimistic Confederate army. All night long, people in both

Ulysses S. Grant had a beard that would make Chuck Norris himself weep with envy. Grant hated military music and claimed he only recognized two tunes. When asked which ones, he said, "One is 'Yankee Doodle.' The other isn't."

Beauregard, meanwhile, sent a telegram to Jefferson Davis announcing "a complete victory." He was ignoring warnings that reinforcements were on their way to help the Union.

The next morning, with reinforcements arriving, the Union had an army of forty-five thousand, with fresh supplies and ammo. The Confederates were down to about thirty thousand and were low on supplies. Beauregard woke up planning to lead an attack but found, to his surprise, that the Union was attacking him.

At the end of that day, the Union had regained the ground they had been forced to cede the day before, and the Confederate army was in retreat. Neither side had really gained any ground, and there were more than twenty-three thousand casualties. Both sides were horrified at how bloody the battle had been—and neither side realized that there were three more years of similar battles still to come.

THE EMANCIPATION PROCLAMATION

In September of 1862, five months after the Battle of Shiloh, the Union attacked General Lee's army in the Battle of Antietam, a one-day battle that was nearly as bloody as Shiloh. While nobody really won, General Lee had to abandon his plans to invade Maryland,

RATIFYING THE AMENDMENT

Three-fourths of the states needed to ratify the Thirteenth Amendment to end slavery before it could be added to the Constitution. It became part of the law of the land within a year after being proposed, but some states that rejected it at the time didn't get around to ratifying it until much later. Kentucky didn't ratify the amendment until 1976, and Mississippi didn't get around to it until 1995!

which made it look like a Union victory.

This "victory" gave the Union a morale boost, and gave Abraham Lincoln the confidence and support he needed to announce the Emancipation Proclamation.

Prior to the war, when called upon to put an end to slavery, Lincoln had claimed that he didn't actually have the authority to do so in peacetime—indeed, many argued that it would have been unconstitutional. However, the special powers granted to him in wartime gave him some extra authority, and on September 17, 1862, he issued the famous proclamation. It stated that all slaves in territories that the Union took over from that day on were free and that unless seceding states rejoined the Union within a year, the slaves there would all be declared free. This proclamation didn't actually end slavery; in fact, it didn't free *any* slaves right away. But it was probably the most Lincoln felt he could get away with.

Regardless of what it *didn't* do, the proclamation did accomplish some major objectives. For one thing, it allowed black soldiers to join the Union army, and about two hundred thousand of them did, making the army even more

✷ ✷

FREDERICK DOUGLASS

Born a slave, Frederick Douglass escaped (which he referred to as "stealing himself") and became one of the most powerful speakers and writers in American history. He held opinions about equality that were way ahead of their time; even most people who argued against slavery wouldn't start to argue for social equality between races for decades after slavery ended. Douglass argued not only for racial equality, social and otherwise, but for equal rights for women and everyone else.

During the Civil War, Douglass helped convince Congress to allow black soldiers to join the army, which turned out to be a very wise move. Afterward, in 1872, he was (probably) the first black vice presidential candidate, having been made the running mate of Victoria Woodhull of the Equal Rights Party, which held the radical notion that people of all races, sexes, religions and backgrounds should be granted equal rights (more on her later).

Late in his life, Douglass met with Hugh Auld, the man who had owned him when he was a slave, and sort of made peace with him. When Douglass died, he was remembered as one of the greatest speakers and reformers of all time. When Auld died, the only reason anyone cared was that he had once known Frederick Douglass.

formidable. The Confederacy wouldn't hit on the idea of letting black soldiers join—or forcing them to—for another couple of years, by which point (spoiler alert) it would be too late.

The Emancipation Proclamation also gave the war a higher purpose. Instead of just being a war to preserve the Union, this was now a war to end slavery. This absolutely killed the Confederacy's chances of getting the official recognition and reinforcements from Europe that it badly wanted. The European countries, most of which had outlawed slavery long before, weren't about to side with the slaveholding states.

Perhaps most importantly, the Emancipation Proclamation put events in motion that led, two years later, to the

Stonewall Jackson: Unlike Grant's well-groomed beard, Jackson's was of the sort that would make him a real red flag for airport security nowadays.

introduction of the Thirteenth Amendment, which officially put an end to slavery, though Lincoln (another spoiler alert) wouldn't live long enough to see it ratified. That happened in December 1865, several months after Lincoln's death. It was the first amendment to be added to the Constitution in more than sixty years.

GENERALS LEE AND JACKSON

One thing most historians *do* agree on is that the war would have probably been a whole lot shorter if General Lee hadn't been fighting for the Confederacy. Nowhere is this more evident than in the South's victory at the battle of Chancellorsville, Virginia, in early May of 1863. Lee and his right-hand man, General Thomas "Stonewall" Jackson, had a force of 60,000 fighting against an incredible 133,000 Union troops. The Union had a better army, better weapons, and a better battle plan in place. It was only through Lee and Jackson's leadership that the Confederacy was able to win the battle.

Stonewall Jackson was at this time the most famous and admired soldier in the Confederacy, having led his army through some rough patches and having earned the respect of his soldiers, who happily did almost inhuman amounts of marching under his orders. He was also known to be sort of a weirdo. He supposedly believed that his right arm was longer than his left (which ended up being amputated, and buried about a week before the rest of him was), and used to ride with it raised in the air to improve circulation. He was also said to fall asleep at the drop of a hat, sometimes with food in his mouth, or while he was on his horse, and he was known to lead his men in circles on occasion. As much as the soldiers and public loved him, most of the other generals thought he was crazy. He was so paranoid that he wouldn't reveal his strategies to anyone,

ROBERT E. LEE

No general on either side of the Civil War has been more mythologized than Robert E. Lee. Lee opposed the South's decision to secede. Most historians believe that he opposed slavery, at least in principle, but like many people of his day, he believed that slavery was God's will and it would end when God willed it to end. He eventually freed his own slaves during the war, though.

Lee was offered command of the Union army, but he felt too great a sense of duty to his home state of Virginia and chose instead to fight for the South, even though he largely disagreed with the cause.

Historians do agree that Lee tried his best to be a gentleman. He didn't drink, smoke, or gamble and refused to speak against the North after the war. His reputation as a general and a gentleman made him a hero in the South, despite the facts that his decision to invade the North, rather than stick around to defend the Mississippi Valley, had probably been a bad one, and that decisions he made at Gettysburg probably cost the South the battle—and the war.

even other generals, and had a reputation for refusing to follow orders. His greatest victory had been at the Battle of Harpers Ferry, where he won because he listened to Lee, for once. But people loved the guy.

He also listened to Lee at the Battle of Chancellorsville, helping bring about a major Confederate victory there. But the victory came at a price. When Jackson approached some of his troops at night, one of them called out "Who goes there?" and, before he could get a response, the order to shoot was given, and Jackson was hit three times, costing the Confederacy their most famous general: Jackson died eight days later. General Lee said that he felt as though he had lost his right arm (whereas Jackson had lost his left).

THE BATTLE OF GETTYSBURG

In 1863, General Lee made a second attempt to invade the North. His goal was to take over Philadelphia and influence Northern politicians to give up

✗ ✗

HISTORICAL MYTHS: BLACK CONFEDERATES

For years, Confederate supporters have claimed that there were thousands of black soldiers fighting for the South. This is often held up as proof either that the Confederacy wasn't fighting to maintain slavery or that slavery wasn't really all that bad, and that black people were happy to fight to preserve it (beg pardon?). This story has been thrown around enough that many people—including some teachers—assume it's true.

The truth is that it has never been proven that any black soldiers fought for the Confederacy. Anecdotal evidence strongly suggests that there were a few with light-enough skin to "pass" who snuck into the army for one reason or another, perhaps because they heard it was better work than what they'd been doing before, but there certainly weren't "thousands." Any black man who tried to join would have been turned away; arming black people was about the last thing that the Confederacy, fearful of slave revolts, wanted to do.

Toward the end of the war, when the Confederacy was on its last legs, states began to allow black soldiers to enlist in exchange for freedom, and many did (or were made to), but they were still in training when the war ended a month or so later.

on the war and just let the South go its own way.

Lincoln began sending armies after him, and Lee's army collided with a Union army led by General George Meade near Gettysburg, Pennsylvania, on July 1, 1863.

By this time, with Stonewall Jackson busily decomposing, Lee had become the South's greatest hero and their last

JEFFERSON DAVIS

In the 1850s, Jefferson Davis served as secretary of war under President Pierce, and once tried to start a division of the cavalry that would ride on camels instead of horses.

Though he opposed secession in general, when states began to secede, Davis, by then a senator from Mississippi, announced his state's secession and resigned his seat in the U.S. Senate.

A few weeks later, he was named president of the Confederate States of America. Immediately, he ordered a peace commission to go to Washington to pay for any U.S. property on Confederate soil, hoping to work out the differences between the regions without a fight. But Lincoln refused the deal, as selling the fort would have been the same as saying, "Okay, you can go be a new country now." So Davis authorized a raid on Ford Sumter, which started the war.

As president, Davis was pretty unpopular. Lincoln said that the only thing that made him feel better when he read nasty things about himself in the papers was picking up Southern papers to see what they were saying about Davis.

Modern colorization techniques made it much *easier to tell blue from gray, which is a real pain in the butt sometimes in black-and-white pictures like this one. Feel free to color in the black-and-white parts yourself, but stay inside the lines. We're trying to run a* classy *history book around here. Really.*

great hope. The idea of the South "winning" the war and taking over the northern states had long been out of the question (only the really hard-core Confederates had ever planned on that to begin with). By now, the most they could hope for was that the North would give up and recognize the Confederacy as a separate country.

On July 1, soldiers from Lee's army of twenty-five thousand successfully pushed twenty thousand Union soldiers back into the small town of Gettysburg. Attacking them that night didn't seem practical, so Lee decided to attack the next day.

Some of Lee's other officers had told him that attacking at Gettysburg was a bad idea—Union forces there, they said, were going to be impossible to defeat. But rumors were starting to go

around that Lee's army was somehow supernaturally invincible, since they had been so successful, and Lee himself was starting to believe it.

Lee planned to attack the Union army's main stronghold at Cemetery Ridge. Once again, many of his men warned that it would be an impossible siege. But Lee pressed on, gambling that one more day of fighting would win him the battle and, eventually, the war.

This was *it*. For both sides, this third day of fighting was crucial. By then, Lee's army of seventy-five thousand was engaged against upwards of ninety thousand men from Grant's army. If the Confederacy won the fight, not only did they still have a chance of surviving the war, but they might also succeed in putting the Union itself in danger. If they failed, the war would be pretty much over for them. When a Confederate general gave the order to charge, he was so overcome with emotion that he couldn't even speak. He simply raised his hand.

That morning, the two sides fired cannons at each other in some of the heaviest fighting of the war. Soon, the battlefield was hardly visible due to all the black smoke.

In the midafternoon, the Union army stopped firing to save ammunition. Thinking that their enemies had run out of ammo, twelve thousand Confederate soldiers formed a mile-long line and began to march toward the Union army and, they assumed, victory. This became known as Pickett's Charge, after General George Pickett, the commander.

The Union, having fooled them good, then opened fire, and the field

THE NEW YORK DRAFT RIOTS

Just after the Battle of Gettysburg, Congress ordered a draft, requiring military service for anyone called up by the government. Many citizens were furious. If they had wanted to join the army, they would have done so already.

Many men were also racist enough to be unwilling to fight in what they saw as a war to end slavery. In New York, the worst riots in American history up to that point broke out. At least a hundred civilians—mostly black—were killed, and more than three hundred were injured. At least fifty buildings, perhaps many more, were burned to the ground. And of those men who were actually drafted, only about 6 percent actually ended up serving.

Not all rioters were opposed to the draft for racist reasons. Some were upset that men could buy their way out of military service for three hundred dollars (somewhere from ten to thirty grand today, depending on which economist you ask). This prompted some to say "This is a rich man's war, and a poor man's fight."

Down South, meanwhile, a similar draft had been instituted in which people could stay home if they owned twenty or more slaves. Annoyed soldiers (almost none of whom actually owned any slaves) complained that the war was a "rich man's war and a poor man's fight."

Of course, most wars are.

was quickly littered with maimed bodies. Many soldiers broke through to their foes, though, and soon the field was full of hand-to-hand combat, guns fired at close range, and bloody men who had been stabbed with bayonets. The Confederates came fairly close to capturing their target, a small cluster of trees on top of a hill, but more Union reinforcements arrived and drove them back down. The attack had failed.

Lee rode out to meet the survivors, saying that it had all been his fault, and began a slow retreat into Virginia. Union general George Meade let him go, too exhausted to chase him down. Lincoln was furious, saying that Meade had missed a "golden opportunity" to capture Lee and win the war once and for all. But this was only one of many such opportunities on both sides that

SONGS

Lots of memorable songs came out of the Civil War, including "The Battle Hymn of the Republic" (Glory, Glory Hallelujah), "The Bonnie Blue Flag" (a really catchy Confederate song that was about defending either liberty or property, depending on which version you were singing), and, of course, "Dixie."

I wish I was in the land of cotton
Old times there are not forgotten
Look away, look away, look away, Dixieland.

No one is sure now who wrote "Dixie"—it's one of those things that historians tend to argue about. Some believe it was written by an Ohio man; others say he stole it from a black man in the South, who wrote the song as a satire, not a tribute (which would explain all the "look away's.") In any case, it became the unofficial anthem of the Confederacy. And naturally, soldiers wrote plenty of humorous verses of their own, such as:

Pork and cabbage in the pot
Goes in cold and comes out hot
Look away, look away, look away, Dixieland.

This is the only known picture of Lincoln at Gettysburg. Can you find Lincoln, three top hats, and a floating head?

were passed up due to exhaustion. They did, after all, march their butts off.

At the end of the battle, twenty-eight thousand Confederate soldiers were dead or wounded, along with twenty-three thousand Union soldiers. It was the bloodiest battle of the war, and the bloodiest battle ever fought in America. But a few Confederate supporters are probably going to be challenging us to a bloodier one after they read this book.

THE GETTYSBURG ADDRESS

For days after the battle, thousands of corpses littered the fields of Gettysburg. The smell of the rotting bodies was remarkably unpleasant, and residents agreed that getting them buried as soon as possible should be made a top priority. To get things moving, a local guy rich was given the job of establishing a cemetery.

SCORE

"Score" means "twenty"—"four score and seven" means "eighty-seven." Lincoln probably said "four score and seven" instead of just "eighty-seven" to echo a line of the Bible that states that a life should last "three score and ten" (seventy years), though it's interesting that Lincoln opened a speech that was known for being short and to the point by finding just about the most complicated way possible to say "eighty-seven." He *could* have said "273.17 divided by pi years ago," we guess.

WHAT DID HE SAY?

We don't know *exactly* what Lincoln actually said at the Gettysburg Address. There are five handwritten copies that he gave away, plus a couple of transcripts written by reporters who were present, and there are slight differences between them. Mainly, some versions include the phrase "under God," and some don't.

The guy, David Wills, planned an elaborate ceremony to dedicate the field and invited a man named Edward Everett to be the main speaker. Everett was regarded as one of the finest speakers of the day. Back then, long, brainy speeches were all the rage. Using one word when you could use twenty was considered very poor speaking, and speeches were often filled with quotes from ancient Greeks and Romans that might or might not have actually had anything to do with the rest of the speech. People just liked to hear quotes from dead Romans. It made them feel really smart.

Everett's speech was meant to be the main event at the ceremony. Abraham Lincoln was only invited at the last minute, when Wills decided it might be nice to have the president say a few words to conclude things. Planners were shocked when Lincoln accepted the invitation.

Everett's speech was thirteen thousand words long and went on for two

WHAT WOULD YOUR LIFE HAVE BEEN LIKE?

Well, it would have sucked. No two ways about it. In fact, this is one of few times in American history where your life would have definitely been wretched even if you were white. If you're a guy reading this book, you're probably old enough that you would have been in one army or the other. Officially, you had to be eighteen to join, but most recruiters weren't that picky about it. In the Union, somewhere along the lines of a hundred thousand soldiers under the age of fifteen fought in the war.

If you were fighting for the North, you'd have been living on a diet of coffee and hardtack biscuits not unlike firecake that were also known as "molar breakers." On a really good day, you might get some rancid meat. If you were fighting for the Confederacy, you might not have even had that. On both sides, the food tended to consist mostly of worms, though most people reported that the worms didn't really taste like anything. So you'd have that going for you, at least.

No matter which side you were on, you would have spent your days marching tremendous distances on an empty stomach. At night, the soldiers often had to "spoon," which is another word for cuddling, in order to keep from freezing to death—and the guy you were spooning probably stank to high heaven, though you wouldn't exactly have been at your freshest yourself.

If you got hurt (and you probably would have), you might have slowly bled to

death on the battlefield, or you might have had to have a limb or two sawed off, which wouldn't have been any less painful than it sounds. Odds are pretty good that you would have deserted (ditched the army and run away)—somewhere between a quarter and a half of all soldiers did. No one particularly blamed them.

Girls didn't have it much better (did they ever?). Though they weren't expected (or allowed) to join the army, they were often in charge of sewing uniforms, nursing wounded soldiers, and other such duties, and they were just as subject to starvation and disease as the boys.

hours. When he finished, the crowd went crazy—though some historians have suggested that they were cheering mainly because it was finally over. Brave souls who try to read the speech today usually get bored and give up in a real hurry.

Lincoln then stepped up to address the crowd and gave a short speech—only ten sentences—that lasted only two or three minutes. You often hear stories that he wrote it on the train on the way to give the speech, perhaps on the back of an envelope, but these stories aren't true. He had put the speech together very carefully in Washington.

When Lincoln finished, the photographer hadn't even set up his camera yet. There was no cheering, only a hushed silence, followed by a short smattering of applause. This may have been because the crowd was so blown away by the speech that they couldn't bring themselves to make a noise. But Lincoln certainly felt that it was because he had bombed. He reportedly said to Everett, "I failed. I failed: and that is about all that can be said about it." This may have just been Lincoln being Lincoln: depressed and cynical.

Everett, however, told Lincoln, "I should be glad if I could flatter myself that I came as near to the central idea of the occasion, in two hours, as you

did in two minutes," and asked for a handwritten copy of the speech. It's true that getting to the point in two minutes certainly wasn't one of Everett's skills.

In the years that followed, though, Lincoln's brief remarks came to be known as one of America's greatest speeches, possibly *because* it was nice and short. Lincoln said the newly buried soldiers were martyrs to a "new birth of freedom" and called on people to see their example and rededicate themselves to the war for the cause of a government "of the people, by the people, for the people."

THE WAR RAGES ON . . . AND ON . . . AND ON . . .

The day after the Battle of Gettysburg ended, General Grant successfully completed a siege on Vicksburg, another major blow against the Confederacy. That same day, Union forces repelled a Confederate assault and gained control of Arkansas. All in all, the first week of July 1863 was a really crappy week for the Confederate States of America.

Throughout 1864, General Grant and his armies chased General Lee's armies around Virginia toward Richmond, the Confederate capital. Along the way, they suffered an astounding sixty-six thousand casualties. Grant's forces finally pinned the Confederates down around the town of Petersburg, beginning nine months of trench warfare that would result in tens of thousands of casualties.

Meanwhile, General Sherman began a march through the South. Sherman told Grant that if he could keep Lee occupied in Virginia, he and his men would march clear to the ocean, take over the Atlantic ports, and end the war. The Confederacy couldn't possibly survive without any ports to bring in supplies.

General Sherman believed in "total war." His strategy was to march through the South, burning every town he came through, destroying crops, food, and buildings, destroying the

ANDERSONVILLE PRISON

Early in the war, most prisoners were just sent home. After Confederate troops (under General Nathan Forrest, who went on to start the Ku Klux Klan) murdered black Union troops who had surrendered, General Grant decided they'd start taking prisoners until such time as the Confederacy treated black and white soldiers equally. The Confederacy refused, and the Union began to hold captured Confederate soldiers in prison camps. The Confederacy, in turn, began to hold Union prisoners.

None of the prison camps on either side were very pleasant places (Camp Douglas, a prison for Confederate troops in Chicago, was known as "eighty acres of hell"), but the most notorious was the overcrowded Andersonville prison in Georgia, in which forty-five thousand Union prisoners were held. More than twelve thousand of them died, largely

due to disease and starvation. By most accounts, the people in charge did their best—the guards got the same rations as the prisoners—but the Confederacy just didn't have the resources to make the prisons safe or sanitary. When the prison was full, Andersonville went from being a tiny town to the fifth largest in the Confederacy.

South's ability to fight back. Even those who agree that this was the only way to finish the war for good have to admit that Sherman must have been a real downer at parties.

Sherman marched from Chattanooga, Tennessee, into Georgia, not bothering to do much fighting along the way. He only made one attack on the Confederate army, which kicked his army's butt at Kennesaw Mountain, not far from Atlanta.

After this, he wisely avoided directly assaulting the armies and instead simply marched straight to the cities. He took over Atlanta (and set fire to it) in early September. This victory made him famous, and helped Lincoln win reelection in a near landslide two months later.

Sherman then took his troops on a march through Georgia to Savannah, a city of great strategic importance due to its location on the Atlantic coast. Along the way, he caused, by his own estimate, about a hundred million dollars in property damage. He also stopped at the state capitol in Milledgeville, where his men held a mock session of the state government in which they repealed Georgia's ordinance of secession.

Contrary to popular belief, Sherman didn't burn every city he came to. To this day, a lot of stories are told about the brutality of Sherman's march.

Many small towns around Georgia have stories about why Sherman didn't burn them down: usually something along the lines of "he thought it was too pretty to burn." Usually, the truth is that he didn't burn it because he was never actually there; he didn't stop in every single city in the state.

Sherman and his men arrived in Savannah in late December and promptly sent a telegram to Lincoln offering him the city as a Christmas gift. Lincoln was pleased but probably would have preferred a pony. He was only human, after all.

GENERAL LEE SURRENDERS

By 1865, the war was winding to a close. Lincoln even met with the Confederate vice president early in the year to discuss terms of ending the war—one suggestion brought up was that both armies be brought together to invade Mexico. But terms couldn't be agreed on, and the war went on.

As Sherman continued marching across the South, burning things down, Lee's and Grant's armies continued to fight each other in and around Virginia. In early April, Grant finally broke through the trenches. Lee was forced to abandon both Petersburg and Richmond and move his army to Appomattox Station, where he hoped to meet a supply train that would take his

William Tecumseh Sherman certainly didn't look like someone you'd want to meet in a dark alley. He said "War is hell," and looked like he knew what he was talking about.

troops to join those led by General Johnston[30] in North Carolina. But on April 8, Union forces captured three supply trains, further crippling Lee's army. The Union now controlled the Confederate capital city, and Lincoln was able to sit in Davis's chair (Davis had escaped by then). Lincoln hadn't told anyone he was coming but found himself mobbed by black Virginians who saw him as their emancipator.

Meanwhile, at Appomattox, Lee sent a message to Grant saying he wasn't ready to surrender just yet. He wanted to discuss how the terms of surrender would affect the South. Grant had a throbbing headache that got worse when he realized Lee wasn't done fighting.

The Confederate army made one last stand in Appomattox the next day. When they were defeated and driven back, Lee knew that his only option was to surrender. A cease-fire was enacted, and Grant and Lee met to discuss the terms of the surrender.

By all accounts, the meeting was an awkward one. At first, all the generals could do was discuss the last time they had met: as comrades in the Mexican-American War. When Lee finally brought the conversation around to the surrender, Grant offered generous terms: the soldiers would have to lay down their arms, but they could keep their horses and baggage and go home, rather than being taken as prisoners. Officers could even keep their sidearms, in case they got attacked by bears or something on the long trip back, and their ancestors could call anyone who said they were fighting to protect and prolong slavery a historical revisionist.[31]

---

[30] This was Joseph E. Johnston, a newer general, not a zombie version of General Albert Sydney Johnston, who died at Shiloh—though that would have been pretty cool.

[31] Okay, this wasn't *really* one of the terms, but it might as well have been. As we've mentioned, we can't wait to see what kind of letters we'll be getting about this chapter (see

Lee accepted the terms and rode away. As he did, Grant's men began to celebrate, but Grant ordered them to stop. The Confederate army had just lost, and he didn't think it was very polite to rub it in. Grant wrote, "I felt like anything rather than rejoicing at the downfall of a foe who . . . had suffered so much for a cause, though that cause was, I believe, one of the worst for which a people ever fought, and one for which there was the least excuse."

The formal surrender was the next day. Lee's soldiers were met by those of General Joshua Chamberlain (whose strategies at Gettysburg had probably won the battle), who then shocked some of his officers by ordering his soldiers to salute the Southern armies.

Lee ordered his army to lay down their arms. Some officers wanted to let their forces slip into the mountains and set up a guerrilla army. Had Lee let them, the guerilla war could have lasted years—possibly to this day. But Lee told his men that the war was over, and when Lee spoke, they listened.

The Smart Aleck's Guide to Getting More Mail). If you wish to write to us to explain the Great Lost Southern Cause of States' Rights or what have you, please just buy a copy of The Smart Aleck's Guide to Shutting Your Pie Hole and save us all the trouble.

DAVIS IN A DRESS?

On May 10, Jefferson Davis was captured by Union forces who assumed—incorrectly—that he had been involved in the Lincoln assassination. The story goes that he was attempting to disguise himself in his wife's Sunday dress when he was captured, but those who were present insisted that this was nonsense.

Lincoln received word that Lee had surrendered. The war wasn't over yet—there were still plenty of Confederate soldiers in the field who hadn't heard about the surrender—but now it was only a matter of time. To relax his stressed nerves, he and his wife, Mary Todd, went to see a play at Ford's Theatre a couple of days later, on April 14, 1865.

THE DEATH OF LINCOLN

A couple of days after Lee's surrender, Lincoln gave a speech from the White House suggesting that soon, some black people would even be allowed to vote. In the crowd stood John Wilkes Booth, an actor, who didn't like this idea one bit. Furious, he is said to have vowed that it was the last speech Lincoln would ever make.

John Wilkes Booth was not a crazy loner, like most of the historical assassins. On the contrary, he was a very famous actor who had performed in theaters all over the country. Some reviewers called him "the handsomest man in the country," and the *Chicago Trib-une* called him a genius. He performed at Ford's Theatre so often that he had his mail sent there. He even gave his final performance there, less than a month before the assassination. He knew the theater, and all of the guards, pretty well.

He had been getting offers to do some pretty big engagements but ended up taking some time off to focus on other interests, such as plotting to kill Abraham Lincoln. He and several coconspirators had hatched a plan to kidnap Lincoln after a play the month before the assassination. However, the president never showed up that night. Instead of going to the play, he went to a gala at the National Hotel, which, ironically, was where Booth had been living.

On April 14, Booth learned that Lincoln would be attending the play *Our American Cousin*. Friendly as he was with the guards, he had no trouble leaving his horse right outside the theater and slipping into the building, right into Lincoln's box.

He snuck up behind Lincoln, drawing a pistol.

Onstage, an actor said, "I guess I know enough to turn you inside out, old gal, you sockdologizing old mantrap . . ."

The crowd erupted in laughter. Booth knew that this was the best line in what must have been a fairly dull play, and had picked the laughter that followed as the moment to pull the trigger. As the crowd laughed, he fired his gun into the back of Lincoln's head.

Lincoln being shot by John Wilkes Booth in a realllly tasteful cartoon. Apparently, people in 1865 had shorter arms than people in most other eras.

WHAT DID BOOTH SAY?

After jumping from the balcony, John Wilkes Booth either said *"Sic semper tyrannis!"* or "The South shall live!" Nobody is totally sure, but it seems a lot more likely that it was *sic semper tyrannis*.

SCENARIO A

BOOTH: *Sic semper tyrannis!*
PATRON A: What did he just say? Was that even English?
PATRON B: I dunno. Probably something about the South.
PATRON A: Yeah, that sounds right. I'll bet it was "The South shall live."

SCENARIO B

BOOTH: The South shall live!
PATRON A: What did he say?
PATRON B: Why, I believe he said "Thus always to tyrants."
PATRON A: No, that's not what it sounded like.
PATRON B: Well, he said it in Latin, so . . .
PATRON A: Did anyone *else* hear what he said?

You can see how someone might think Booth said "The South shall live," but how could anyone have come up with that Latin phrase if he didn't say it? Still others, however, maintain that he didn't say a thing; he just ran like a bat out of New Jersey to his horse, which would have been the smart thing to do.

Booth then jumped eleven feet from the box seats onto the stage—breaking a bone in his leg in the process[32]—and shouted, *"Sic semper tyrannis!"* It was the

---

[32] Actually, he probably broke it later on during the escape but said that he broke it in the jump to make it seem more dramatic. You'd think the guy had read *The Smart Aleck's Guide to Lying!*

Lincoln's funeral train goes through New York. One of the kids looking out the window is thought to be a young Theodore Roosevelt, the *next* truly memorable president. It's either him or some kid who snuck into the Roosevelts' house to watch the funeral train go by.

state motto of Virginia, Latin for "Thus always to tyrants."

Everyone was so surprised by what happened, and so confused as to what exactly *had* happened, that no one was able to stop Booth as he ran out of the theater, jumped on his horse, and rode away. He was captured and shot to death in a barn eleven days later, never having brought about the Confederate comeback he thought he would be facilitating.

Booth had assigned friends of his to kill Vice President Andrew Johnson and Secretary of State William Seward the same night, but both assassination attempts were unsuccessful, and Johnson was quickly sworn in as president.

All the coconspirators were arrested and executed . . . or were they? Lots of people believed that others had been involved but were never captured. Mary Todd Lincoln herself was sure that Vice President Johnson had been involved.

RECONSTRUCTION

After Lee surrendered, there were still 175,000 troops in the field, but everyone who heard about Lee knew that the war was basically over. Johnston surrendered to Sherman less than two weeks after Lincoln's assassination. On May 5, 1865, Jefferson Davis met with other officials to officially dissolve the Confederate government. About six weeks later, the last Confederate general in the field surrendered, officially ending the war.

Lincoln had known that, even with the war over, uniting the country again and helping the South regain its footing was going to be a massive task. Between the naval blockade, the destruction brought by Sherman's army, and the sheer cost of a war in which 18 percent of the young men in the region had died, the South was in bad, bad shape. The fact that slavery—previously the backbone of their economy—was now outlawed didn't help them too much, either. The Southern states immediately enacted "black codes" that would more or less keep slavery going, even though it was outlawed on paper.

Seeing that the Southern states weren't going to cooperate with the whole emancipation business, Congress had to crack down hard. They passed the Civil Rights Act of 1866,

✷ ✷

WOULD THE SOUTH HAVE ENDED SLAVERY?

Most historians agree that slavery wouldn't have lasted forever in the South even if they had won the war. Some even say that it was already on its way out. The cotton gin was making owning slaves a lot less profitable than it had been before.

It is likely, though, that overturning slavery in the Confederacy would have taken decades. After all, any future Confederate president who wanted to outlaw slavery would have had a hard time, as doing so would have been clearly unconstitutional in the Confederacy.

which made blacks (and anyone else born in the United States, except for "Indians not taxed," who, of course, continued to get a raw deal) citizens and prohibited states from denying them their rights. President Johnson vetoed the act, but Congress overrode the veto.

Congress then set out a series of acts that required states that wanted to come back into the Union to recognize blacks as citizens and allow black men to vote. Many states were not happy in the least, but they needn't have worried. Most of these acts were vetoed by President Andrew Johnson before they could become law. Johnson was, by all accounts, one annoying little booger.

Most generally think Reconstruction was a failure, partly because it failed to rebuild the Southern economy and partly because the South largely refused to cooperate. The states enacted as many laws as they could to restrict black rights. Many of these "Jim Crow laws" stayed on the books for over a century. We know of neighborhoods in the South that didn't allow nonwhites to move in as late as the year 2000.

But another view of Reconstruction is that the South was let off easy. The Union didn't classify the ex-Confederates as traitors, they simply let them go home. They didn't even execute the leaders, which is generally the

Either a 1917 reunion of Civil War soldiers in Washington, D.C., or a Colonel Sanders look-alike contest.

first thing a country does after crushing a rebellion. Compared to other losing sides, the South got a pretty good deal.

CONCLUSION

To this day, there are people who claim that the South very nearly won the war. Saying that the two powers were pretty evenly matched makes the stories that much more dramatic. In reality, though, the Confederates never had a chance. That they lasted as long as they did was actually quite a feat.

From the beginning, the deck was stacked against the Confederacy. The Union had twice as many people, five times as many factories (to make guns and other weapons), and almost all the railroad equipment in the country. The only things the Confederacy had were a lot more slaves (who they refused to let fight, at least until the very last days of the war), and a *lot* more cotton. But you just can't win a war by throwing cotton at your enemy. Not anymore.

Very early on, Lincoln had ordered a naval fleet to block all the Southern ports. The blockade kept the Southern states from being able to sell cotton overseas, which essentially ruined their economy. And yet they fought on.

Many people still argue that neither side was actually *right,* per se—certainly, neither side can be proud of everything they did. And one way of looking at it is that nobody really *won* the war—more than six hundred thousand lives were lost, in addition to almost unimaginable damage to land, property, and national morale.

But at the end of it, slavery had been abolished, closing the book on one of American history's greatest embarrassments. If there's a lesson to be learned here, perhaps it's that sometimes, two wrongs *do* make a right.

WHAT BECAME OF . . .

Short version:

They all died.

Robert E. Lee: Worked to repair relations between the North and the South and criticized Jefferson Davis for holding a grudge. Suffered a stroke and died in 1870.

Jefferson Davis: Was in prison for two years on a somewhat trumped-up charge before his bail was posted (partly by a man who had earlier been a primary funder of John Brown's war on slavery). He became president of a life insurance company (a bit of a step down, but at least he was out of jail) and retired to write books about the Confederacy, arguing persuasively that the states that had seceded had every right to do so.

Ulysses S. Grant: Became one of the most famous men in the country, and heard so many people say he should be president that he decided they must be right. As a president . . . well, he was a pretty good soldier. See the next chapter.

General Joseph Johnston: Became a commissioner of railroads, and respected Grant and Sherman (to whom he surrendered) so much that he was a pallbearer at their funerals. By the time of Sherman's funeral, Johnston was eighty-four and feeble but insisted on keeping his hat off as a sign of respect, even though it was raining. He caught a cold, or possibly pneumonia, and died shortly therafter.

William Tecumseh Sherman: When asked

to run for president, he said, "If nominated I will not run; if elected I will not serve." He was reputed to be a brutal, heartless fighter, but at the end of the war he openly spoke of being sick to death of violence and spent his later years studying Shakespeare, attending plays, and painting. In 1879, he famously told the graduating class of a military academy that "there is many a boy here who looks on war as all glory, but boys, it's all hell."

Sherman, postwar.

BAD GUYS FROM THE NORTH

There were really no completely good or bad guys in the war. Here are some bad things about the Union:

- Lincoln suspended the writ of habeas corpus, the constitutional right to a fair trial. This allowed him to jail thousands of suspected Confederate sympathizers for years without giving them a trial. Really uncool.

- While Lincoln's views on race—especially by the end of the war—were very liberal for his day, some of his earlier speeches in which he claimed that he absolutely didn't support social equality or interracial marriage are quite racist by today's standards. He even once suggested that the best thing to do was send black people back to Africa, though he gave up on that idea pretty quickly.

- The Union initially refused to let black soldiers join the army. Even when they did, black soldiers were paid less than white soldiers.

- Though slavery was widely hated in the North, Northerners weren't much less racist than Southerners on the whole. Slavery was actually still legal in some states fighting for the Union (the Emancipation Proclamation only covered slaves in Confederate states, not slaves living in the Union at the time—they would have to wait for the Thirteenth Amendment to free them).

SOME OF THE STUFF WE MISSED

Ambrose Burnside: A Union major general notable for having facial hair that made it look like he had a fuzzy Frisbee stuck in his face (see above).

Clara Barton: A nurse who founded the American Red Cross.

James Longstreet: A Confederate general who became a big supporter of Grant and a critic of the Confederacy after the war. Some say that his actions at Gettysburg cost the South the battle.

Joseph Hooker: Another Union general, best known for losing to Lee at Chancellorsville.

Acoustic shadows: A scientific phenomenon that causes sound waves to act all weird. At Gettysburg, for instance, people ten miles away couldn't hear the battle, but people 150 miles away in Pittsburgh were said to have heard it clearly. Cool, huh?

The rebel yell: A Confederate battle cry. Since they didn't have as many soldiers or supplies as the Union, the Confederate soldiers yelled to scare their foes, which probably worked but wasn't that wise when they were trying to be sneaky. Oddly, no one knows exactly what it sounded like today (besides the fact that it sounded like a yell). There's a video going around (see our Web page, www.smartalecks guide.com), but its accuracy is in dispute (naturally).

Carpetbaggers: Northerners who went south to take advantage of Southerners during Reconstruction, when the poor economy and political upheaval left them rather vulnerable.

Bounty jumping: The practice of joining the army, taking the bounty (money offered to men who enlisted), then running away and joining another army. One guy pulled this off thirty-two times!

John J. Williams: Said to be the last man to be killed in the war, a month after Lee surrendered.

Hiram Revels: The first black senator. He took over Jefferson Davis's old seat, having been elected by the state legislature (which is how people became senators in those days—they wouldn't be elected by the voters until well into the twentieth century).

William Seward: Lincoln's secretary of state. He was stabbed—nearly fatally—the night Lincoln was shot by one of Booth's coconspirators.

END-OF-CHAPTER QUESTIONS

MULTIPLE CHOICE

1. **What was the Civil War all about?**
   a. Slavery.
   b. States' rights.
   c. Money.
   d. Your face.

2. **Which Civil War guy had the best nickname?**
   a. Guzzlin' Grant.
   b. Stonewall Jackson.
   c. Honest Abe.
   d. "Jeff" Davis.

3. **Which Civil War historical site has the best gift shop?**
   a. Gettysburg.
   b. Appomattox.
   c. The Cyclorama (a thing in Atlanta that is connected to the Civil War somehow, we think).
   d. Fort Sumter.

4. **What does it mean when someone waves a "rebel" flag today?**
   a. "I am a proud Southerner."
   b. "I am a racist."

The Confederate battle flag, which is now waved around by Confederate supporters even though it was never the official flag of the Confederacy. It was also known as the second Confederate Navy Jack.

   c. "I'm not a racist, I just don't care if you *think* I am."
   d. "I don't understand the difference between the flag of the Confederacy and the battle flag."
   e. "Lynyrd Skynyrd rules!"
   f. Something about NASCAR.

ANSWERS: AW, SHUCKS, WE DON'T KNOW. WHAT ARE YOU ASKING US FOR? DON'T YOU HAVE ANY TEACHERS AT YOUR SCHOOL?

The actual flag of the Confederate States of America—or one of the flags, anyway. This design lasted two years before being replaced by one that was plain white except for a Stars and Bars in the top left corner.

DISCUSSION

1. In 1982, the Florida Keys got upset about a government road block, seceded from the Union to become the Conch Republic, and immediately declared war on the United States. About a minute later, they surrendered and requested a billion dollars in financial aid. They didn't get the money, but the roadblock was taken down, and now the Conch Republic runs some pretty sweet gift shops all over the Keys that might, in fact, have generated a billion dollars in tourist cash by now.

Keeping this in mind, think of another way the Southern states might have reacted to Lincoln's election and explain why it would have been better than what they really did.

2. What are some good ways to defend yourself against Civil War reenactors who disagree with your interpretation of the war? Keep in mind: some of these guys never wash their uniforms so they can get that authentic odor. If you come up with a good answer to this, send it in. Fast. Please. And keep in mind that we've *tried* restraining orders and holographic ghosts of Abe Lincoln.

EXTRA CREDIT!

Here's a political cartoon (right) from the end of the war, when some people still thought that the leaders of the Confederacy were probably going to be hanged. Can you find . . .

- John Wilkes Booth actin' all sneaky-like?
- At least one instance where the artist seems to think an urban myth about Davis was true?
- An angel with a giant shoehorn?
- Two "mourners" who are going to survive their hanging? (Hint: at least two of those nooses are never going to work.)
- Abe Lincoln apparently being elected to his first term as God?
- A guy in polka-dot pants?
- What appears to be a naked stick-figure woman running out of prison in a panic?
- Both faces on the evilest tree this side of Oz?
- A demon who looks like the Creature from the Black Lagoon?
- Palm trees a long way from their natural environment (we're assuming that this is in Virginia, since Libby Prison is in the background)?
- At least three guys we never even mentioned?

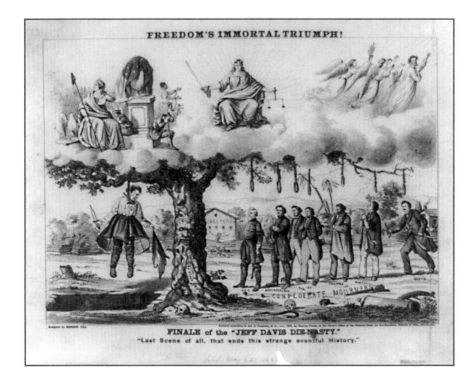

CHAPTER

THE GILDED AGE
(OR, SCREW THE POOR!)

The caption on this poster reads, "History repeats itself—the robber barons of the Middle Ages and the robber barons of today."

> "What is the chief end of man?
> —to get rich. In what way?
> —dishonestly if we can; honestly
> if we must."—Mark Twain

INTRODUCTION

Following the crappy, crappy years of the Civil War, America burst forth into the Gilded Age. It was an age when everything seemed shiny and beautiful and full of promise for a great future—as long as you were rich and appropriately corrupt. Otherwise, your life probably sucked as much as ever. More, if anything, except that you'd be a lot less likely to spend all day marching.

America very rapidly became an industrial empire, and one of the major powers in the world. New factories, mills, and oil fields were changing the face of the country. Lots of inventions, like lightbulbs, movies, and telephones, were starting to appear. But, behind the scenes, the labor involved in building many of these things was deadly, and the pay was crap. Thousands of workers died—many of them immigrants, women, blacks, or others who had no real voice or power in the country.

The rich got richer in this era. Lots, lots richer. But the life of the poor,

Even during the colonial days, the only people in America who ever wore beards were pioneers and hillbillies. But quite suddenly, facial hair came into fashion around 1850. Abe Lincoln became the first president to sport a beard after an eleven-year-old girl wrote him a letter encouraging him to do so (he probably decided to grow it on his own but used the letter as an excuse). Andrew Johnson was beardless, but after that, there wouldn't be a clean-shaven president for years. For nearly half a century, men needed whiskers to be taken seriously. Men with facial hair could still plausibly stand for office throughout the first half of the twentieth century, until, around the 1950s, it was suddenly only acceptable for beatniks and hippies to wear beards. Above, Walt Whitman, one of America's greatest poets, shows off the Santa Claus look chicks really go for.

which had never been a picnic,[33] got harder and harder. The West was being "tamed" (meaning that it wasn't really the "wild" west anymore), but an awful lot of Native Americans got killed in the process.

---

[33] Well, maybe if you count the picnic at the Battle of Bull Run.

General Custer: Lip-readers feared his name. Indians, not so much.

If presidents such as Garfield, Arthur, McKinley, Harrison, and Cleveland sound obscure, it's because they are. Everyone knew who was really in charge of the country in these days: it wasn't the president, it was a handful of rich jerks. Many of these rich jerks were about as corrupt as a person can possibly be, and they knew full well that they could do anything they wanted—and step on anyone they wanted—without fear of getting in trouble. The laissez-faire ("let 'em do whatever the heck they want") attitude that governments in America and England took toward big business in this era led to an age of great advancement and a bright future for many, at the expense of great misery for others.

CUSTER'S LAST STAND

It was during this era that the great American frontier began to vanish as the "Wild West" was "won."

Lacking a war to keep it occupied, the army busied itself with killing every Native American it could find. About three hundred thousand Native Americans were left in the West at this point, having been kicked all over the country for years, and the U.S. government spent twenty-five years in a war against them. Tribes were sent to one reservation or another, under the authority of the Bureau of Indian Affairs (which, of course, was pretty openly corrupt). "Reservations," for the record, was usually a polite way of saying "death camps." Reservations were poorly supplied, on poor land, with little access to luxuries like medical care. But if someone found gold or some valuable use for the land the reservation was on, the tribes were ordered to go someplace else. Sometimes they hadn't been *moved* in the first place so much as *slaughtered*.

George Armstrong Custer had become a general at the age of twenty-three during the Civil War. When the war was over, he embarked on a career of tromping around the country hassling Native Americans and, most likely, waiting to turn thirty-five so he could run for president.[34] Having

---

34 The Constitution sets thirty-five as the minimum age for presidents. What's the point of this, do you think? Could someone younger even get elected to begin with?

found out that there was gold in the Black Hills of South Dakota, the government ordered the Cheyenne and Sioux tribes who were living there to get lost. Instead, they decided to fight back. When Custer and his men attacked, they were outnumbered by something like ten to one. Only one soldier survived the battle, and it wasn't Custer or even a person. It was a horse.

This battle, known as the Battle of Little Big Horn, was the last victory the Native Americans would have over the army. Americans were furious when they heard about this—after all, the newspapers made it look like Custer and his heroic, innocent men had been savagely wiped out by the horrible Indians. Everywhere, cries were heard to kill every Indian left, and about half of the U.S. Army was sent to do exactly that. All over, Natives were either killed or pushed onto reservations.

No one knows how many Native Americans were in the country before the Europeans arrived—some estimates say it was about four million; other estimates go as high as eighteen million. In 1910, there were about a quarter of a million left. There's really nothing funny we can say about this. But we *can* make fun of cowboys, so proceed to the next section.

Nineteenth-century novels and plays depicted cowboys as clean, which they weren't. They also depicted Indians as eager to be strangled, which, obviously, they weren't.

COWBOYS

Around the same time that people were thinking of Native Americans as dangerous, blood-thirsty maniacs, they were also starting to romanticize cowboys. Of all the smelly people in American history (and if we've taught you anything, it's probably that there were plenty of those), the real cowboys may have been just about the smelliest. The cowboys shown in books of the day (and in movies and TV shows of the twentieth century) had very little in common with the real ones.

During the late nineteenth century,

cowboys played a major role in what was starting to be called the Wild West. Most of the stories told about the Wild West—the shoot-outs at high noon, the outlaws, and the battles between cowboys and Indians—were entirely untrue.

In fact, there weren't all that many cowboys to begin with. Even in their heyday, cowboys were outnumbered by farmers about a thousand to one. Cowboys' lives consisted mainly of driving cattle across the prairie, and their idea of a good time was probably stopping off in a small town for a night of drinking. They probably did smell terrible, and were hugely unpopular before they started to become a part of the new mythology America was creating for itself.

Shoot-outs between cowboys and outlaws were actually uncommon. In fact, there's no evidence that there was ever a single shoot-out on a main street at high noon anywhere in the West. Dodge City became famous for its shoot-outs, but in its worst year, there were only five shootings. And that thing in movies where the person who draws his gun and fires first shoots the other guy and wins? That's just nonsense. In reality, according to Wyatt Earp, a Wild West bigshot who ended up living in Hollywood and hanging out with several early cowboy-movie stars, the person who survived a

Ranchers identified cows by their brands, the symbols burned onto them. Unbranded cattle were called mavericks, after Samuel Maverick, a rancher who refused to brand his cows. No one is sure *why* he rejected the practice; some say he planned to claim all unbranded cattle as his own. If that was his idea, he failed, but you can't blame a guy for trying, and besides, the cows probably appreciated his stance.

shoot-out was invariably the one who took the time to aim.

But towns like Tombstone, Dodge City, and Deadwood became famous for the dramatic shoot-outs for one major reason: to attract more settlers and tourists, the locals went along with the stories written about them in dime novels. To this day, these towns all have booming gift shops.

And people ate the stories up. Robbers and murderers like Jesse James and Billy the Kid came to be viewed as Robin Hood—type characters. Guys like Buffalo Bill Cody, who ran a popular "Wild West show," even ended up writing books about themselves—and Cody's wife cheerfully admitted that most of his stories were complete

The Farman flying machine, 1909. Look at how excited these guys are! How can it even be possible that air travel would be so, so boring only a century later?

hooey. Cody stuck to his story that he had been wounded 137 times in fights with Indians, but after his death, his wife said that at least 136 of those wounds were made up.

It's easy to imagine *why* these stories might seem so attractive. America was a new country, with relatively few heroes or myths of its own. It had been settled (by white people, anyway) for only about 250 years, and, as we've seen from the first chapters of this book, most of the first 150 were so dull that history books just skip right over them. The best story about the Pilgrims involved them heroically eating a meal. And people were still sharply divided on which figures from the previous hundred years—including the Civil War and the dull years before it—were

heroes and which were villains. These mythical cowboys had no real political leanings: they simply fought for courage, honor, and rugged individualism, three qualities that most Americans could agree were good. And sitting at home, reading a dime novel about shoot-outs between cowboys and outlaws, you couldn't tell what the prairie smelled like. But it's easy enough to imagine if you think about it—cattle ranches would have been filled with, well, a whole bunch of bull.

THE AGE OF INVENTION

With the Gold Rush over, and most of the free land grabs taken, countless Americans hit on a new way to get rich: inventing things. New inventions were appearing all the time in the late

An inventor with a doohickey. ✻

nineteenth century, and several of them were things we could hardly live without nowadays.

Countless people invested every cent they had trying to get inventions off the ground—and even many of the successful inventors ended up in poverty. Charles Goodyear became absolutely obsessed with making a new kind of rubber that wouldn't melt or stink the way most rubber did, and the fact that he didn't know the first thing about chemistry didn't hold him back one bit. He sold everything he owned and borrowed money from everyone he knew to buy more rubber for experiments, nearly died of the fumes more than once, and even ended up in jail once before finally coming up with the new kind of rubber that neither melted nor stank. Unfortunately for him (but fortunately for rubber fans everywhere), his formula was easy to copy, and he died poor and disappointed. The Goodyear company that makes tires and stuff was named after him, but he never got any money from it.

Another guy named Walter Hunt invented a sewing machine, but decided not to patent it for fear that it would put seamstresses out of work. He then invented the safety pin and sold all the rights to it for four hundred bucks. That was decent money at the time, but the guy who bought the rights got seriously rich.

Other people *did* strike it rich because of, and became famous for, their inventions. Alexander Graham Bell, along with his assistant, Thomas Watson, invented the telephone. Four years later, there were sixty thousand phones in the United States. In those days, you couldn't actually dial phones—you picked up the phone and said, "Hello, Central, get me Henry Whittington, Esquire, please. I want to tell him his wife is ugly and his feet smell," and the operator at Central would connect you. Anyone else who happened to be

Alexander Graham Bell was really disappointed when people started answering the phone by saying "Hello." He wanted people to say "Ahoy."

on the line could listen in, too, if they felt like it. Listening to people over the phone on these "party lines" (which remained common in small towns, in particular, for decades) became a good way to pick up gossip—and was entirely legal, if not particularly polite. You could even chime in and say you happened to know that Henry's wife smelled like roses, if you wanted.

But no inventor became more famous than Thomas Edison, who held 1,093 patents. The irony here is that he didn't really invent much of anything. Many of the inventions were actually made by his staff. Others were things that other people invented; Edison just modified them slightly and took all the credit for them.

There are plenty of nasty things you can say about Edison: for example, when he wanted to show the world that his competitor's brand of electricity was dangerous, he electrocuted an elephant. He also encouraged the use of electricity to execute a condemned criminal. Then again, it can't be denied that the inventions he's credited with (and certainly helped promote) still benefit us today; in fact, odds are pretty good that you can see this page because of an electric light. And in addition to getting the credit for inventing the bulbs (at least twenty people invented versions of lightbulbs before

Thomas Edison will show them. He'll show them all! Mu-hahahahahaa!

him—his was simply better), Edison played a huge role in wiring the country for electricity in the first place. Providing electricity to cities is where Edison made his real money.

In the nineteenth century, there were inventions and discoveries that led, eventually, to just about every major technological breakthrough of the twentieth century, from television to computers to all sorts of weapons. Not bad, considering that many people back then still thought that if you left some corn on a rag in the corner of a barn, the corn kernels would turn into mice.

IMMIGRATION

In 1830, only one in a hundred Americans had been born in another country. In 1850, it was one in ten. The number of people who came to America between 1815 and 1915 was roughly the equivalent of the entire

Ellis Island gets a bad rap these days, but it does seem like it would have been a breeze for anyone who's been through security at Midway Airport in Chicago.

can" name, if they were lucky enough not to be turned away. Actually, while the place was crowded (it was built to process about a thousand people per day but often had to process about five times that many), only about one in fifty people were turned away (mostly due to illness), and very few people were actually *forced* to change their name. Millions, however, did *voluntarily* change their names—sometimes to make them easier to spell, and sometimes to forget their past and start fresh in their new home.

A great many immigrants had no choice but to stay in whatever city they landed in, since they couldn't afford to travel any farther. Hence, New York became a major immigrant center. For example, about a third of all Jews in Europe came to America (European countries were in the habit of kicking Jews out); most stayed in New York. And there were soon more Italians in New York than in most Italian cities.

Most of these immigrants, especially

modern populations of Norway, Sweden, Ireland, Denmark, Austria, and Switzerland combined: somewhere around thirty-five million.

The government set up several processing stations to handle all the necessary paperwork and examinations of new arrivals, the most famous of which was on Ellis Island, just outside New York City. Seeing the Statue of Liberty looming on the horizon after weeks in a smelly boat must have been pretty amazing—certainly more inspiring than seeing the butt end of the statue from the New Jersey turnpike is today. But there were plenty of horror stories about arriving at Ellis Island. Fresh off the boat, immigrants were thoroughly examined, poked and prodded, then often assigned a new, "more Ameri-

THE VICTORIAN ERA

The late 1800s are known as the Victorian era because Victoria was Queen of England. She wasn't queen of America, of course, but we still call Americans from that era Victorians, because there was no American president worth naming an era after at the time.

the ones who weren't white, had a rough time in America. But white immigrants didn't get treated that well, either. In the late 1800s, many stores that needed to hire someone put signs in their windows saying "No Irish Need Apply." Anti-Irish prejudice was rampant.

If one group can truly claim to have been worse off than everyone else, it's probably the Chinese. In 1882, the government passed the Chinese Exclusion Act, which banned Chinese immigration. Its real purposes were to keep the Chinese from coming to California and getting the gold that white people were already digging for and to keep the Chinese who were already present from becoming citizens. The act wouldn't be repealed for sixty-one years.

Those Chinese who were already present had been treated very badly from the start. In some places, especially in the West, mobs attacked Chinese settlements, killing some and wounding others. Those who fought back weren't even allowed to plead self-defense in court if they were arrested for fighting a white person. There may not have been signs saying "No Chinese Need Apply," but that was only because it went without saying.

MORE PRESIDENTS YOU'VE NEVER HEARD OF

Andrew Johnson was a conservative

We here at the Smart Aleck's Guide aren't sure we fully understand this cartoon, but we're pretty sure that it's horribly offensive. ✷

Democrat who was made the running mate of Lincoln (a Republican) merely to balance the ticket. If anyone in the Republican Party at the time had thought he'd actually become president, they never, ever would have given him the vice presidential slot. After Lincoln won the election, Johnson arrived for the inauguration drunk as a sailor on shore leave.

When Johnson became president after Lincoln's death, Congress hated his guts, and many Americans even thought that he had been in on Lincoln's assassination. Probably the most racist president ever (and this will sound like a pretty bold statement after you see the excerpts from Nixon's Watergate tapes), he vetoed many bills that would have given rights to former

Who's buried in Grant's tomb? No one. Grant and his wife are *interred* there, but not buried. ✗

slaves and became the first president to be impeached.

Johnson was impeached for a violation of the Tenure of Office Act, a boring law dealing with firing cabinet members that Congress enacted mainly because they knew Johnson would break it. Break it he did, by firing the secretary of war, and he was put on trial before the Senate. A single vote allowed him to stay in office for a few more months, but the Democratic Party decided not to nominate him for reelection. Instead, they went with Horatio Seymour, who lost—though he probably wasn't whipped as badly as Johnson would have been—to Ulysses S. Grant, the war hero.

Johnson was long regarded as a good president by racist historians who thought giving black people the right to vote was a big mistake, but today he's generally thought of as a big jerk. If he did one thing right, it was letting Secretary of State William Seward purchase Alaska from Russia. People thought Seward was nuts at the time, since gold hadn't been discovered in Alaska yet, but having Alaska as an American territory may have saved our butts from getting nuked by Russia a century or so later since it gave us a convenient place close to Russia to put our missiles. Johnson spent the rest of his life trying to get elected to the Senate in Tennessee. He finally managed it in 1875, but made only one speech as a senator before dying of a stroke.

Ulysses S. Grant spent two terms trying to put the country back together while also trying to help America stay afloat through one financial crisis and scandal after another. Running the White House like a general leads his troops, as he tried to do, couldn't keep the corruption out. If he hadn't been a war hero, there's no way he would have ended up on the fifty-dollar bill.

Rutherford B. Hayes came in next, despite the fact that he didn't actually win the election. The winner of the popular vote was a guy named Samuel Tilden (Tilden won the popular vote 51 percent to 48 percent, as a matter of fact), but Tilden didn't have enough electoral votes to be the official winner, and the committee that picked the president went with Hayes. No one knows exactly how he convinced the committee to name him president, but most people agree on two things: he probably didn't win fair and square, and the administration he formed as a result was so forgettable that it's a wonder he even bothered.

After Hayes came James Garfield, who was in office only six months. A man named Charles Guiteau (see inset next page) repeatedly asked Garfield to make him consul to Paris, despite the fact that he was in no way qualified for the job, and was repeatedly turned down. When being an annoying little booger didn't get him the gig, Guiteau decided to move to plan B: shooting Garfield in the back.

Garfield might have survived if his doctors had been better, but the treatment he got was lousy even by the standards of the day. Doctors stuck

Johnson became president without ever spending a day in school. Before you point this out to your teacher, keep in mind that he sucked as a president.

143

CHARLES GUITEAU

Charles Guiteau may have been the strangest of all presidential assassins. He's an interesting example of a guy who failed his way through life.

He was born in 1855, and as a young man he joined a religious sect that was into free love. Even the free-love people just couldn't find it in their hearts to love him, though, and they nicknamed him Charles Get Out. He was eventually kicked out and moved to Chicago, where he lied his way into being a lawyer. He wasn't successful at it, but he attracted a lot of attention just by being really annoying. He then tried his hand at theology, and published a whole book on the subject, though most of it was plagiarized.

Deciding to try his hand at politics, he wrote a speech in support of James Garfield that he delivered to two small crowds. When Garfield won the election, Guiteau convinced himself that Garfield had only won because of his speech, and demanded a job as consul general to Paris. He made a nuisance of himself at the White House until the secretary of state told him to get lost and stay lost. So he decided on *another* career move: shooting Garfield. For once in his life, he succeeded.

After his arrest, Guiteau's bizarre trial became the social event of the season. Everybody who was anybody went to see it. Guiteau was known for wild outbursts and antics during the trial (as could probably be expected). The spectators stared at Guiteau like he was a monkey in the zoo, and he appeared to love it.

The media circus around his trial delighted him. Even after two people tried to shoot him, he considered himself highly popular, and was so sure that he would be found innocent that he made plans to run for president himself. After all, he noted, "The doctors killed [Garfield]. I did not kill him."

The fact that this was true didn't get Guiteau off the hook, and he was convicted and sentenced to be hanged. While in prison, he wrote an autobiography that ended with a note saying that he'd like to meet a nice "Christian lady of wealth under thirty." Guiteau used his hanging as a chance to promote his new career as a songwriter, and sang a song called "I Am Going to the Lordy" just before they hanged him (it was even worse than it sounds). He had asked for an orchestra to play along as he sang, but the request was denied.

Guiteau is mostly forgotten today, but he probably had more folk songs written about him than any other assassin before or since. Songs about hangings just never seem to go out of style among folk balladeers.

their bare fingers into the wound to get the bullet, and one of them accidentally poked him in the liver. This doctor is probably the only person ever to touch a sitting president's liver. If he's not, it's still probably a pretty exclusive club.

Alexander Graham Bell even showed up to help doctors find the bullet in Garfield's chest. He invented a sort of metal detector to locate the thing, but the tests were inconclusive; no one realized that the metal frame and springs in the president's bed were screwing up the metal detector until it was too late. Oops!

When Garfield died, Chester A. Arthur, a New York big shot who had been about the only person willing to take the job of vice president, took over. He entered office widely despised—many believed he'd had a hand in Garfield's murder, which is just something vice presidents who take over for

Rutherford B. Hayes. Researchers on staff have been unable to determine whether he was actually cross-eyed or just had a real talent for looking confused.

murdered presidents have to live with. It seemed like not a single person trusted the guy while he was in office,

EXPERIMENTS TO TRY AT HOME!

You can't normally feel your liver floating around, so would it hurt to get poked there? Find out! You'll need a biology textbook, a pair of good scissors, and some rubber gloves. If you don't want to poke your own liver, put an ad in the paper asking for a research assistant (or an intern, if you don't want to have to pay anybody). Don't come running to us if, unable to tell we're kidding, you end up really hurting yourself or others.

James Garfield was a smart guy. You could ask him a question in English, and he'd write the answer in Latin with his right hand and in Greek with his left, at the same time. Ask your teacher to demonstrate!

Chester A. Arthur was a hard partier and a power shopper. As president, he was considered competent, which was about all anyone could ask in those days. He died in 1886, barely a year after leaving office. ✗

✗ ✗ ✗ ✗ ✗ ✗ ✗ ✗ ✗ ✗

but most people ended up feeling that he actually did a pretty good job, under the circumstances. Not so good that his

✗ ✗ ✗ ✗ ✗ ✗ ✗ ✗ ✗ ✗

Grover Cleveland kinda reminds us of Cap'n Crunch. ✗

party would nominate him for a full term, but then he didn't try that hard to get the nomination. By the time the 1884 election rolled around, Arthur was dying of kidney disease. Knowing that he didn't have long to live may have been what allowed Arthur to do such a good job as president—he was above party politics and didn't care who he annoyed. What could they do, kill him? Not caring who he annoyed allowed him to get a lot done.

Still, Arthur's refusal to toe the party line led the Republicans to nominate a guy named James Blaine for the next election. Blaine lost to Grover Cleveland, who spent a full term doing little besides, apparently in his own words, "blocking other people's bad ideas." After failing to get reelected, he waited four years and *then* won a second term, making him the only man ever to serve two nonconsecutive terms. This can really screw with people making lists of presidents in chronological order, or counting how many presidents there have been, since you never know whether to count Cleveland twice.

Between Cleveland's terms was Benjamin Harrison, whose four years weren't much more memorable or productive than those of his grandfather, William Henry Harrison (the guy who died in thirty days), unless you're the kind of person who thinks tariffs and attempts to pass antitrust legislation are really exciting.

Since you're not, we'll move right along to the guy who came after Cleveland: William McKinley. McKinley imposed even *more* tariffs and established the gold standard, which meant that paper money was backed only by gold, not both gold and silver. Par-tay!

McKinley was only a year into his second term when he was shot to death by an anarchist named Leon Frank Czolgosz. It was right around this time that people started to figure out that maybe, just maybe, presidents could stand to have a few more bodyguards.

RICH INDUSTRIAL JERKS

The huge growth of industry, including factories, steel mills, and railroads, made a handful of people filthy, stinking rich. There's a reason they call it filthy, stinking rich, and not shining, happy rich. There were accounts of these guys hanging around smoking cigarettes rolled in hundred-dollar bills and buying their dogs necklaces that cost fifteen thousand dollars—about the amount their employees would earn in forty years of hard work. But they weren't just decadent, they were also remarkably corrupt—so much so that they came to be known as robber barons.

J. P. Morgan, a banker, started making money through various schemes to

Will beards just hurry up and go out of style already? We're tired of beard jokes. Harrison was the last president to sport one—at least so far! He was also afraid of light switches, having once gotten a bad shock from one. True story.

profit from the Civil War (in which he didn't serve–he was one of the guys who paid to get out of it). There was barely a big financial deal in the country that he wasn't involved in, and, at

McKinley, smiling.

the height of his wealth, he and his companies were by one estimate worth more than everything in the country west of the Mississippi River. He owned almost half of all the railroads in the country, and the rest were owned by his friends.

Meanwhile, John D. Rockefeller amassed one of history's largest fortunes by forming the Standard Oil Company, which soon became so powerful that it could—and did—buy off large chunks of the government. Monopolies, companies that controlled an

✱ ✱

THE CROSS OF GOLD

One thing from this era that you hear about a lot is William Jennings Bryan's "Cross of Gold" speech. By 1895, the number-one issue in the country was bimetallism: using both silver and gold, not just gold, to back money. Some people thought this would really boost the economy (though it probably wouldn't have), and others feared it would keep the rich from getting richer. Boring as this sounds, it was *the* debate of the day. At the Democratic Convention of 1896, a thirty-six-year-old named William Jennings Bryan (pictured below) made a speech about it, saying that you could

tear down the cities and they would grow back up, but if you tore down the farms, the country was done for. He ended by extending his arms, as though he were nailed to a cross, and saying, "You shall not crucify mankind upon a cross of gold!" The speech was such a success that Bryan became the Democratic nominee for president. The Democrats only had three hundred thousand dollars to spend on a campaign, however, while the Republicans may have spent as much as seven million for their nominee, William McKinley. McKinley won.

entire industry, were illegal, but one of Rockefeller's attorneys came up with the idea of making the company into a holding company, a collection of smaller companies that could get away with more than one big one. Rockefeller thus became the richest man in the world—some say the richest of all time. If you measure how much he had as a percentage of the total economy, nobody today, not even Bill Gates, comes close to being a rich as Rockefeller was.

These new trusts were able to take over entire industries, and soon about five thousand major companies had been organized into about three hundred trusts that pretty much ran the country. Without any competition, these trusts kept prices high and wages low. And the presidents at the time couldn't do much about it. After all, the government was very much under the control of the jerks who ran the trusts.

It didn't stop there. Newspaper barons such as William Randolph Hearst hit on the notion that if nothing exciting was going on, they could just make something up. They used sensational stories in their newspapers to push the country into the Spanish-American War strictly because they knew that wars sold newspapers.

J. P. Morgan practices his lightsaber skills.

LABOR

Rich and jerky though these guys were, they were also noted philanthropists, giving huge amounts to charity and establishing museums that we still visit today (many of which have above-average gift shops!). At the same time, many of them treated their employees like dirt.

People in those days sometimes worked sixteen-hour days in factories that were dark and dangerous, and when the unsanitary conditions made you sick, you couldn't take a sick day or expect any health benefits—you either showed up to work or got fired. Life expectancy for factory workers tended to be low, and the pay was lousy. Many companies only "paid" in the form of credit to the company store, which often had higher prices than anyone could really afford. After sixteen hours of work, workers still

The Haymarket Riot, a Chicago rally for an eight-hour workday that ended badly when police charged on it. Someone threw a bomb, killing seven policemen and injuring an unknown number of ralliers. Rather than find out who threw the bomb, police arrested eight of the protestors. Five were sentenced to hang at the urging of local rich people such as Marshall Field, who wanted to make an example of them so poor people would learn not to fight for better conditions. Note the guy who appears to be looking at his watch and saying, "Look at the time! I have to get back to work!"

wouldn't have made enough to cover the day's expenses, and ended up even further in debt. And there are countless stories of workers getting together and asking for a raise only to be fired on the spot just for asking.

Even worse, there were no real child labor laws in those days, and many of the nastier jobs were held by kids. At one point, something like 20 percent of all kids in the country were working in a place like a factory or mine. It paid better than going to school but was far less pleasant.

Every now and then, workers would try to get organized and form a union, threatening to quit if conditions weren't improved. Often, entire work-forces were fired just for bringing up the idea. Other times, strike breakers—guy with clubs and rifles—were sent in to attack the strikers and force them back to work. Irish coal miners formed a group called the Molly Maguires, and after being accused of violence, nineteen or twenty of their leaders were executed. A couple of years later, when railroad workers went on strike after having their already-tiny salaries cut, more than one hundred workers were killed, and thousands were put in jail. As strikes got bigger, robber barons used their influence to get the government to send the army to break up the strikers.

One of the most common arguments against labor organizations was the claim that they were run by socialists or anarchists. Often this was true. Many of the groups had plans beyond just improving conditions for workers; they wanted to reorganize society itself. Their followers are still hanging around outside of rock concerts, passing out pamphlets and looking generally unclean. These wide-eyed plans ended up doing most of the organizations more harm than good, and the ones that went off the deep end with plans for a "new society" or "worker's paradise" didn't get much done at all.

Less radical groups got more accomplished. The American Federation of

Labor, for instance, focused on more practical matters, like better pay, better safety, an eight-hour workday, and a five-day work week. These guys were much more successful at getting fair labor laws passed, but the robber barons and the trusts were still in charge of the country. And everyone knew it.

THE SPANISH-AMERICAN WAR

The Spanish-American War of 1898 didn't happen *just* because the newspapers made up stories to provoke such public outrage that citizens would demand that the country go to war. That might have been one of the major reasons we ended up getting involved, but there were legitimate reasons as well.

At the time, Cuba was still controlled by Spain, and Spain was rejecting the Cubans' request to become independent. As tensions between loyalists (who wanted to stay Spanish) and rebels got violent, a battleship called the USS *Maine* was sent to Cuba, only ninety-odd miles from Florida, to protect American interests there. The *Maine* sank in Havana Harbor the next month. What caused it to sink has never really been determined. The Americans said it was a gunpowder explosion, and the Spanish believed there had been some sort of internal explosion. But newspaper editors, most notably William Randolph Hearst, had no qualms about telling people that

YOUR LIFE IN THE LATE NINETEENTH CENTURY

Your life probably would have stunk in the years *after* the Civil War, too. You wouldn't have been getting shot at once the war was over, but you probably wouldn't have been in school, either, and your life as a factory worker wouldn't have been much more pleasant—or much safer, for that matter—than life as a soldier or slave.

If you had been a slave, you would be free now, but not much better off. Employment opportunities for former slaves were pretty scarce; odds are good that you'd still have been working at the same plantation where you'd been a slave, doing pretty much the same work for pretty much the same pay (i.e., none). But you would have at least been free to leave if you wanted to, which was certainly progress, and you would have had the opportunity to pick out a last name (which most slaves didn't have—even their first names were often assigned by their owners). Many people say that most slaves took on the last names of their former owners, but it was actually more common for them to pick names that sounded "American," such as Jackson and Washington.✶

Colonel Theodore Roosevelt and his men on top of San Juan Hill. Their hats may be silly, and their mustaches even sillier, but we wouldn't pick a fight with them.

the Spanish officials had sunk the ship, and American voters began to cry a slogan written for them by the newspapers: "Remember the *Maine,* and to Hell with Spain!" Gradually, as the situation between the loyalists and the Cuban rebels became more and more of a civil war, the American government, then led by William McKinley, decided to support the rebels. In April of 1898, the United States declared war on Spain, with the intention of driving them out of Cuba.

Theodore Roosevelt, a historian (like us!) who had worked as a cowboy, been appointed to the United States Civil Service Commission, taken control of (and cleaned up) the New York Police Department, become a political rock star, and ended up assistant secretary of the navy, resigned his commission to fight in the war. He helped organize a group of cowboys into a volunteer band of soldiers known as the Rough Riders, which he was eventually put in charge of.

In the most famous battle of the war (in fact, probably the *only* famous battle of the war), Roosevelt led the Rough Riders in a charge up San Juan Hill. The Spanish surrendered only four months after the war began, and Roosevelt became a national hero. He returned home and became governor of New York, but he never stopped referring to the Battle

Roosevelt was born into a rich New York family. After graduating from Harvard, he became a cattle rancher in the Dakotas. Other ranchers initially made fun of him (few of them would shout things like "Hasten forward quickly!" at their cowboys), but his energy, work ethic, and sense of adventure won them over. Cowboys described him getting dragged through freezing mud and shouting, "Good God! This is fun!"

of San Juan Hill as his finest hour. For the rest of his life, he preferred to be called "Colonel," even though (spoiler alert) "Mr. President" would have been more appropriate.

The Spanish-American war may have been short, and ultimately forgettable, but it *did* help heal the still-festering wounds of the Civil War. For the first time since the 1860s, Northern and Southern soldiers (not to mention black and white soldiers) fought alongside one another toward a common goal. During Roosevelt's later political campaigns, groups of Confederate veterans were known to sing "The Battle Hymn of the Republic," while bands of Union veterans played "Dixie," in a remarkable showing of mutual respect.

THEODORE ROOSEVELT

These qualities won the American public over, too. When Roosevelt was still in his twenties, he became a noted historian, and the numerous magazine

Theodore Roosevelt: trust-buster, intellectual, soldier, reformer, conservationist, reader, author, historian, cowboy, explorer, butt-kicker.

Roosevelt's daughter Alice (posing here with an accessory dog) was almost as popular as he was. Women at this time were still expected to be "proper," but Alice smoked, drank, partied, gambled, and often burst into the Oval Office to give her father advice. Her antics and pranks got her banned from the White House during the Taft and Wilson administrations, and she was known as a witty figure in Washington until her death at age ninety-seven. Her most famous line may be "If you can't think of anything nice to say, come sit next to me!"

articles he wrote gave him the status of a nationally known intellectual. By the time he became governor of New York, at barely forty years of age, he was one of the most admired men in the country.

Other members of the Republican Party, of which he was a member, were a bit afraid of him. By this time, the long process by which the Republican Party became the more conservative party (while the Democrats became the more liberal party) was well under way, and Roosevelt, who was really into reforming the country by standing up to the robber barons and other rich jerks, was considered dangerously progressive by the party leaders.

So the party decided to give him a job where they didn't think he'd be able to bother anybody: they made him vice president. The vice presidency had been little more than a political tomb for years (though not for Andrew Johnson and Chester A. Arthur, of course). Roosevelt became vice president for McKinley's second term but served only a matter of months before McKinley was assassinated. Roosevelt then became president, and overnight, he put an end to the long era of forgettable presidents. Some people said Roosevelt was a dangerous radical, some said he was a fraud, and some said he was a maniac, but nobody said he was boring.

Roosevelt promised to carry on McKinley's work, and did—at least at

GUZZLIN' ROOSEVELT
Roosevelt didn't drink alcohol, but he drank roughly a gallon of coffee per day. It's a wonder he got any work done, considering how much time he must have spent getting up to pee.

TEDDY BEARS

While he was president, Roosevelt went on a hunting trip in Mississippi. When he couldn't find anything to shoot, a group of people chased a black bear down, clubbed it half to death, tied it to a tree, and offered Roosevelt the chance to shoot it. Roosevelt refused, feeling that shooting a tied-up, injured bear was unsportsmanlike. The event was memorialized in political cartoons, and a toy store owner began selling stuffed bears he called Teddy bears, after the president. Soon, every other toy store was copying him. ✶

first. But after he won the 1904 election, he moved to the left politically and began aggressively taking on the trusts and robber barons, issuing lawsuit after lawsuit against major corporations.

He was a popular character, known for being a rough-and-tumble sort of guy—kind of like Andrew Jackson, only smarter, less corrupt, and not as intent on screwing Native Americans over. He had so much energy that some of the people around him joked that he was like a six-year-old. He knew he was popular, and loved attention. His daughter Alice famously said that he wanted to be "the bride at every wedding and the corpse at every funeral."

But he was famous not only for his personality but also for his policies. Roosevelt took on the robber barons and finally ended the long period during which rich business owners were allowed to do whatever they wanted. He

was also the first president to take an active role in conserving the environment. If it hadn't been for him, for example, developers would have filled in the Grand Canyon, robbing the country of a national treasure (and a whole pile of awesome gift shops). The man got an awful lot done as president—and still found time to horse around with his children *and* read upward of two or three books *per day*.

Roosevelt realized, perhaps better than anyone, that the world in the twentieth century was going to be a very different place, and that America's place in it was going to change. When his parents were born, America was still seen as a quirky little experimental country where other countries could send the "wretched refuse of their teeming shores." When Roosevelt was a boy, the Civil War was raging, and America was often seen as a failed experiment.

But in the twentieth century, Roosevelt knew, America was going to be a force to be reckoned with. During his presidency, the United States became one of the most admired and respected countries in the world. He pushed endlessly for innovation and reform to shape America into a twentieth-century power.

Roosevelt campaigns for the Bull Moose Party.

ROOSEVELT AND THE BULL MOOSE PARTY

After his second term came to an end, Roosevelt went on safari in Africa, leaving the country in the hands of William Taft, his handpicked successor, who is best known today for being, by a wide margin, our fattest president. But while Roosevelt was in Africa, news of how Taft was doing angered him. The new president wasn't nearly as progressive as Roosevelt had hoped. So he returned to America and ran for the Republican nomination for a third term. He managed to win the primaries handily, but primaries in those days didn't really mean a thing; the party nominee was chosen by delegates at the convention in Chicago, no matter who won the primaries.

It's interesting to imagine what might have happened if Roosevelt had been nominated. It's generally believed now that he would have won the gen-

eral election, and that the Republican party would have become the party of reform. However, the nomination went to Taft (many felt that he stole it fair and square), and the once-radical Republicans solidly became the party of conservatives.

When it appeared that the nomination was going to Taft, Roosevelt decided to leave the Republican Party altogether. He formed the more liberal Progressive Party, which came to be known as the Bull Moose Party after Roosevelt quipped that he felt as strong as a bull moose.

The Progressive Party was *way* ahead of its time—or way ahead of the other parties, anyway. It was the first major national party that allowed women to serve on its board, and

ROOSEVELTISMS

Roosevelt was one of our most quotable presidents. A couple of his famous lines:

- "Speak softly and carry a big stick, and you will go far."
- "The only man who never makes a mistake is a man who doesn't do anything."
- "A man who has never gone to school may steal from a freight car, but if he has a university education, he may steal the whole railroad."
- But his most famous saying was a simple word: "Bully." This basically means "Great!" As in, "Mr. President, they're having a sale on monocles down at the haberdashery." "Bully! Let's go!"

Roosevelt declared that he was absolutely, unconditionally in favor of women's rights. The Progressive Party platform was filled with talk of social justice, social welfare, and economic reforms that wouldn't actually come to pass for decades.

Though even *he* had little chance of winning the election as a third-party candidate, Roosevelt threw himself wholeheartedly into the campaign, going on a grueling speaking tour while Taft, knowing that he'd never beat Roosevelt (and not really wanting to—he didn't care much for being president anyway), went on vacation. Roosevelt's campaign rallies were likened to religious revivals, with Bull Moosers screaming in ecstasy, interrupting the speeches to break out in spontaneous renditions of "The Battle Hymn of the Republic," and Roosevelt himself declaring, "We stand at Armageddon, and we battle for the Lord!" Having lost the battle for the soul of the Republican Party, he felt that he was battling for the soul of America itself.

Less than a month before the election, while on a campaign stop in Milwaukee, Wisconsin, Roosevelt stood up in a car to wave to the crowd. As he did, a man some seven feet away pulled out a gun and shot him in the chest. The bullet went through a glasses case and a fifty-page speech in Roosevelt's

William Howard Taft, Roosevelt's successor, really only became president because his wife, a tireless social climber, wanted him to. At about 330 pounds, he was by far the heaviest president up to that time. He didn't really seem to *want* to win re-election in 1912 and barely campaigned at all, unwilling to speak against his friend Teddy Roosevelt any more than he had to. He was thrilled to leave office and ended up as chief justice of the Supreme Court, the job he'd really wanted to begin with.

pocket; the length of the speech probably saved his life, as its bulk narrowly kept the bullet from piercing his heart.

Roosevelt, always ready to act tougher than was probably necessary (or safe), didn't even cancel an appearance that was scheduled for that morning. With the bullet still in his chest and his shirt getting bloodier and bloodier, he made a ninety-minute speech, which he opened by saying, "I don't know whether you fully understand that I have been shot, but it takes more than

Taft, looking terribly jolly at the inauguration of his successor, Woodrow Wilson, who appears to be due for a dental appointment. Note the grinning goofball in the background.

that to kill a bull moose!" He would have gone on longer than ninety minutes, but blood was still gushing out of his chest as he spoke, and eventually he got woozy enough to agree to get off the stage and go to the hospital. He let the bullet stay in his chest for the rest of his life, preferring not to risk the good old-fashioned liver-poking that could have resulted from having doctors try to remove it.

But the wound kept him from being able to campaign much more, and in the end, the Republican vote was split. Most of the Republican voters went to Roosevelt, but many stayed with Taft, and neither of the two garnered enough votes to beat Woodrow Wilson, who became the first Democratic president in sixteen years.

The Bull Moose Party was effectively out of business after that (Roosevelt eventually made peace with the Republicans), but they had formed a template for what the Democratic Party would become under the leadership of Roosevelt's fifth cousin Franklin Delano Roosevelt, who was elected president twenty years later.

Roosevelt was depressed by the loss, and dealt with his depression by going

If we here on staff may paraphrase Roosevelt, our motto is: A student who studies a bit may get a good grade, but a smart aleck who studies more may take over the whole class.

on another safari, this time in South America. While on this safari, he and his crew explored a previously uncharted 625-mile river named the River of Doubt, in a dangerous expedition that pitted him against deadly rapids, poisonous snakes, starvation, murderous crew members, and possibly violent natives (a dog was killed by a blow gun, but the natives were never seen). He survived to see the river renamed the Rio Roosevelt in his honor, but he never fully recovered from the diseases he contracted in the jungle; he later estimated that the trip took ten years off his life.

The Freedmen's Bureau, a government agency established to help former slaves, had its work cut out for it, as no amendment to the Constitution was about to make white Southern voters happy about working alongside freed slaves. Congress shut the bureau down in 1872.

The remains of the Progressive Party tried to nominate him again in 1916, but Roosevelt told them that the best thing Progressives could do was back Charles Evans Hughes, the Republican who ran against and lost to Woodrow Wilson that year. At the time of his death, Roosevelt was laying the groundwork to run for the Republican nomination again in 1920. Most people believe that had he lived, he would probably have won a third term at last, and the Republicans would have become the liberal party after all.

Roosevelt is often ranked among the top five presidents, despite not being associated with any major wars. This fact seems all the more remarkable considering how *un*remarkable nearly every president—other than Lincoln—had been for the previous few generations. Today, candidates of both parties quote him endlessly.

SOME OF THE STUFF WE MISSED

The Panic of 1893: A major economic depression that lasted until 1897.

The World's Columbian Exposition: A World's Fair held in Chicago in 1893 that showed everyone how America had come up in the world.

Bourbon Democrats: A name for conservative Democrats, mainly applied to those who supported Grover Cleveland.

Scalawag: An unfriendly term given to white Southern voters who became radical Republicans during Reconstruction.

The Great White Fleet: A new navy that Roosevelt pushed for (and got). He sent it all around the world to show off how tough America had become.

The RMS Titanic: A giant luxury

ship that was said to be unsinkable in 1912. It sank on its first voyage, which was to be from Southampton, England, to New York, and more than fifteen hundred people died. The government quickly passed laws requiring ships to have enough lifeboats for everyone.

The Eastland: A cruise ship that tipped over in 1915 in the Chicago River, killing more than eight hundred people. The extra lifeboats they'd tied to the top in accordance with new laws (see above) may have contributed to the tipping.

The Panama Canal: A canal that allows ships to pass through Central America instead of having to go clear around South America. Roosevelt was a big supporter of building this canal. He went so far as to help overthrow the Colombian government to make Panama an independent country and help the plan along.

Boss Tweed: The guy who ran the Tammany Hall political machine (the political group whose name is still synonymous with corruption—mentioned in a Chapter 3 sidebar, in case you've forgotten). He eventually stole about a hundred million dollars (billions in today's money) from New York taxpayers.

The Pullman strike: An 1894 strike of workers of the Pullman Palace Car Company, which led to sympathy strikes and protests nationwide. More than ten thousand U.S. soldiers were deployed to break up the strike.

The Philippine-American War: A largely forgotten war (officially from 1899 to 1902, though there were still fights as late as 1913) between the United States and insurgents in the Philippines. Ended with the Philippines becoming a U.S. territory.

END-OF-CHAPTER QUESTIONS

MULTIPLE CHOICE

1. How do you pronounce "Czolgosz"?
   a. "Coal-gash."
   b. "Cuh-zuhl-gosh."
   c. "Cuz-ole-ghosh."
   d. "Coal-gosh."

(ANSWER: IT'S A, FOR THE RECORD, THOUGH WE'VE ALSO HEARD PEOPLE USE D, AND AREN'T SURE WHO TO BELIEVE. THEN AGAIN, SOME PEOPLE ALSO SAY THAT JOHN WILKES BOOTH PRONOUNCED HIS NAME "BOWTH" (RHYMES WITH "MOUTH"), WHICH MAKES YOU WONDER HOW MUCH IT REALLY MATTERS HOW IT WAS PRONOUNCED BACK THEN.)

2. Which president was the least effective?
   a. Benjamin Harrison.
   b. Grover Cleveland.
   c. William McKinley (pre-assassination).
   d. Grover Cleveland (second term).

(ANSWER: ANY ANSWER IS ACCEPTABLE HERE,

IF YOU'RE PREPARED TO JUSTIFY IT IN AN ESSAY!)

3. Which would be better for the country?

   a. The gold standard.

   b. The silver standard.

   c. No standard (which is what we have now, despite the objections of a few fanatics).

   d. Forget gold and silver—how about a pickle standard?

(ANSWER: NO ONE CAN SAY FOR SURE, SO WE'LL LET YOU HAVE CREDIT FOR ANY ANSWER EXCEPT D.)

ESSAY

1. Were robber barons good or bad for the economy and the growth of the nation? Why?

2. How might the nation be different today if Roosevelt had won a third term in 1912?

3. Who would win in a fight, Theodore Roosevelt or Giles Corey?

Charles Guiteau, singing his little heart out.

ASSIGNMENT!

Be like William Randolph Hearst! Write an editorial that could push the nation into war against Freedonia.[35] Send it to your local paper and see if you get any reaction! Use of facts is optional.

MORE STUFF TO HELP YOU REMEMBER

Here's the song Charles Guiteau sang on the scaffold before he was hanged. He'd written it that very morning (all by himself). He apparently sang the first verse but ended up just chanting the rest, not being much better at singing than he was at songwriting, poetry, politics, preaching, law, or free love.

> *I am going to the Lordy, I am so glad,*
> *I am going to the Lordy, I am so glad,*
> *I am going to the Lordy,*
> *Glory hallelujah! Glory hallelujah!*
> *I am going to the Lordy.*
> *I love the Lordy with all my soul,*

---

[35] Freedonia was the name of the country Groucho Marx ran in the movie *Duck Soup*. In 1992, *Spy* magazine asked several members of Congress about the situation in Freedonia, and they all talked about it as though it were a real place. They didn't want to admit that they'd never heard of it. If the government can be fooled, the people who read your paper can, too. Give it a shot!

Glory hallelujah!
And that is the reason I am going to the
  Lord,
Glory hallelujah! Glory hallelujah!
I am going to the Lord.
I saved my party and my land,
Glory hallelujah!
But they have murdered me for it,
And that is the reason I am going to the
  Lordy,
Glory hallelujah! Glory hallelujah!
I am going to the Lordy!
I wonder what I will do when I get to the
  Lordy,
I guess that I will weep no more
When I get to the Lordy!
Glory hallelujah!
I wonder what I will see when I get to the
  Lordy,
I expect to see most glorious things,
Beyond all earthly conception
When I am with the Lordy!
Glory hallelujah! Glory hallelujah!
I am with the Lord.

ASSIGNMENT

Using only stuff from this chapter, complete this sentence:

"I Am Going to the Lordy" sucks even more than _____.

A few sample responses:
- working for J. P. Morgan.
- being a capitalist at one of Leon Czolgosz's dinner parties.
- getting poked in the liver.
- being General Custer in a field of Indians.
- being Rutherford B. Hayes's optometrist.
- showing up at Ellis Island with a rash.
- getting Woodrow Wilson's dental bill.
- standing downwind of Taft on three-bean casserole day.
- trying to get anyone to notice you when Teddy Roosevelt is in the room.

CHAPTER

6

WORLD WAR I:
"THE WAR TO END ALL WARS"[36]

---

36 Ha!

"God grant we may not have a European war thrust upon us, and for such a stupid reason, too."—Mary, wife of King George V of England

INTRODUCTION

You don't hear a whole lot about World War I these days. There are many reasons for this. One is that practically everyone who was involved in it is dead by now,[37] and unlike the case of, say, the Civil War, their surviving descendants seem to be over it. Hence, there's no one who is all that eager to come to your class and "make World War I come alive" for you.[38] Most of the best twentieth-century war movies are either about World War II or Vietnam (though there are plenty of good sci-fi movies about World War III and the unholy monsters and motorcycle gangs that will stalk the earth afterward). World War I mainly survives in popular culture through things like the novels of Ernest Hemingway, and if teachers assign those, parents might complain. Hemingway was a pretty rowdy fellow.

Also, there's simply nothing pleasant about World War I. Nothing. No war is a lot of jolly fun, but at least the Revolution freed us from England, the Civil War ended slavery, and World War II defeated Hitler. It's hard to be all that proud of World War I, since no one can really explain what we accomplished—or why we fought it to begin with.

See, that's probably the biggest reason you don't hear much about World War I these days: no one wants to go to the trouble of trying to explain what it was all about, why it happened, or who fought who, because they know they can't do it without confusing the snot out of you. Many history books take the easy way out and just gloss over the whole affair. Even if you went back in time and went out to the front lines (which, incidentally, we don't recommend) and asked someone who was actually *fighting* in the war, there's a pretty good chance that they themselves

---

[37] There were about ten surviving World War I veterans in the world as of the beginning of 2009.

[38] K. A. Chelsea, Smart Aleck staff entrepreneur, used to have a business in which she dressed up in World War I garb, dug a trench outside a school, and lobbed grenades and poison gas at students, but the little brats *still* didn't think history was fun. Some things are so unpleasant that it's best not to want to make them "come alive"—see *The Smart Aleck's Guide to Being Careful What You Wish For.*

would only have a loose grasp of just who was fighting who.

SO WHAT WAS THAT WHOLE THING ABOUT?

What happened was that a whole bunch of countries started to form alliances with one another. And when one country declared war on another one, that set off a chain reaction in which a whole bunch of countries declared war on a whole bunch of other countries.

What was it all about, exactly?

We'll try to make it short. See, around the beginning of the twentieth century, the world was changing very quickly. The Industrial Revolution (the growth of factories, machines, and mass-produced goods, etc., in the nineteenth century) didn't just change the way societies were shaped, it led to lots of new kinds of weapons like battleships, tanks, airplanes, submarines, machine guns, and other stuff that made every army in the world obsolete. Countries that thought of themselves as major powers in the world suddenly found themselves vulnerable; their armies were now useless. Any country that could build up a big, modern arsenal could, at least in theory, become the greatest power in the world, and any country that couldn't keep up with the Joneses risked becoming an extra on the world stage.

So countries like England, France,

Propaganda, a form of advertising that goes out of its way to manipulate opinions, made it look as though the army really took care of its veterans and that soldiers would come home in better shape than ever. As Bob Dylan sings: "Propaganda all is phony."

Russia, and Germany got into an arms race. As with any arms race, though, it sort of went beyond just modernizing their armies and started to veer into a "who has the biggest thingie"[39] contest. By about 1910, countries across Europe had lots and lots of shiny new weapons, and it seemed like they were all just itching to use them.

Many of these countries began teaming up with each other, and pretty soon Europe was divided, more or less, into two teams: the Allied powers, which included England, France, the Russian

---

[39] And by "thingie," we mean "stamp collection."

165

Empire, Japan, and eventually Italy, and the Central Powers, which had Germany, Austria-Hungary, and the Ottoman Empire, which extended to the former home of the Barbary pirates.

Meanwhile, democracy had been slowly spreading across the globe, but much of Europe was still controlled by kings, kaisers, czars, and other autocrats who wanted to flex their muscles to show that they were still in charge, even though they were becoming more obsolete by the minute. They could probably see the writing on the wall and thought that a big-enough military display might erase it.

It was the assassination of some nobody in 1914 that kicked the war into gear.

On June 28 of that year, Archduke Franz Ferdinand, heir to the throne of Austria, was killed in Bosnia. There was a group in Bosnia known as the Black Hand that was dedicated to turning a bunch of Austrian provinces into independent countries. These guys became really, really determined to kill the archduke. Ferdinand and his wife managed to survive having a bomb thrown into their car but were then shot to death by an assassin. If they'd only had a Pope-mobile, the whole war might have been avoided–but it probably would have just been delayed. World War I was really an accident waiting to

happen. If the assassination hadn't started it up, something else would have sooner or later.

As a result of the assassination, Austria-Hungary declared war on Serbia. And then Germany joined in on Austria-Hungary's side, and soon everyone was declaring war on everyone else.

Meanwhile, over in America, people got confused right away; no one could really keep track of who was fighting who. All most Americans knew was that none of it concerned them. Unfortunately, the war was so big that America eventually had no choice but to join in.

We tried to stay out of it. We really did. In 1915, the Germans sank the *Lusitania,* a British passenger ship that happened to have 128 Americans aboard, and people began to call for America to enter the war (England was kind of miffed that we hadn't yet). But President Wilson declared that America was too proud to fight. To win reelection in 1916, he even promised to keep America out of the war. But most people felt that Wilson, too, was just itching to get into the fight. William Jennings Bryan, the "Cross of Gold" guy, who was now secretary of state, resigned over Wilson's warmongering.

Wilson had the idea to organize all the big countries into a League of Nations, an international organization that would push to get rid of the weapons, promote global welfare, and avoid war (Theodore Roosevelt had pushed for a League of Peace years earlier). Wilson knew he was going to need a seat at the table when all of the countries got together at the end of the war to figure out how the world was going to work for the rest of the twentieth century—and he felt like he'd have a much better seat if his country had been fighting. He also believed a theory going around at the time that this war was going to turn into "the War to End All Wars." The idea was that this war could somehow resolve all conflicts and make future wars unnecessary. Seriously.

In 1917, the British intercepted a telegram (later known as the Zimmermann Telegram) sent from Germany to Mexico. In the telegram, Germany told Mexico that if America got into the war, they should team up with Japan and declare war on America. The telegram promised that at the end of the war, Mexico would regain control of Texas, Arizona, and New Mexico if they played ball. Wilson made a big deal out of this.

Furthermore, while Wilson talked about being neutral, he had been quietly sending merchant submarines over to England with weapons and other supplies. When a bunch of the submarines were sunk by Germany, Wilson asked Congress for a declaration of war. They gave it to him in April 1917.

HIT SONGS OF THE DAY

Some popular songs from World War I include "How Ya Gonna Keep 'Em Down on the Farm After They've Seen Paree?" "Over There," and "It's a Long Way to Tipperary." Soldiers in the trenches kept themselves amused by making up songs that spread from trench to trench, like this one:

"WHEN THIS LOUSY WAR IS OVER"

(sung to the tune of "What a Friend We Have in Jesus")

When this lousy war is over, no more soldiering for me!
When I get my civvy clothes on, oh how happy I will be!
No more church parades on Sunday, no more begging for a pass.
You can tell the sergeant major to stick his passes up his . . .[40]

Of course, there were also somewhat naughty versions of the popular songs of the day going around, as there always are in wars. There was a popular parody of "It's a Long Way to Tipperary" going around the trenches entitled "That's the Wrong Way to Tickle Mary." More songs from the war are linked from www.smartalecksguide.com.

Of course, there was another reason for America to go to war: money. American businessmen knew that a

---

[40] At this point, the historical record is damaged. No one knows what the last word is. According to multiple sources, every time the song was sung, two soldiers would cough, another would drop a book, and a machine gun would go off right when they got to the last word. Really.

Trench warfare. Please, no "Still beats being in school" cracks. It doesn't.

A flying ace was a pilot who had killed five or more people. This is Baron Manfred von Richtofen, a German pilot better known as the Red Baron, who led a squadron known as the Flying Circus. He is credited with shooting down eighty enemy planes—but he never got that beagle!

The guy who tried to sell the navy a submarine was named Lodner Darvantis Phillips. He was a shoemaker by day and a submarine inventor by night. He is said to have had successful models of subs, which he used to take his family on underwater picnics, in the Great Lakes as early as the 1840s.

good old-fashioned war would be good for the economy. The seat at the table that Wilson wanted would help them with international business deals in the postwar world, and while the war was on, they could make a fortune building tanks, sewing uniforms, and selling miniature flags. They did not, however, stoop so low as to make war-themed trading cards. No one would go *that* far until 1991.[41]

America didn't have much of an army at that point, but almost four million men were soon in the armed services. Practically overnight, America became one of the greatest powers in the world.

Wars hadn't changed much in the centuries that came before World War I. But in the early twentieth century, new technology made wars deadlier than ever. No one knew just how bad their new weapons would make World War I, which introduced the world to several new ways for soldiers to be killed or maimed.

First of all, there was submarine warfare. Countries had experimented with submarines before, but as late as the Civil War, when a guy tried to sell the U.S. Navy on the idea of submarines, they told him, "Our boats go *on* the water, not under it." But in the fifty-odd years since then, submarine technology had advanced, making subs into viable weapons, not just metal tubes for people who liked to cheat death by having underwater picnics.

---

[41] The first Gulf War had barely started when Topps issued Gulf War trading cards, teaching a whole generation that war was all kinds of fun—and profitable, too! See *The Smart Aleck's Guide to Really Tacky Attempts to Cash In.*

More significantly, this was the first war in which airplanes played a major role. But flying planes in those days was ridiculously dangerous; they were clunky contraptions that had a tendency to catch fire even when they weren't being shot at.

Then, of course, there was gas.[42] Chemical warfare was hardly a new idea, but it really came into its own in World War I. By the end of the war nearly two hundred thousand tons of gas had been used in chemical weapons. Some of this was regular old tear gas, but there were more damaging formulas. One was mustard gas, which causes some pretty nasty blisters and can have deadly long-term effects, like causing cancer. Most of the gases weren't very effective when it came to killing, but they could put soldiers out of commission for quite a while.

But the most notorious sort of fighting in World War I was trench warfare. The practice of digging a trench and firing at the other army from inside it also wasn't new, but it became deadlier than ever in an era with machine guns, gas, and more sophisticated explosives.

The idea of trench warfare is that one army digs a big ditch and hides out in it. The opposing army digs a trench

EXPERIMENTS TO TRY AT HOME!
Make your own mustard gas! You will need:

4 tablespoons of margarine
1/3 cup of milk
1/2 cup of corn syrup
3 ounces of unsweetened chocolate
4-1/2 cups of confectioner's sugar
1 tablespoon of water
1 teaspoon of vanilla extract

Melt the margarine over medium heat and stir everything else in slowly. Pour the mixture into an eight-inch-square baking pan, cool, cut into squares, and serve. You will notice that this doesn't look, smell, or taste anything *like* poison gas. You see, we *do* know how to make poison gas, but our lawyers said that even though we've already told you to hire interns and poke them in the liver, saw off your friends' legs and hang them, and all sorts of things that we assume you know are just jokes, providing an actual recipe for poison gas might violate international law. So we replaced it with a recipe for fudge. Everyone just loves fudge!

of their own on the other side of the field. The two armies hang out in the trenches, shooting at each other as well as they can. In World War I, armies were often holed up in trenches for months at a time. The space between the trenches, littered with dead bodies that no one could safely remove, became known as no-man's-land. Sitting around in a ditch staring out at dead bodies and waiting for someone to throw a grenade at you is just about as pleasant as it sounds. To make matters

---

[42] Yeah, yeah. We're not going to make that kind of joke here. For once.

worse, it's hard to feel as though your army is making any progress when all you do is sit in a trench all day. Add to the equation the fact that many of the soldiers only had a vague idea of what the heck they were trying to accomplish (other than staying alive longer than the guys in the other army) and you can imagine that the soldiers were a pretty unhappy bunch.

American involvement in the war lasted for just about a year and a half before Germany and the rest of the Central Powers gave up. It was really already winding down by the time America joined in. The Allies were already winning, and getting a sudden infusion of four million soldiers was all they needed to put them over the top.

THE CHRISTMAS TRUCE

The war was hell. No nicer way to put it. And a great many of the soldiers were only fighting because they'd been drafted—they didn't really have anything against the soldiers on the other side personally. Soldiers rarely do.

On Christmas 1914 came the Christmas Truce. In the early hours of the morning, German soldiers in a trench in Ypres, Belgium, began decorating the area around their trench and singing Christmas songs. British soldiers began to respond by singing songs of their own. Then the two

STUPID HATS OF HISTORY: WWI GERMAN HELMET WITH A SPIKE ON IT

The helmets used by German officers in World War I were known as (get this) *Pickelhaubens*. Do not forget that you left one of these on your chair. It's a mistake you'll only make once.

armies were shouting Christmas greetings back and forth. Soon, they even began climbing out of their trenches and walking across no-man's-land to exchange gifts of cigars, booze, and whatever else they could scare up. Religious services were held, and bodies that had been festering in no-man's-land were finally buried.

The truce spread all around the lines. The two armies even organized soccer games in no-man's-land.

In most places, the truce only lasted for one day, but in some sectors, no

Archduke Ferdinand, a guy who might as well have had a sign reading KILL ME on his back. Medical aides were a bit tripped up when they tried to help Ferdinand; he had had his suit sewn shut to make himself look thinner, or to avoid wrinkles, depending on who you believe.

ARMISTICE

Armistice was declared on the eleventh hour of the eleventh day of the eleventh month of 1918—you'll want to make a note of that, because most teachers expect you to remember it. When the armistice was declared, soldiers from both sides ran out of the trenches and had a big party. Their commanding officers had warned them not to fraternize with their former enemies, but seeing as how the war was over, they weren't that concerned about getting in trouble anymore.

In a way, battlefield celebrations were holdovers from old-style warfare, when people imagined that war was an honorable contest fought by equals who respected one another. It was still true that the soldiers on opposing sides didn't really have anything against each other, and were only too happy to party together as soon as the orders to stop shooting started coming in.

At the end of the war, four major European empires (the Russian Empire, the German Empire, the Austro-Hungarian Empire, and the Ottoman Empire) had been broken apart. Borders were redrawn; dynasties were ended. The Russian czar was gone, replaced by Communists.[43] Germany's kaiser was

one fired a shot until after New Year's Day. Many commanding officers on both sides were furious with the soldiers who had participated and vowed that no such truce would ever take place again. They began rotating soldiers around more to keep them from getting overly familiar with enemy troops, and started ordering heavy bombing on Christmas Eve the following year to make sure that the fighting would still be going on the next day. But informal truces sprang up at various points on Christmas.

---

43 The idea of Communism, in a nutshell, is that no one is rich and no one is poor. The government

gone; even Germany itself had been turned into the Weimar Republic.

Twenty million or so people had been killed, and at least another twenty million had been wounded. And just to make things worse, toward the end of the war, the Spanish flu broke out, beginning an epidemic that would kill another fifty million people around the world.

When Wilson sailed over to Europe for his seat at the table that would carve up Europe, he became the first sitting president ever to travel overseas. He was greeted as a hero by crowds in the street; the decisive victory that America brought the Allies sealed America's reputation as the most trustworthy of all nations. Roosevelt's popularity had made it an admirable nation, and America was seen as having won the war for the Allies.

Most of the other countries at the conference were sold on Wilson's League of Nations, but there was one problem: Congress wasn't wild about it. When Wilson got home, he went on a tour to promote the idea, hoping that if he could get the public behind his

Daddy, what did YOU do in the Great War?

The government (the British one, in this case) found all sorts of ways to guilt people into joining the army. This is a good example of war propaganda.

controls the economy, and "the people" control the means of production. See *The Smart Aleck's Guide to Communism, Standardized Testing, and Other Things That Work Pretty Well in Theory but Not Necessarily in Practice.*

plan, Congress would feel like they had to approve it. Unfortunately, in the middle of the tour, he suffered a stroke. For the next six weeks, his wife, Edith, essentially ran the country for him while he recovered.

Congress eventually refused to ratify the treaty, which kept America out of the League of Nations. Without American help, the League proved to be pretty much useless. Wilson died feeling that the whole war had been for nothing.

And just to add insult to injury, World

"War profiteers" were sometimes criticized just for making money off the war. Imagine! ✶

✶ ✶ ✶ ✶ ✶ ✶ ✶ ✶ ✶ ✶ ✶

War I didn't end all wars. Not even close. And the wars to come would wipe away any remaining illusion that there was anything dignified about war.

Another propaganda poster. As history book writers, we suggest you do *read history. Being propaganda, the poster plays down the notion that if you went off to war, you could be* history.

SOME OF THE STUFF WE MISSED

A lot of stuff about World War I was left out of this chapter, mostly because it happened a long time before America got involved in the war. But here's some stuff longer history books probably talk more about.

Newton D. Baker: The smart-looking U.S. secretary of war (pictured above).

Battles: Goodness gracious, we barely mentioned these! There were lots of them, of course, though most of them were already fought by the time America entered the war. Some of the more famous battles of World War I are the Battles of Gallipoli, Ypres, the Somme, and the Marne.

"In Flanders Fields": The most famous poem about the war, by Colonel John McRae, a Canadian.

The Sedition Act of 1918: An act that made "disloyal" statements illegal. In other words, it was against the law to protest the war.

The October Revolution: The midwar revolution in which the Bolsheviks, led by Vladimir Lenin, took over Russia to make it a Communist country.

Remembrance Day: The international holiday on November 11 commemorating the armistice. Rarely noticed in the United States, where it's now called Veterans Day. By this time, we're already too busy getting ready for Thanksgiving and Christmas.

William Fitzsimmons: Said to be the first U.S. officer killed in the war.

END-OF-CHAPTER QUESTIONS

MULTIPLE CHOICE

1. **What kind of poison gas was common in the war?**
   a. Mustard.
   b. Ketchup.
   c. Onion.
   d. C'mon, you *know* we're building up to another bad joke about pickles, right?

(ANSWER: A.)

2. **What is it with the Smart Aleck staff and pickles, anyway?**
   a. Pickles are like monkeys, feet, and butts: always funny.
   b. It's a running gag, just go with it.
   c. The Smart Aleck headquarters is right above a deli.
   d. Ask Sigmund Freud.

(ANSWER: ALL OF THE ABOVE.)

3. **Why did people still think there was anything dignified or noble about war?**
   a. The army recruitment film sure made it *look* that way.
   b. They hadn't heard that speech that Sherman made about its being hell.
   c. Jean Renoir's brilliant World War I film *The Grand Illusion,* which condemned that whole idea, wouldn't come out for nearly another twenty years.
   d. They were old-fashioned and still clinging to stupid ideas.

(ANSWER: MOSTLY C AND D.)

4. **What was the best part about trench warfare?**
   a. Being packed in tight with dozens of other guys who you might or might not have gotten along with and who hadn't showered in weeks.
   b. The convenience of not having to travel far to use the bathroom.
   c. Staying alert for grenades, which really helped your hand-eye coordination.

d. Going home when the lousy war was over.

(ANSWER: D.)

ESSAY

1. How would you like to be named Lodner?

2. Think of a nice thing to say about Woodrow Wilson!

3. What sort of mustache would *you* have grown during the war? (Girls: You have to answer this one, too. We're just trying to be fair.)

4. So . . . what was World War I about?

MUSTACHES OF WAR

Kings were no safer than their soldiers during the war—less so, given how many of them were exiled or executed by the end of the whole thing. But royalty in Europe was still a big deal before World War I, and who was in charge of what was a complicated business. One thing the war *did* accomplish was that it put a lot of old-fashioned dictators out of a job. Match the name to the mustache!

1.

2.

3.

4.

5.

6.

a. Wilhelm "Kaiser Bill" II, King of Prussia and Emperor of Germany, was the go-to bad guy of the war—which ended with him abdicating (giving up the job). He was exiled to the Netherlands, where he lived until his death in 1941. You can just imagine him curling that mustache in his finger while tying a damsel to the railroad tracks.

b. Czar Nicholas II of Russia, who was also King of Poland and Grand Duke of Finland, sported both a handlebar 'stache *and* a beard that would make Grant proud. After the midwar Bolshevik uprising in Russia, Nicholas and his family were imprisoned for a year before being executed in 1918. Also known as Bloody Nicholas (for things that happened *during* his reign, not because of how his corpse looked) and now considered a saint by some religions, St. Nick[44] was one of the richest people who ever lived. Rumors that his daughter Anastasia was still alive went around for years.

c. David Lloyd George, prime minister of England, who promised to punish the bad guys, reward the

---

[44] *No, he's not that St. Nick.*

good guys, and make England a place "fit for heroes to live in." He was insanely popular–even conservatives seemed to admire him, though he was a liberal. He had one of the more sensible mustaches of the day, as well, though the similarity to the one Hitler ended up wearing has made it very unpopular since the 1940s.

d. King Peter of Serbia wore a white handlebar 'stache that made it look like he *really* needed to blow his nose. He wasn't that active in the war, but he did go to the trenches to visit his troops now and then. In 1918, just after the war, he was declared King of the Serbs, Croats, and Slovenes. After this declaration, he was never seen in public again (being seen in public wasn't really the safest thing for monarchs to do at the time). He died three years later.

e. Sultan Mehmed V of the Ottoman Empire kept his mustache fairly bushy. Known as a peaceful guy himself, he didn't much want to get into the war but was pushed into it by the guys who really called the shots in the empire. By the time of his death in 1918, the Ottoman Empire was in tatters.

His brother, Mehmed VI, took over just in time to surrender, and the sultanship was done away with altogether in 1922.

f. King George V of England, who looked an awful lot like Nicholas II of Russia, right down to the handlebar/beard combo–funnily enough, the two were cousins. King George V visited the front lines of the war often, and broke his pelvis when a horse rolled on top of him during one of the visits.

(ANSWERS: 1–D, 2–B, 3–E, 4–C, 5–F, 6–A.)

ASSIGNMENT

Woodrow Wilson was the first president to form an official propaganda department. The posters above are propaganda for the war effort *and* for Wilson himself. Your assignment: Make a propaganda poster advertising your teacher. Send it in to us at www.smartalecksguide.com!

CHAPTER

THE ROARING TWENTIES

Young women doing the Charleston in front of the Capitol—the last photograph taken before civilization ended.

> "All of you young people who served in the war . . . You are a lost generation. . . . You have no respect for anything. You drink yourselves to death."
> —Gertrude Stein

INTRODUCTION

Soldiers came back from World War I ready to party, and happy to ignore new prohibition laws. These laws banned the sale of alcohol in the United States starting in 1920, which turned out to be the best thing that ever happened to gangsters, who made a fortune selling "bootleg" alcohol. The 1920s became known as the Jazz Age. If you're studying the Jazz Age, get ready for your teacher to assign *The Great Gatsby,* by F. Scott Fitzgerald.

Prohibition was one of the most widely ignored laws in history. We'd venture a guess that only speed limit laws have been obeyed less often. In fact, by most estimates, people drank *more* than they had when alcohol was legal, even though the price of booze skyrocketed. Owners of speakeasies—illegal bars—had to bribe the cops to keep from being shut down, but the cops, who were often not that inclined to uphold prohibition anyway, were only too happy to take the money.

Two former cops drinking until they're pretty, which doesn't work. This caption brought to you by Mothers Against Drunk Driving.

By this time, though, America was known as one of the greatest powers in the world. New technology was making life more and more exciting all the time, and the feeling of "changing times" was electric. They don't call it the Roaring Twenties for nothing.

WOMEN'S SUFFRAGE

It's hard to believe now that as World War I wrapped up, women *still* weren't allowed to vote in most of the United States.

Women's rights wasn't a new issue, of course. In the nineteenth century, Susan B. Anthony had made a lot of headway in getting the country used to the idea of women being allowed to vote. She isn't in this book much, because there's simply nothing very funny you can say about her without taking a swipe at the fact that she always looks really, really sour in her

Once again, civilization comes crashing to a halt, as it often did in the 1920s, according to people who were less thrilled than others about the changing times.

A suffragette promotes the then-radical concept of female police officers. Perhaps the idea of women in pants was too much even for some suffragettes. ✶

pictures, and even *we* think that's a cheap shot. She wanted to vote and couldn't—how happy could she be?

Other women had also agitated for women's rights—and not just voting. Take Victoria Woodhull, for instance. She and her sister, who had the somewhat unfortunate name of Tennessee, published a newspaper that advocated not only voting rights but also free love. For women to hold such positions in 1870 was a pretty big deal. Woodhull even ran for president in 1872, with Frederick Douglass as her running mate (though she didn't bother to tell Douglass about this), as the candidate of the Equal Rights Party. Some historians make a really big deal out of this, but in reality, whether she ever actually appeared on any ballots seems to be debatable, and she's only known to have gotten one vote for sure. Not only was she unable to vote for herself on election day, she was also unable to go to the polling place. She spent election day in prison after being arrested for passing obscene material (her newspaper) by mail. So Woodhull wasn't exactly a serious candidate (in fact, she wasn't even thirty-five, the minimum age for a president according to the Constitution), but it's hard to imagine she would have been any worse as president than Grant turned out to be.

As is often the case, people who were against giving women the vote had what seemed to them perfectly sound reasons for their opinions. One idea brought up regularly was that if women had the right to vote, it would just be giving husbands a second vote, since women would vote for whoever their husbands told them to. This sounded perfectly reasonable to many people back then.

But in the twentieth century, women began focusing on getting voting rights state by state, rather than pushing for new national laws, and were fairly successful. By the time the election of 1912 arrived, women were voting in a handful of states and, more importantly, voting *against* Woodrow Wilson in pretty large numbers. Had more women been allowed to vote, the Bull Moose Party might have had a better shot.

A newspaper portrays Victoria Woodhull as Mrs. Satan. Over a century later, we *still* haven't had a president who openly advocated free love (though a handful of them certainly did get around in private). At least a few presidents have been known to carry on extramarital affairs, and several more are suspected to have. But no one's about to brag about this during a campaign.

But Wilson won anyway, and after his reelection, women began to picket outside the White House all day and all night. Now, the government was not particularly fair to the protesting women at first. Some had been imprisoned, and the public was starting to sympathize with them, enough so that an amendment eventually managed to pass Congress, if only barely. It was passed on to President Wilson in 1919. Knowing that women would start to turn against the Democratic Party just because he was in it if he refused to sign the amendment, Wilson decided to support it. The Nineteenth Amendment was added to the

Constitution in August of 1920.

Some people thought this would be

"By what right do you refuse to accept the vote of a citizen of the United States?"—Victoria Woodhull.

Did she just mean *adult* citizens?

Today, people say that citizens under age eighteen shouldn't be allowed to vote because they'd just vote for whoever their parents tell them to, or that kids just aren't smart enough to vote. Sound familiar? Many of the arguments against letting kids vote are the same ones that people used to stop women and black people from voting in centuries past. Some people say that the voting age should be lowered, and we here on the Smart Aleck staff are all for it.[45] Some of us on staff (Adam, for instance) have been paying income tax since the age of fourteen. And we could all have been tried as adults in court at twelve. And while some might point out that kids aren't always savvy enough to make wise political decisions, we can surely point out that most adults aren't, either. So why keep the voting age at eighteen? Why not let anyone who pays income taxes vote? Make noise. Act up. Call your congressman.✻

---

[45] Except for Professor Rosemont, who isn't really wild about letting anyone vote.

the end of society. They thought that if you gave women the right to vote, it would lead to outright anarchy. If you gave women the vote, they said, next they'd be drinking, smoking, sleeping around, and wearing short skirts.

THE FLAPPERS

In the 1920s, women started drinking, smoking, sleeping around, and wearing short skirts. Of course, they'd always done these things (except for the skirts part—right up through World War I, women kept their ankles pretty well covered), but in the 1920s, women, particularly those known as flappers, became much more open about them.

This wasn't because the women got the right to vote, though a few jerks probably said it was. It was just a natural progression for society after the war and the famously stuffy Victorian era.

Soldiers returned from the war disillusioned (every history book has to say something like this, even though it probably ought to be obvious that soldiers who saw their friends maimed, gassed, and killed, then decided it hadn't really accomplished much would be a little ticked off). When they returned, many decided to just kick up their heels, forget about their cares, and party down. And women decided to party right along with them.

If history has taught us one thing (and

if it hasn't, we here at the Smart Aleck's Guide are out of a job), it's that periods of repression like the Victorian era, which come about every now and then, are always, always, followed by periods in which anything goes. Throughout the Roaring Twenties, people acted up in ways that their Victorian parents could never have imagined.

Historians have come to call the 1920s the Jazz Age (in addition to its other nicknames). Old-fashioned ideas about morality, modesty, and stuff like that were thrown aside. Jazz replaced depressing parlor songs as the popular music of the day, which was certainly progress.

The illegal drinking of the 1920s introduced a whole generation of disaffected youth to the joys of breaking the law. If the Great War had been the real beginning of the twentieth century, the era of prohibition was solid proof (for those who just didn't trust that sneaky ol' calendar) that the nineteenth century was over. People from the nineteenth century—the Victorians—are famous today for their modesty and repression. Many people would have been terribly embarrassed to say words like "toes" or "pants" out loud in mixed company. This isn't to say that sex didn't exist in the Victorian era—in fact, it was a regular boom time for prostitution—but people were supposed to keep quiet about it.

A flapper giving away the secret hiding place for her liquor. Is this your great-great-grandmother? Of course, *most* people who were sneaking alcohol around illegally didn't pose for photographers. It's just common sense. The fact that this one did shows just how open people were about ignoring the prohibition laws. ✻

With this new sense of freedom and abandon came a new kind of woman, known as flappers. Flappers kicked butt.[46]

Flappers were wild and crazy. They were often living on their own, which was a very new concept for women, who, in earlier times, would have been shipped off to live in someone's attic if they weren't married by the time they were about twenty-five or thirty. They smoked cigarettes, danced to jazz

---

[46] Well, some of them did, and some of them didn't. Some of them were sort of prototype feminists, but many of them—perhaps the majority—were just vacuous drunks who jumped on the bandwagon and became an early version of Valley Girls.

FLAPPER SLANG!

Flappers had a rich vocabulary all their own. Some of their slang terms, like "nookie," "knocked up," "hootch," "java," and "necking," are still in use today, but others have, sadly, fallen by the wayside. It is up to you, the new generation, to bring 'em back! Here's a sample:

applesauce: nonsense

barney mugging: sex. How the heck did *this* term die?

cake basket: limousine

cake eater: ladies' man or lounge lizard

corn shredder: one who steps on women's toes while dancing

cuddle cootie: man whose idea of a good date is to take a girl for a ride on the bus. Par-tay!

dead soldiers: empty bottles

dogs: feet

dog kennels: shoes

ducky: excellent

egg: one who lives the life of Riley (see below)

egg harbor: a dance

getaway sticks: legs

handcuff: engagement ring

"I have to see a man about a dog/horse": another way of saying "I have to go buy some liquor" or "I have to pee" (The exact meaning of each varied from city to city.)

to "know your onions": to know what you're talking about (as in "those guys at the Smart Aleck's Guide really know their onions!")

life of Riley: high life

"mind your potatoes": mind your own business

pearl diver: dish washer

petting pantry: movie theater

quiff: cheap prostitute

snugglepupping:[47] somewhat more illicit form of snuggling than the normal kind, practiced at "petting parties," precursors of makeout parties

snugglepuppy: girl who enjoys snugglepupping (The male version was "snugglepup.")

"That's the bee's knees!": "That's fantastic!" A variation of this was "That's the cat's pajamas!"

---

47 Neat fact: In Chicago, Lillian Collier, a teenage flapper who ran the Wind Blew Inn, a tearoom that also served illegal liquor, was arrested for holding petting parties at her establishment. She coined the term "snugglepupping" when she told the judge that there was "no snugglepupping at the Wind Blew Inn." The judge sentenced her to read a book of fairy tales so she'd learn proper values. Seriously.

music with people they had no intention of marrying, treated sex fairly casually, and drank hard liquor. Some said these women would be the end of society, but others said they were ushering in a new era when women would be "liberated." Nearly a century later, we can at least say that the appearance of women who drank and swore openly wasn't the end of the world.

FADS OF THE TWENTIES

For a couple of decades after 1899, the world still seemed to be about the same as it had been in the nineteenth century, but by the 1920s, the new century had truly arrived. Mass communication, particularly in the form of radio, really took off. Movies had existed for a while, but talking movies began to appear in this decade; before then people had known how to match the sound up to the picture, but theaters hadn't had the capabilities to amplify the sound well enough for anyone to hear it. The proliferation of both movie theaters and automobiles gave young couples great new places to make out. Telephones became more common, making communication a whole lot easier. Practically no one owned a television, but TVs began to be tested and demonstrated in the 1920s.

And strange fads began to go around. One was flagpole sitting, the practice of sitting on top of a flagpole for a really long time. Crowds would gather to watch people do this and pray that inventors would hurry up and get televisions on the market so there'd be something better to watch. After all, they had to find *something* to distract them from the famously boring Teapot Dome Scandal, which dominated the newspapers (we'll explain later and apologize in advance).

Today, we generally remember the Roaring Twenties as one big party. But it had its dark side as well. For instance, the 1920s ushered in an era of . . .

THE ALGONQUIN ROUND TABLE: SMART ALECKS

Throughout the 1920s, a group of the sharpest literary minds in New York met every day at a big round table at the Algonquin Hotel to eat lunch and crack jokes, which they then worked into their books, plays, and newspaper columns. They ushered in what Dorothy Parker, a founding member of the group, called the Terrible Day of the Wisecrack. They were a clever bunch, but if they'd been half as clever as they thought they were, they probably could have cured all disease and landed a man on the moon by 1930.

. . . EVEN MORE FORGETTABLE PRESIDENTS!

The 1920s began with the election of Warren G. Harding, who, following the end of World War I, ran on a platform of a "return to normalcy." He died before he could finish his first term, but during the time he was in office, he did a pretty lousy job. In fact, through the end of the twentieth century, he routinely topped

✱ ✱

HENRY FORD

Henry Ford did not invent the automobile. He didn't invent the assembly line, either. But he was an inventor—he held more than 150 U.S. patents. And he used the assembly line and the automobile to become one of the richest men in the country.

Ford attracted the best workers to his company by offering five dollars a day in pay—more than twice what most mechanics made—and, eventually, a forty-hour work week, for which labor unions had been clamoring for years. But this is not to say that the guy was a good employer—in fact, in the view of many historians, Henry Ford was one of the most colossal jerks ever to walk the face of the earth.

From 1918 to 1927, Ford published a newspaper called the *Dearborn Independent*. To call the *Dearborn Independent* anti-Semitic (anti-Jewish) would be to put it pretty mildly; the view expressed freely in the paper was that Jews were the world's biggest problem. Hitler was a big fan; he reportedly hung a picture of Ford on the wall of his office. Exactly how anti-Semitic Ford was personally isn't really known. Some say that he had several Jewish friends, and he certainly didn't write any of what was in the *Dearborn Independent* himself. In fact, he claimed that he didn't know what it said, he only read the headlines. But the idea that the paper could run for eight years without anyone telling him that it was violently anti-Semitic suggests that either he was lying or unbelievably ill-informed about his own business.

Just to end on a happy note, we'll point out that he also enjoyed square dancing. Yee-haw!

lists of the worst presidents of all time.

So, what was so bad about the guy? Well, he *did* once lose a set of White House china dating back to the Benjamin Harrison administration (which may have been about the only proof that Harrison was ever there to start with) in a poker game. Some say the only reason he even managed to get elected was that people thought that he just *looked* like a president.

But the real problem wasn't *him*, it was

THE HARLEM RENAISSANCE

When people prior to the 1920s thought of "black culture," they usually thought of minstrel shows, traveling shows in which white performers would paint their faces black and sing, dance, and act like buffoons.

While minstrel shows did introduce white audiences to "Negro music" (some of which was authentic, some of which was not), they also promoted an awful lot of awful stereotypes. Well into the twentieth century, they were insanely popular; in fact, the first widely released movie with sound (which the hipsters of the day called a "talkie") was *The Jazz Singer,* in which actor Al Jolson performed in blackface.

But even as minstrel shows spread the idea that black people were obnoxious, ignorant, horny, and hilarious, the 1920s also saw the first great explosion of African American culture in what came to be known as the Harlem Renaissance, named for Harlem, a predominantly black neighborhood in New York City. During this period, black writers produced art, novels, poems, plays, and philosophical works that challenged everything people thought they knew about black people. Black pride and the idea of black intellectuals were still pretty new concepts. For artists such as the men pictured here, writers Langston Hughes, Charles S. Johnson, E. Franklin Frazier, Rudolph Fisher, and Hubert Delany, the Harlem Renaissance represented a chance to show the world exactly what they could do and to loudly demand equality. The renaissance helped lay the early foundations for the civil rights movement in the decades that followed.

Warren G. Harding, often said to be the worst president ever.

his staff, who turned out to be pretty corrupt. After Harding's death, a member of his staff leased government land at the Teapot Dome oil reserve in Wyoming to a private oil company. The resulting Teapot Dome Scandal was almost without question the single most boring thing that ever happened in the United States of America. To this day, comedians who want to refer to something boring in American history often go with the Teapot Dome Scandal.

Some people probably found the whole thing fascinating, but to most, it was so boring that they actually elected Calvin Coolidge, the vice president who had taken over when Harding died, to a full term in 1924. Coolidge, nicknamed Silent Cal, was known for his tendency to be quiet, polite, and dull at all times. While Theodore Roosevelt's motto had

been "Speak softly and carry a big stick," Coolidge's motto seemed to be simply "Sit down and shut up."

According to legend, when a D.C. woman sat next to him at dinner, she said, "Mr. President, I made a bet that I can get you to say more than two words at dinner tonight." He turned to her and said, "You lose." Yes, even dull people who aren't very good presidents can be smart alecks.

In 1928, when he decided not to run for another term, he gathered reporters and, rather than making a big speech, simply said, "I do not choose to run for president in 1928." He wasn't a bad president, exactly, but he seemed to go out of his way not to say or do anything particularly memorable. He even took off for three months to go fishing!

Since Coolidge didn't want to run for another term, the Republicans nominated Herbert Hoover. At the time, Hoover was one of the most respected men in the world for his tireless work for famine relief. He was known overseas as the great Humanitarian for his heroic efforts to keep most of the world from starving to death during World War I, and his face was one of the first ever to be broadcast on television. In England, he had even been offered a spot in the British Cabinet, which is not something they offer to just anyone.

Everybody wanted Hoover to run for

president—everybody in both parties, in fact, since Hoover had bounced back and forth between parties. He'd been a Republican but then left the party in 1912 to be in the Bull Moose Party with Theodore Roosevelt. The Democrats had tried to recruit him in 1920, but he declined, supposedly on the grounds that the only Democrat in his hometown had also been the town drunk. As a Republican again, he won the 1928 election by the biggest landslide in history. However, less than a year into his term, the U.S. economy was crippled by the Stock Market Crash of 1929, which ushered in the era of the Great Depression (see the next exciting chapter). Rich people became poor overnight and went from selling stocks on Wall Street to selling apples on the street corner. Hoover didn't *cause* it, but people blamed him for it, and for the fact that the economy didn't turn right back around (like he kept saying it would). Many of the newly homeless set up little cities of shacks and boxes that they called Hoovervilles in his honor. The old criminal court and jail buildings in Chicago were converted to a homeless shelter that was nicknamed the Hotel Hoover.

Hoover responded immediately to the sudden change in the economy. He spent more on unemployment relief than all the presidents who had come before him combined. But it wasn't nearly

Calvin Coolidge: At least as boring as he looked. His real motto was not "Sit down and shut up," it was "The business of America is business." His policies of letting business owners do pretty much whatever they liked, with minimal regulation, probably helped set the stage for the Great Depression.

enough, and his somewhat radical idea of focusing many relief efforts on the

Herbert Hoover: Poor guy.

Many people dream of having their picture in the history books, but few dream of getting there by sitting through the Teapot Dome hearings, like these poor saps. ✗

✗ ✗ ✗ ✗ ✗ ✗ ✗ ✗ ✗ ✗

rich—the idea being that they'd pass the money on to the poor by creating jobs for them—didn't work as well in real life as it seemed like it would on paper. But the real nail in his coffin was . . .

. . . THE BONUS ARMY

Sometimes, we here at the Smart Aleck Staff feel sorry for ol' Hoover. Everyone loved him and thought he was a hero before he became president, but by the time he left office, he was

Burning the shacks put up by the Bonus Army. Not something you want your people to do in front of photographers when you're running for office. That's a tip, kids. Write it down.

seen as a regular villain. That's the way it goes: it sometimes seems that people start hating presidents the minute they get voted in.

The Depression alone might not have actually been enough to ruin Hoover's reputation, though. The last nail in his political coffin was his handling of the Bonus Army in 1932.

In 1924, army veterans had been granted certificates that entitled them to the equivalent of their pay, plus a bonus payable in 1945. When the Depression hit, many veterans decided to ask for their pay early on the grounds that if they didn't come up with some cash, they weren't going to *live* until 1945. In June of 1932, a group of about seventeen thousand veterans got together and began a march to Washington, D.C., to demand immediate payment of the bonus. They became known as the Bonus Army.

The marchers set up a Hooverville of their own near Washington, D.C., hoping to pressure Congress into granting them their money.

Led by General Douglas MacArthur, who would eventually become famous for being a pain in presidents' butts, the U.S. Army attacked the camp, setting fire to the shacks, shooting off tear gas, and making noise to get the veterans to disperse. Normally, the army is not allowed to be used for general law enforcement, but it was okay in Washington, D.C., which wasn't—and still isn't—part of any state. MacArthur was convinced that the Bonus Army was part of a big Communist plot to overthrow the government and figured that using force was totally justified. Hundreds of the veterans were injured and quite a few of them were killed.

This whole incident shed light on the extent to which the government was ignoring the veterans of World War I. They had sent them off to fight a war that turned out not to have had too much of a point, then, having chewed them up, promptly spit them out. While vets wouldn't manage to get the bonus for a few more years, the public outrage at their being attacked led to the creation of the G.I. Bill of Rights and the Veterans Administration.

Public outrage also whisked away the last bit of support Hoover had. The fact that the whole thing happened just months before the 1932 election made it into a regular nightmare scenario for him. Franklin Delano Roosevelt, Hoover's successor, wasn't in favor of early payment, either, but the very fact that he wasn't Hoover got him elected. Hoover had been swept into office in what was then the biggest landslide in history, but he was swept out in an even bigger one.

The Bonus Army makes itself right at home.

SACCO AND VANZETTI

For decades, there were two kinds of people in America: people who thought Sacco and Vanzetti were innocent, and people who thought they were guilty, no-good foreigners.

Despite the Harlem Renaissance, the 1920s was an era when bigotry and racism still ran rampant. See if you can find copies of "banned" cartoons from that era, and you'll notice that cartoon audiences of the 1920s seemed to be very much in favor of every form of prejudice you can name.[48] Most of the

---

[48] These cartoons aren't actually banned; they just don't usually get aired on TV nowadays. People like to say that they're banned so they can whine about political correctness, though.

Sacco and Vanzetti.

cartoons of the day that weren't about animals seem to base their humor on ethnic stereotypes. One of the first live television demonstrations featured a guy making jokes about black and Irish people.

When a "foreigner," or immigrant, was accused of a crime, people tended to assume that he or she was guilty. Some said that whenever a terrible crime was committed, the police's first order of business was to find someone foreign to blame it on.

In 1920, Nicola Sacco and Bartolomeo Vanzetti were arrested for the robbery and murder of a shoe factory employee and a security guard, who were carrying the factory's payroll. To many Americans of the day, these guys

just *looked* guilty—in addition to being Italians with funny names, they also happened to be anarchists. By 1920, most people were so busy being afraid of Communists that they had forgotten all about anarchists. Communists had just taken over Russia, and a lot of people were afraid that if they could take over Russia, they could take America over, too. Anarchists were yesterday's news. But Sacco and Vanzetti brought antianarchist sentiment roaring back.

To be fair, these were *real* anarchists, not the posers who listen to punk rock, make fun of people who wear name-brand clothes, and complain about big corporations and think that makes them anarchists. They were followers of a particular group of Italian anarchists that favored the violent overthrow of society through bombings and assassinations. But the fact that they were into that sort of thing didn't mean they were the robbers and murderers in this particular case, and neither of them had a criminal record.

The trial was a pretty big story, and was full of action and drama. The prosecution claimed to have proved that one of the four bullets used in the murder had to have come from Sacco's gun, and the defense asked where the others had come from. Some thought that the prosecution had planted the bullet in question. One of the prosecution's biggest pieces of evidence was a hat found on the scene that they claimed was Sacco's, but when he tried it on, it appeared to be too small to have been his.

Witnesses' stories were contradictory. Some people said they had seen Sacco and Vanzetti on the scene, but even more couldn't identify them. One witness described Sacco exactly, but it turned out that all she had seen was a quick glimpse of the getaway car from half a block away. Seeing as how she didn't have super vision, this didn't seem like very reliable testimony.

But the jury only deliberated for five hours before returning a guilty verdict. The appeals in the trial dragged on for a good six years, with many people claiming that the judge and jury had been prejudiced against Sacco and Vanzetti because they were Italian and that they hadn't been given a fair trial. As time went on, it became clear that the trial hadn't been exactly fair, as key witnesses came forward and admitted that they'd been coerced into lying on the stand. It also turned out that the evidence had been tampered with, and a story went around that the judge who had presided over the trial had been calling Sacco and Vanzetti "long-haired anarchists" and bragging that he'd "get them good and proper," which sort of implies that he wasn't exactly impartial.

Sacco and Vanzetti wrote a bunch of letters from prison swearing that they were innocent and demanding a new trial. Scores of intellectuals, writers, and celebrities of the day also argued for them to get a new trial with a judge who wasn't so biased and evidence that hadn't been tampered with. Folk singers wrote song after song about them. But the judge denied every request for a new trial. Though more and more evidence backing up their claims of innocence was coming to light, in 1927 Sacco and Vanzetti were both executed in the electric chair.

Riots and strikes erupted, and anarchists took the convictions as cues to throw some bombs around. The judge became so unpopular with people who advocated the violent overthrow of the

American system—who were not necessarily the safest people to anger—that he had to be protected by armed guards twenty-four hours a day for the rest of his life.

This was one of the first national cases that led to widespread public demand for retrials of people convicted of a crime, which would become more and more common. For years, what you thought of Sacco and Vanzetti sort of defined your political leanings: liberals thought they were innocent, or at least deserving of a second trial, and conservatives thought they were guilty. In the end, it seems that the truth lay somewhere in between. Modern forensic testing has indicated that Sacco was probably guilty but Vanzetti was probably innocent.

SOME OF THE STUFF WE MISSED

Hooverball: A sport played daily by

A game of Hooverball keeps Hoover's staff from having to work.

Hoover and his staff. Find out how to play it on www.smartalecksguide.com!

Ziegfeld Follies: A series of musical revues on Broadway that featured many of the biggest stars of the day.

The Lindy Hop: A dance based on the Charleston and named after Charles "Lucky Lindy" Lindbergh.

Palmer Raids: A series of raids on suspected political radicals, launched by A. Mitchell Palmer, the attorney general under Wilson. The raids led to the largest mass arrests in U.S. history.

Bonnie and Clyde: A couple of lovers/murderers who became alarmingly popular with people who thought their story was charming.

The Scopes Monkey Trial: A famous trial over whether John Scopes could teach human evolution in a Tennessee school; the lawyers were Clarence Darrow, probably the greatest lawyer of the day, and William Jennings Bryan, the "Cross of Gold" guy, who spent a good chunk of his later years arguing against evolution.

Admiral Richard Byrd: An explorer who made the first flights over the North Pole in 1926 (though some doubt that he actually made it that far north) and over the South Pole in 1929.

"On with the Show": The first all-color, all-talking movie. Featured the song "Lift the Juleps to Your Two Lips."

George Gershwin: A phenomenally

popular songwriter who also wrote "Rhapsody in Blue," an American classical piece.

END-OF-CHAPTER QUESTIONS

MULTIPLE CHOICE

1. What did Coolidge say to that woman at that dinner when she said she'd made a bet that she could get him to talk?

a. "You lose."

b. "I do not approve of gambling, young lady."

c. "Are you going to eat that pickle?"

(ANSWER: A.)

2. Who would have made a better president than Harding?

a. Roosevelt in 1920 (he would have run if he hadn't died the year before).

b. Victoria Woodhull.

c. Gouverneur Morris.

d. David Lloyd George.

e. Any of the above, even though three of them were dead and one was busy running England.

(ANSWER: BE REALISTIC; IT AIN'T E. ANY OTHER ANSWER WILL DO, BUT BE PREPARED TO JUSTIFY IT.)

3. All the regulars at the Algonquin Round Table thought very highly of themselves—they certainly thought they were better than _you_. Who was really the best writer of the bunch?

a. Dorothy Parker.

b. Robert Benchley.

c. Alexander Woollcott.

d. Franklin Pierce Adams.

(ANSWER: PROBABLY PARKER, IN THAT SHE'S THE ONLY ONE WHOSE WORKS ARE STILL WIDELY READ—AND THE ONLY ONE MENTIONED IN THIS CHAPTER!)

4. Flappers had all sorts of hats, few of which were really all that stupid. What did they call the ones with enormous peacock feathers stuck in them?

a. Caps.

b. Bobtops.

c. Turbans.

d. Macaroni.

(ANSWER: NONE OF THE ABOVE; WE JUST WANTED TO THROW IN ONE MORE "STUCK A FEATHER IN HIS HAT" CRACK—BECAUSE THAT'S THE WAY WE ROLL, SON.)

DISCUSSION

1. Does your mom vote for whoever your dad tells her to?

2. Think of the oldest people you saw at your last family reunion. Were they flappers back in the day?

3. Here's a serious one, just for

good measure: jazz is sometimes said to be the first truly American art form. Why?

ASSIGNMENT!

The Teapot Dome Scandal was pretty boring. But it's not as bad as we made it out to be—it represents a land-mark scandal involving big oil compa-nies trying to buy the presidential administration (and the rest of the country), something that they'd work hard at for years to come. Take a look at this picture:

See if you can find out:
a. What in the world is going on here.
b. Exactly when it was that big oil companies succeeded in their quest to take over the world.

CHAPTER

THE DEPRESSING THIRTIES

Every textbook's go-to image of the Depression.

> "Prosperity is just around the corner."—Herbert Hoover

INTRODUCTION

Calvin Coolidge's idea that "the business of America is business" led to a big economic boom in the 1920s. As the decade began, people had more money to spend than ever before, and it was a good thing, too, since illegal alcohol cost a fortune. But there was a problem, too: more than 5 percent of the country was unemployed. Some economists said that a crash was inevitable if big business and the government didn't get their act together. But

New York in the 1930s. The rent on the beam this guy is sitting on is now $1,050 per month, plus utilities. No pets. The landlord calls it a "prewar vintage efficiency with free heat, skyline view, roof access."

others ignored those economists and poured every cent they could into something they thought was a sure bet: the stock market.

Then, in October of 1929, the market crashed. On October 24, stock certificates that had made people rich the day before were worth significantly less than toilet paper. By 1932, it seemed like *everyone* was dirt poor and out of work.

Many people blame the Great Depression on the stock market crash, but the crash didn't *cause* the Depression all by itself. It was just another accident waiting to happen as a result of bad economic policies that had been in the boiler for years.

They didn't call it the Great Depression for nothing—life really sucked back then. Any time some old guy starts talking about what life was like in the Depression, you can pretty well guess that he's not going to tell you that life those days was just bags and bags of fun. Well, unless his father was J. P. Morgan or a Hollywood movie star. *They* did all right.

Most people, however, were not so lucky. Herbert Hoover, as we mentioned earlier, would have been better off if he'd just stayed home instead of becoming president. Every couple of months, he'd tell people that the worst was over and that things would be better from now on. Then things would

Just when you thought this book was finished with taking cheap shots at smelly people . . .

get worse. Hoover also avoided setting up government programs to help the poor specifically, which didn't really endear him to anybody, least of all . . .

. . . HOBOES

With so many people out of work and no jobs to go around, countless people took up the life of a hobo: wandering from city to city, looking for work anywhere they could get it. Some hitchhiked to get from town to town. Others, finding it awfully hard to find drivers who would give a ride to someone who looked as though he'd never been introduced to a bar of soap, jumped onto freight trains illegally. They hid in railroad yards, jumped onto empty boxcars, and went wherever the trains went. It was dangerous as all get-out (there are tons of ways to get killed while jumping onto, and hiding out on, a moving train), but it got

DANCE MARATHONS: BEFORE WE HAD REALITY TV...

One of the more sadistic pastimes of the 1920s and 1930s was going to watch dance marathons. These were contests in which couples danced forty-five minutes per hour, twenty-four hours per day, until all but one couple had collapsed or been disqualified. They could go on for weeks. Dancers, some of whom competed in marathons for a living, got free food and shelter as long as they were in the competition, and spectators enjoyed watching people who looked even more miserable and dirty than they were. Many of the dancers hoped to use the marathon to become movie stars, but others just needed a job.

Promoters made up backstories for couples. For instance, there would often be a couple dancing to earn money to get an operation, a couple who'd fallen in love at the marathon, and a girl from Belching Hollow, Indiana, who'd come all the way to the marathon to be a star. Spectators got involved in the stories, picked their favorite cou-

ples, and came back night after night to cheer them on. As the weeks wore on, promoters would spice things up by having contests like races and "grinds"–long periods during which there were no rest periods–to bring in more spectators and eliminate couples dramatically.

By the time the marathon had gone on for a month, people would pile in nightly to watch the couples, who, by this time, were not exactly dancing so much as just pathetically moving their feet, looking dirty, tired, and miserable. Many even learned to sleep while dancing. As they became dirtier and more miserable, the crowds got more and more excited. It was very much like modern reality TV, and like much of reality TV, the marathons were often rigged.[49]

---

[49] We here on the Smart Aleck staff would like to state, at the request of a couple of tough-looking guys with brass knuckles, that reality TV is never rigged.

you where you wanted to go, and you got to enjoy the company of other hoboes who were just as dirty as you and could teach you folk songs and recipes for mulligan stew.

At some towns, hoboes would set up hobo jungles, which were pretty much the same things as Hoovervilles. In towns where no such jungle existed, hobos developed a system of signs that they would draw on walls and sidewalks to show other hoboes where the good houses to beg were.

It's hard to document exactly how many hoboes there were in the country during the Depression; it's not like you had to sign up to become one. Most historians estimate that the number was well into the millions, though.

You don't see as many hoboes these days, now that the Depression is long over and most of the trains just run from paper mill to paper mill. You see plenty of panhandlers downtown in our major urban centers, but they're not quite the same thing. Practically no one writes folk songs about panhandlers.

FRANKLIN D. ROOSEVELT:
A MEMORABLE PRESIDENT AT LAST

In 1932, when he ran for president, Franklin Delano Roosevelt offered voters what he called the New Deal. Under this deal, he'd offer relief to people

FDR, looking much more vigorous than he does on the dime.

who couldn't get work, try to create more jobs so people would have more money to put into the economy, and save the banks, which had fallen into a nasty habit of failing and taking people's money with them. He also promised to repeal Prohibition, which by that time was something of a national embarrassment, as it seemed to be doing more harm than good. When the election came around, Roosevelt mopped the floor with Hoover.

One of the main differences between Roosevelt and Hoover was that Roosevelt didn't try to tell people things were about to get better. He told them straight up that it was going to take a while to get out of the Depression but that "the only thing we have to fear is fear itself." People who were afraid of starving to death, getting run over while trying to hop a freight train, or catching the latest diseases might have

Franklin D. Roosevelt was fifth cousin to Theodore Roosevelt, which is a pretty distant relationship: you find that practically everybody is related to everyone else, when you really do the research. In fact, one of FDR's other fifth cousins was Eleanor Roosevelt, his wife (above). ✸

taken exception, but the message was clear: If we don't starve to death, we can rise above this.

Exactly how close Franklin and his wife, Eleanor, were is sort of up for debate. We now know that Franklin had a handful of affairs, and that after about 1918, he and Eleanor started living in separate rooms. They most likely stayed married mainly because of politics; being divorced was pretty uncommon in those days, and could have derailed both of their careers.

Roosevelt's staff always went to great lengths to cover up the fact that he was frequently seen nipping off to secluded spots in the White House for some red-hot action with Lucy Mercer, his secretary, but covering up his sex life was nothing compared to the trouble they had covering up the fact that Roosevelt was in a wheelchair. He had been stricken with polio (or some similar disease; new theories pop up now and then) around 1920, which left him paralyzed from the waist down.

Hiding Roosevelt's disability was a lot easier in those days than it would be today, since nobody had a television set, but it was still no picnic. When Roosevelt appeared in public, he'd have to be propped up against one of his staff members. With the use of a cane and leg braces, he was able to teach himself to walk by swiveling his hips and shaking his legs around. The reason for all this effort was simple: Roosevelt believed, probably correctly, that not enough people would vote for a guy in a wheelchair. Today, many people think Roosevelt was just about the best president we ever had but that he would never manage to get elected today, when covering up the fact that a candidate is paralyzed from the waist down would be impossible.

Roosevelt's plan to tackle the Depression had three parts: relief, recovery, and reform. Relief and recovery would be getting people out of the box-cars, into a bathtub, and then into a job to get the economy humming again. Reform would be fixing the problems that had led to the Depression in the first place; Roosevelt blamed greedy bankers, bosses, and robber barons for a pretty good chunk of it.

He started to work right away. On the day of his inauguration, the country was in the middle of a bank panic. Since banks had been losing everyone's money, people were demanding to withdraw all their money. The next day, Roosevelt declared a bank holiday, shutting all the banks down for four days and setting up a system to keep them from going under. In his first few days in office, his many relief bills passed through Congress easily. He created laws regulating business and creating jobs for hundreds of thousands of workers, which beat the living heck out of just telling people that the Depression was almost over, like Hoover had done.

The massive number of bills Roosevelt managed to pass in his famous first hundred days in office didn't come close to ending the Depression, but they were a good first step to making life better. People who might have starved to death survived the decade and grew up to spend their later years talking endlessly about how much you

EXPERIMENTS TO TRY AT HOME!
Can makeshift toy tractors be fun? Find out!

You still run into the occasional old person who will ramble on about how he and his nine siblings used to make toy tractors out of broken pencils and old spools of thread. Given that tractors are about the least exciting piece of machinery ever, we decided to make our own toy tractors to see if they could *possibly* be any fun.

Our results are pretty inconclusive; *we* sure didn't manage to have any fun, even when we tried to mix things up by getting some Star Wars action figures involved. We had Darth Vader try to invade the rebel base (an old cardboard box) on his spool-and-pencil tractor, and had Obi-Wan Kenobi be a crotchety old guy who hangs around outside the base, talking about how cheap things used to be and turning the hose on invaders, but though we were amused for a minute, we couldn't get past the fact that a starship would have been a lot more practical than a tractor as an invasion vehicle.

We realize that during the Depression, sometimes a pencil and a spool were all you had, but we have still not yet determined why, of all the vehicles in the world, anyone would want to make these items into toy tractors when they could just as easily be toy tanks, spaceships, or monster trucks.

The lesson here: Don't believe everything old people tell you about the olden days!

Hitler and Mussolini, the most famous fascists of the day, as photographed by Hitler's girlfriend. The Black Hand could've come in mighty handy at this parade.

could get for a nickel back in the olden days. Having to go a whole year sharing three ears of corn among eight brothers and sisters and walking eight miles to get to school (uphill both ways) gave them conversation topics that would last them a lifetime.

MEANWHILE, OUTSIDE AMERICA

Franklin D. Roosevelt seemed willing to try pretty much anything to help people out—but not everything he tried worked. One of his more famous efforts was the National Industrial Recovery Act (NIRA), in which he attempted to give himself the power to regulate business and other things.

Two years later the Supreme Court unanimously decided that parts of it were unconstitutional.

Meanwhile, Europe was inching toward another major war. Germany was in bad, bad shape after World War I. People were humiliated by their loss, inflation was out of control, and, around

A TERM POPULAR IN HISTORY BOOKS

Fascist: An authoritarian, nationalistic dictator. Some teachers get a kick out of being called a fascist, but most aren't amused by it in the slightest. Call your teacher one at your own risk.

1930, a depression similar to the one that had hit America took hold in Germany. Adolf Hitler, who was Austrian by birth, spent about fifteen years crawling his way to the top, eventually taking over Germany completely in 1933.

Hitler took a lot of cues from the Fascists who had taken over in Italy as he rose to power. Through a series of speeches, propaganda, and various underhanded tricks, he gave people in Germany reason to be optimistic again, telling them that Germany was the greatest country in the world, and that they (well, most of them) were the "master race." And he gave them people to blame for all their problems: mostly Jews, Communists, and minorities.

Hitler had a big plan to reunite all the German-speaking countries that had been divided up after World War I and turn them into one big country, and he started with his native Austria. He didn't even have to start a war there; the Anschluss, or annexation, occurred when Austria just sort of let him take over without a fight in 1938.

Next on his list was the Sudetenland, a German-speaking area of Czechoslovakia. At a conference in Munich, the prime ministers of England and France agreed to let Hitler take over the Sudetenland if he promised not to pick a fight with them next. British prime minister Neville Chamberlain thought

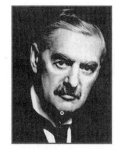

Neville Chamberlain: Not a fascist, but also not the guy you want to hear on the other end of the phone when you call the Psychic Hotline.

that that would be the end of that, and proudly came back to England saying there will be "peace in our time."

Winston Churchill, another British politician, said, "Britain and France had to choose between war and

From the evidence of this statue of Churchill in London, we can state that while he may have had foresight, alas, ladies and gentlemen, the man had no neck.

Woody Guthrie's "This Land Is Your Land" was written as an angry response to the song "God Bless America." There are a few verses they surely didn't teach you at camp, including "In the shadow of the steeple / I saw my people / By the relief office / I seen my people; / As they stood there hungry, / I stood there asking / Is this land made for you and me?"[50] Note the writing on his guitar, which reads, "This machine kills fascists." Kabong!

dishonor. They chose dishonor. They will have war." Obviously blessed with better instincts than Neville Chamberlain, Churchill ended up becoming prime minister and eventually got a rather dumpy-looking statue of himself put up in London.

As it turned out, Hitler was not content with just marching into the Sudetenland. Six months later, in 1939, he took

over the rest of Czechoslovakia, and started to seem intent on taking over the whole world. In September, he took over Poland. Never having agreed to let him do this, England and France finally declared war on Germany.

Hitler ordered his Nazi troops into France and took over Belgium, the Netherlands, Denmark, Norway, and Luxembourg along the way, giving him a pretty large collection of European countries. In June of 1940, he invaded France. Unable to take on an army the size of the one Hitler had amassed, France surrendered in less than three weeks.

In July, the Nazis began bombing England and came pretty close to taking over. Around this time, Italy formed an alliance with Germany. Italy was being led by Fascists, too, after all, and it looked like siding with Hitler would put them on the winning team.

So where were we in all of this? America, for the most part, just sat around, twiddling its proverbial thumbs, listening to the "Little Orphan Annie" program on the radio and going around repeating such catchphrases as "leapin' lizards."

Roosevelt wanted to get into a war with Hitler—partly because it was the right thing to do and partly because he knew how much it would benefit the ailing economy. But most Americans

---

50 Though this and a couple other verses were left out of most versions for years on the grounds that they were dangerously radical, Pete Seeger and Bruce Springsteen sang a version with every verse at a concert to celebrate President Barack Obama's inauguration in 2009.

were opposed to getting involved, on the grounds that what was happening in Europe was none of our business. In fact, Hitler wasn't totally disliked in America. A lot of prominent people (such as Henry Ford) thought he was pretty keen.

The general mood in America was one of isolationism. Americans knew that war wasn't exactly bad for the economy, but recent investigations had shown that weapons builders had made a mint in World War I, and people were pretty ticked off about it. They began to believe, not without reason, that these builders had pushed America into the war just to make money. Responding to people's concern that it would happen again, Congress had passed a neutrality act in 1935 that wouldn't even allow Roosevelt to take sides.

In 1940, England was starting to run out of money and supplies. Roosevelt was starting to get desperate, and began to sell them "surplus" weapons, which was not, technically, something he was allowed to do. Finally, right around the end of 1940, Congress passed the Lend-Lease Act, which allowed him to aid nations whose defense was vital to America. Under the act, he could loan weapons to countries as long as they promised to return them (or something of equal value)

after the war. This allowed America to make money off the war and help the allies without getting the military involved.

Factories were cranked into production to make bombs, guns, battleships, and airplanes to lend to England. The jobs created pretty much brought an end to the Depression, but it would be nearly a year before the United States finally entered the war.

SOME OF THE STUFF WE MISSED

Penny auctions: Sometimes when farms were foreclosed on and auctioned off,

Charles Lindbergh was the first guy to make a solo flight across the Atlantic, making him one of the most famous and admired men in the world. As Hitler began taking over Europe, Lindbergh started an isolationist group called America First, which advocated the idea that Americans shouldn't have anything to do with any other countries. Folk singer Woody Guthrie wrote a song about *that,* too. He said, "They say America first, but they mean America next."

The Empire State Building: A particularly awesome Art Deco skyscraper that opened in New York in 1931. Even now, landlords can jack up the rent on an apartment just by saying it's in an Art Deco building in the listing.

other farmers would get together, buy stuff for pennies, and give it back to the original owner. Anyone who tried to interfere and buy stuff at a fair price would be dealt with severely. Awesome.

Smoot-Hawley Tarriff: Like most tariffs, this is terribly boring to talk about, but Smoot-Hawley is lots of fun to say out loud. And if there's not a punk singer named Holly Smoot, there should be.

John Dillinger: A bank robber who revolutionized the bank robbing industry and became the Robin Hood of the age when the end of Prohibition made most gangsters much less interesting. Stories that he was robbing from the rich to give to the poor were complete applesauce, and most people probably

knew it, but banks were *very* unpopular at the time, and robbing them seemed like a win for the common man.

The Twenty-first Amendment: The amendment to the Constitution that repealed the one banning alcohol. One of the first things Roosevelt pushed through Congress.

Cole Porter: A hugely popular songwriter of the day, author of such standards as "You're the Top," "I Get a Kick out of You," and "Begin the Beguine." To this day, knowing a handful of Cole Porter songs is an easy way to show people that you're sophisticated and classy.

Amelia Earhart: A spectacular female pilot who disappeared over the Bermuda Triangle.

The Spanish Civil War: Another war going on at the time. If you want to find out what it was all about, get yourself a *world* history book, kids.

The Golden Ages: Old people often refer to the 1930s as the Golden Age of comic books, radio, Hollywood, and whatever else they enjoyed back in the good ol' days.

Huey "Kingfish" Long: A Democratic senator who may have been trying to challenge Roosevelt for his party's nomination in the 1936 election but was assassinated by a doctor named Carl Weiss. What Weiss had against Long isn't quite known, as Long's bodyguards pumped the doctor full of lead before he could say anything. Many people think Weiss was framed.

The Hindenburg: A zeppelin (blimp) that crashed in New Jersey.

The Dust Bowl: A section of the Great Plains that suffered from a severe drought in the early 1930s. Woody Guthrie wrote many songs about it.

The Grapes of Wrath: A novel about the Depression and the Dust Bowl era by John Steinbeck. Tom Joad's last speech is a real showstopper, but you can learn just as much about how bad life during the Depression was from the scene in the movie where Grandpa dreams of one day "scrooging" his butt around in a washtub full of grapes.

Robert Johnson: A blues singer rumored to have sold his soul to the devil before his death in 1938. His influence on rock and blues music is incalculable. Even if you know the quadratic formula.

Jazz music: Jazz had been around for some time, but the version known as swing caught on in the 1930s and nearly ended civilization (like most self-respecting musical genres).

END-OF-CHAPTER QUESTIONS

MULTIPLE CHOICE

1. What does your history teacher do during the summer?

a. Tour obscure battlefields along the Eastern Seaboard.

b. Square-dance competitively under the name Dixie Calhoun.

c. Chain-smoke while playing bingo with other teachers.

d. Sit around and eat firecake.

e. Get a washtub full of grapes, sit down in it, and "scrooge around."

(ANSWER: B. WE HAVE PROOF.)

2. Why all the references to Woody Guthrie?

a. His songs captured the Depression era better than those of, say, Cole Porter, whose songs in the 1930s were usually about rich people (though they were excellent songs).

b. The Smart Aleck staff is full of Commies.

c. The Smart Aleck staff is trying to get a backstage pass to the next Woody Guthrie Folk Fest in Okemah, Oklahoma.

d. We know you teens just *love* folk music!

(ANSWER: LET'S GO WITH A.)

3. What should you do if you see a hobo?

  a. Stop, drop, and roll.

  b. Hide any pickles you might be carrying.

  c. Get back in the DeLorean and go back to the future.

  d. Start singing "I've Been Workin' on the Railroad" to entice him to share his stew.

  e. Bow deeply.

(ANSWER: DEPENDS ON THE HOBO.)

4. How did people survive during the Depression?

  a. By doing hard work and not complainin'.

  b. By borrowing money from Al Capone (or whatever gangster ran their neighborhood).

  c. They survived because they had *values* in those days, by gum!

  d. By dropping out of school in fourth grade and going to work in the mines.

(ANSWER: ANY ANSWER IS ACCEPTABLE; GANGSTERS *DID* OFTEN OFFER LOWER INTEREST RATES ON LOANS THAN THE BANKS DID.)

OTHER WOODIE GUTHRIE SONGS YOU SHOULD LOOK UP AND WRITE A REPORT ON

- "Deportee"
- "So Long, It's Been Good to Know Ya"
- "Going Down the Road"
- "I Ain't Got No Home"
- "Jesus Christ"
- "Do Re Mi" (not to be confused with the show tune of the same name)
- "Jarama Valley"
- "Grand Coulee Dam" (The Grand Coulee Dam people paid Guthrie to write songs about the dam. Yes, even Guthrie was a sell-out.)
- "Pastures of Plenty"

THE BIGGEST EXPERIMENT OF ALL!

We can give you all sorts of rhymes and wisecracks about pickles and stoves, but the truth is that the best way to learn something is to experience it for yourself. To help you learn about the Depression—and to make sure you remember what you learn—we suggest you find out for youself what it was like.

First, get a railroad. Make it run. Make it race against time. And build a tower while you're at it. Build it up to the sky.

Then lose it. Lose everything.

Drop out of school and get a job at a factory (plenty of them still play fast and loose with child labor laws), then get fired after an on-the-job injury makes it impossible for you to do your job (plenty of them also still find ways to step around the concept of workers' compensation).

Stand in line for bread. Get as dirty as possible, then sit around on the corner asking passersby for change. Sell them apples, if you can get any. Complete the effect by calling "Say, don't you remember me? I'm your pal!"

By now, you should be pret-ty depressed. Write some poetry about how no one likes you, then hop a freight train. Eat stew when you can get it.

If that doesn't teach you any lessons, at *least* find out what song we're alluding to in this section. We'll put a few versions of it on www.smartalecks guide.com.

CHAPTER

WORLD WAR II (OUT OF . . . ?)

> "I know not with what weapons
> World War III will be fought,
> but World War IV will be fought
> with sticks and stones."
> —Albert Einstein, who worked
> on the atomic bomb (and
> really regretted it)

INTRODUCTION

Obviously, World War I turned out not to be the War to End *all* Wars. In fact, in many ways, it was just a warm-up for World War II, which was even deadlier than World War I. For the first time, civilians were in just as much danger as soldiers.

All the old-fashioned ideas about the nobility of war were swept away. The war ended with the first, and to date the only, use of an atomic bomb in warfare. It didn't end all wars, either, but warfare would certainly never be the same.

DECEMBER 7, 1941: A DATE THAT USED TO LIVE IN INFAMY

Roosevelt badly wanted to get into a war with Hitler but wasn't able to rally the country around the idea until America was attacked on December 7, 1941, when the Japanese bombed Pearl Harbor, an army base in Hawaii (which was not yet a state). Generations of Americans remembered the date of December 7 the same way people today remember September 11.

Lots of people today[51] say that

In our desperate quest to say something snarky, we'll just wonder how that one guy from the 1778 side ever managed to keep his clothes so sparklingly white. Whatever detergent he was using, we'll buy.

[51] And not just conspiracy theorists—anyone who wants to make Roosevelt look bad ends up hovering around this theory sooner or later.

FIRE BALLOONS

Though no battles were fought on the U.S. mainland, the Japanese did manage at least a couple of mainland attacks. In 1942, one sea plane was catapulted from a submarine and flown over Oregon, where it dropped a couple of incendiary bombs intended to start massive forest fires. It might have succeeded if the forest hadn't been too wet for a fire to get started. The Japanese also managed to float a few bombs across the ocean attached to balloons; about nine thousand "fire balloons," or "balloon bombs," were launched in 1944 and 1945, and around 10 percent actually made it across the ocean. A few even managed to kill people, though this was a well-kept secret at the time. A few are still thought to be out there in the forests of the Northwest—still armed and dangerous. ✦

Roosevelt knew that the Pearl Harbor attack was coming and did nothing to stop it in order to get the country into war. Whether this is true, however, will probably never be known. There's plenty of proof that Roosevelt knew the Japanese were planning an attack, but he doesn't seem to have believed they could actually pull it off.

Roosevelt may have been a great president, but he was still living with the prejudices that were common at the time. Neither he nor any of his advisors seemed to believe that the Japanese could successfully attack, not just because they were far from being a world power at the time, but probably also partly because of a belief that they weren't biologically capable of it. Even after the bombing, General MacArthur, who was well on his way to being the country's most famous pain in the butt, insisted that the pilots must have been mercenaries, on the grounds that the Japanese didn't have good enough eyesight to fly airplanes. And *this* is the guy they put in charge of fighting the Japanese.

Japan was being run at the time by a group of people who were really, really into warfare and expansion. While Hitler stomped around Europe, Japan was stomping around the Pacific, looking to expand its territories, and Roosevelt had been trying to stop them, or at least slow them down, by building U.S. military bases around the Pacific. Roosevelt didn't want a war with Japan, he wanted a war with Hitler. Though he knew that the Japanese were ticked off at him, he surely hoped they wouldn't really attack.

But attack they did. On December 7, a fleet of more than three hundred Japanese planes attacked Pearl Harbor, killing more than twenty-three hundred American soldiers and wounding over a thousand more. Only sixty-five Japanese soldiers were killed in the process.

That night, Roosevelt took to the airwaves, famously describing December 7, 1941, as "a date which will live in infamy," and told people that we were now at war with Japan. The next day, Roosevelt asked Congress to declare war, and they almost unanimously approved. A few days later, Germany and Italy, which were allied with Japan, declared war on America. World War II had "begun."

Actually, it had begun years before. Hitler had been throwing everything he had at basically everyone in Europe, and America had sat on its hands, pretending it was someone else's problem, for years. Low-rent smart alecks in America love to gloat that we saved England's butt in World War II, but the English rightly point out that it certainly took us long

General Douglas MacArthur was one of only about five guys ever to achieve the rank of general of the army. He earned more medals than any other officer in World War I, and often led his men into battle while refusing to wear a gas mask. After achieving the rank of general, MacArthur rose to national fame by attacking the Bonus Army in 1932. The attack was actually made in defiance of President Hoover, but defying orders had always been a habit of MacArthur's. His tendency to attack what he wanted, where he wanted, when he wanted, no matter what the president wanted him to do, would make him one of the most admired—and most controversial—of all U.S. military figures.

enough to realize that it was our problem, too, not just England's.

As the army began to prepare for war, Americans on the home front decided to do their part by beating the crap out of anyone who looked remotely Japanese. Grocery stores owned by Japanese Americans were vandalized, and Warner Bros. rushed to the studio to create cartoons such as "Bugs Bunny Nips

Uncle Sam: "Seriously . . . pull my finger!"

the Nips"[52] and "Tokio Jokio" that made the racial stereotypes in earlier cartoons seem downright tame.

Roosevelt did his part by ordering all resident aliens to be registered with the government about five weeks after the attack. This was the beginning of the biggest smear on Roosevelt's record: a month after the order was given, Roosevelt approved a plan to remove Japanese Americans from their homes and make them live in camps in states like Colorado and Utah, to keep them from aiding the enemy. Eventually about a hundred thousand Japanese Americans were forced to give up their homes and

---

52 "Nip" was a racist term for the a Japanese person.

possessions and move to these camps. They weren't nearly as bad as some of the camps in Germany, but they weren't exactly the Ritz, either. Only one elected official—Ralph Lawrence Carr, the governor of Colorado—had the stones to stand up for Japanese citizens during the war. It cost him his job.

In the early days of the war with Japan, things didn't go very well. American forces had a tendency to be absolutely routed by Japanese forces, and were eventually driven out of the Philippines and forced to set up a base in Australia until more troops could be amassed. Having been forced to retreat, General MacArthur dramatically stated, "I shall return." Roosevelt asked him to change the statement to "*We* shall return," but MacArthur refused to comply. At times, it seemed that if Roosevelt had ordered MacArthur to refrain from picking his nose, MacArthur would have started digging.

WAR BRIDES
Australian women *loved* the U.S. soldiers stationed in Australia during the war. As many as fifteen thousand of them ended up marrying soldiers. Australian men, as a whole, had been glad when the U.S. Army showed up to keep the Japanese away, but after they started losing their girlfriends, men around Australia complained that the U.S. troops were "overpaid, oversexed, and over here."

Command of the Philippines was given to another general, Jonathan Wainwright, but MacArthur continued to try to run the war himself from afar. Though he ordered Wainwright not to surrender the Philippines, Wainwright eventually had no choice, and in May 1942, he surrendered all U.S. forces in the Philippines to the Japanese army, which sent about sixty-six thousand Filipino soldiers, along with about ten thousand American soldiers, on a brutal sixty-mile march that came to be known as the Bataan Death March. Around ten thousand of the soldiers died during the march. General Wainwright and his men remained prisoners of war for three years.

A week later, though, U.S. planes began to bomb mainland Japan. They didn't do much in the way of real damage with these bombing raids, but the raids helped build U.S. morale, which was pretty badly hurt after the loss in the Philippines.

MEANWHILE, BACK ON THE HOME FRONT

Exactly how many Americans ended up serving in the war is one of those questions to which different people will give you different answers, but it was somewhere along the lines of sixteen million. That sixteen million, however, only represents the number who

Rosie the Riveter, one of the best pieces of war propaganda ever (and one we can still be proud of today). As the men of America went off to war, women took their places in the factories on the home front, showing that they could do anything men could do. Of course, after the war ended, they were expected to head right back to the kitchen.

served in the military. Everyone in the country was involved in the war whether they liked it or not. Opposition to American involvement in World War II dried up very quickly; guys like Charles Lindbergh who initially said it was none of our business shut their big yaps pretty quickly after Pearl Harbor.

To keep the army from running out of supplies, common household items were rationed, and therefore hard to get. People were encouraged to turn in anything made of tin, steel, rubber, or aluminum so it could be used to build weapons.

Taxes during the war were high; practically everyone agreed that paying higher taxes during wartime was necessary for the war effort. Roosevelt's attempts to impose a hundred percent income tax for income over $25,000 (meaning that $25,000 was the maximum anyone could earn—if you earned $100,000, $75,000 would have gone to taxes), however, were unsuccessful. No one was *that* patriotic.

There was no question that the war was good for the economy. Countless factories were converted for military use, and anyone who was out of work could sign up for the army—the military would take pretty much anybody. The last lingering effects of the Depression were wiped away.

Americans at home weren't quite as affected as the home-bound British, who were getting bombed back to the Stone Age as Hitler launched a series of blitzkriegs, or bombing raids, on London. Initially, Hitler had ordered the Nazis *not* to attack London, but, after someone got the wrong memo and did it anyway, the Royal Air Force countered by bombing Berlin. The Germans countered by bombing London again. And the Royal Air Force countered by . . . well, you get the idea. Over the course of the war, these bombing raids claimed the lives of thousands of innocent civilians on both sides.

In England, the entire country participated in blackouts. Windows were covered in thick black fabric, and outside lights were painted black to make it more difficult for German planes to find anything to bomb. City parents, fearful of bombings, sent their children to live with strangers in the country; anyone with an extra room was expected to house an evacuee. People carried gas masks wherever they went. And people were encouraged to eat

Few people worried that Japan could ever attack the mainland United States, seeing as how it was protected by the Pacific Ocean. According to legend, Jack Warner of Warner Bros. worried that his studio looked too much like Lockheed, the aircraft manufacturer that was a likely target of any theoretical bombings, from the air. To ensure the safety of his studio, he painted a big arrow with the words LOCKHEED THATAWAY! on the roof. This is probably just an urban myth, though. If it's true, no one seems to have thought to get a picture of it.

potatoes, skins and all, as often as humanly possible, because potatoes contain a lot of nutrients and didn't have to be imported. Lord Woolton, the British food minister, never seemed to shut up about potatoes. A popular rhyme of the day reminded people to eat potatoes with the skins still on, "knowing that the sight of peelings / Deeply hurts Lord Woolton's feelings."

Rationing was a lot harsher in England, too. At one point, people were allotted only one slim bar of soap per month and only five inches of water per bath. Nylon stockings were outlawed, since nylon was needed for parachutes; some women simply painted their legs brown to make it look like they were wearing stockings. Many even painted a seam. Clothing factories were eventually shut down to free factory workers to join the army.

But while it wasn't quite as rough in America, where only people on the West Coast had to worry even a little about being bombed, everyone was expected to pitch in, and people found all sorts of ways to help the war effort, from going to work in munitions factories to turning in household goods made of metal for use in tanks.

AND IN EUROPE

While soldiers in the Pacific set up camp around Asia to prepare for an

The "Big Three": Winston Churchill, FDR, and Stalin. Stalin was at least as big a jerk as Hitler, but was on the Allies' side at this point.

attack on Japan, millions were sent to Europe and North Africa to help stop Hitler.

In early 1943, Roosevelt met up with British prime minister Winston Churchill to put together a strategy for the eventual invasion of Europe. All they were prepared to do at the time was defend England and the other countries that Hitler hadn't taken over yet, but they knew that sooner or later they were going to have to launch an invasion to liberate the countries Hitler had taken over and eventually take over Germany itself.

Hitler, meanwhile, had invaded Russia, which was a huge mistake. The Battle of Stalingrad, in which Germany and its allies fought Russia for control of the city, raged for a good six months and is sometimes considered the bloodiest battle in human history. Casualties reached something like a million and a half.

The Nazis were able to handle the

TOP HITS OF THE DAY

This was the era of the Big Band and singing groups such as the Andrews Sisters. One thing the whole Smart Aleck Staff agrees on is that World War II had the best music of any major war. Very few songs *about* the war are remembered today, though a few, such as "Remember Pearl Harbor" and "Praise the Lord and Pass the Ammunition," were popular in their day. Some other good songs from the war include "Boogie Woogie Bugle Boy," "We'll Meet Again," "Lili Marlene" (which was popular with both the Allies and the Nazis), "Miss Pavlichenko" (an upbeat tune by Woody Guthrie—go find out who Miss Pavlichenko was!), and "Right in der Fuhrer's Face," recorded by comedian Spike Jones (this became the sound track for a cartoon rarely shown nowadays in which Donald Duck dreams he's a Nazi). Go on our Web page for audio clips!

Soldiers, meanwhile, continued their custom of writing naughty and gory parodies of popular songs. One, "Blood on the Risers," which is set to the tune of "The Battle Hymn of the Republic," tells in great detail the story of a parachuter whose chute doesn't open:

> *He hit the ground, the sound was "Splat," his blood went spurting high,*
> *His comrades all were heard to say: "A hell of a way to die!"*
> *He lay there rolling round in the welter of his gore,*
> *Now he ain't gonna jump no more!*
> *Gory gory, what a hell of a way to die.*
> *Gory gory, what a hell of a way to die.*
> *Gory gory, what a hell of a way to die.*
> *He ain't gonna jump no more!* [53]

Meanwhile, back on the home front in England, schoolchildren sang "Hitler Is a Jerk" to the tune of "Whistle While You Work," including verses so naughty that we can't print them if we don't want parents outside Smart Aleck Headquarters with torches, but you are, as usual, free to look them up yourself. Many of them were first heard on school playgrounds, after all.

Russian army, but not the Russian winter. In late January, when the Russian army captured a group of about ninety thousand German soldiers, it was the first time a German officer had surrendered to any army. The soldiers were taken prisoner, and all but about five thousand died; starvation and freezing caused massive amounts of German fa-

talities. The Allies still probably would have won the war eventually (spoiler alert: they did), but it would have taken a lot longer if Hitler hadn't invaded Russia. Napoléon had made the same mistake back in 1812. So let this be a lesson to those of you who plan to take over Europe in a ground war: don't plan on Christmas in Moscow.

AND IN FRANCE

Crack all the jokes about the French

---

[53] For the complete lyrics, see www.smart alecksguide.com.

you want (actually, we here at the Smart Aleck's Guide don't recommend making *any* ethnic jokes, even about the French), but people who worked for the French Resistance during World War II were tough as nails.

While the Nazis occupied their country, most French people just lived their lives the same way they had before the Nazis had shown up—or at least they tried to. The rations and curfews imposed by the Nazis were awfully harsh, but the French, like the British, rolled up their sleeves and tried to make do. They had to be awfully tough just to keep going.

People from every possible walk of life joined underground resistance groups that worked to aid the Allies, establish escape routes, and generally annoy the crap out of the Nazis. As the Nazis imposed harsher terms on the

Hitler gets his picture taken at the Eiffel Tower in 1940. Ten bucks says he cut in front of everyone else in line at the gift shop. That's just the kind of guy he was.

French—including censoring their news, bombarding them with propaganda, and occasionally razing entire villages that they decided they didn't like—the number of people serving in the Resistance grew.

One of the biggest jobs of the Resistance movement was spying. Resistance spies would check out what sort of fortifications the Germans had set up around the shore and relay the information to the Allies in the form of coded messages that were broadcast over the radio.

Sabotage was also important. One of the most effective ways the French found

THE NAME OF THE WAR

At first, no one called the war World War II; most people just called it the war. When he had to give it a specific name, Roosevelt would usually call it the Tyrants' War or the War for Survival of Democracy. Eventually, in 1945, when the war was nearly over, he asked Secretary of War Henry Stimson to pick an official name, and his choice, World War II, stuck. We here at the Smart Aleck's Guide think it was a stupid idea on his part. When you give something a name like World War II, it sort of implies that there's going to be a third one sooner or later.

to antagonize the Nazis was to destroy the railroads so that the Germans couldn't use them. At first, the Resistance movement built their own bombs, but eventually found it easier simply to steal dynamite from the Nazis. Quite a bit of track was blown up before they figured out that removing the bolts holding the rail to the ground worked just as well in the long run.

And make no mistake—this was seriously dangerous business. By one estimate, the life expectancy of anyone actively working for the Resistance in France was about six months.

D—DAY: JUNE 6, 1944

The most difficult task facing Allied

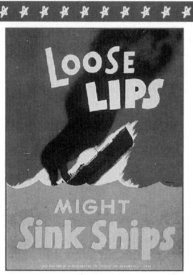

The invasion of Normandy had to be kept a closely guarded secret.

troops was invading Europe itself. Throughout 1943 and early 1944, bombing raids were carried out all over Europe, but bombing a country from an airplane and actually taking it over via ground invasion are two different things.

Invading and taking back France and the rest of Europe had been a major war goal since the beginning of the war, but the French coastline was heavily fortified by German artillery. The Allies were faced not only with the task of preparing one of the most massive military operations in history but also with doing so in such a way that the Germans, stationed only miles away from the British coastline, wouldn't know what was going on.

At the 1943 conference in Tehran to plan the invasion, Churchill noted that the plans must be protected by "a bodyguard of lies." To keep the Germans guessing, the Allies set up a couple of invasion plans: Operation Bodyguard, which was designed to make the Germans think the Allies were invading later than planned, and Operation Fortitude, which was to make them think Norway would be invaded first.

The real invasion was named Operation Overlord. Quite a few pieces of information about the operation were leaked. For example, the word "overlord" appeared in a crossword puzzle in British newspapers the day of the

General Eisenhower gives the troops the ol' thumbs-up. Apparently, what he's actually saying here is "Go get 'em, Michigan," to a soldier from that state.

invasion, which seemed like quite an alarming coincidence to officials. They quickly brought the guy who wrote the puzzle in for questioning. However, while the Germans knew that something called Operation Overlord was going on, they had no details about it and eventually brushed it off as just another phony plan meant to distract them.

General Dwight D. Eisenhower, who was in charge of the invasion, was nervous about the whole thing. He felt that there was only about a 50 percent chance that it would be successful. But on June 5, he rallied the troops, and early the next morning, 150,000 men sailed and parachuted onto the beaches of Normandy. Within a couple of weeks, more than 600,000 troops had stormed the beach, bringing with them over 200,000 tons of supplies.

Casualties were high; about ten thousand Allied soldiers were captured, wounded, or killed. But in the end, the invasion was a succcess. The Battle of Normandy was a decisive victory for the Allies. Churchill announced that while the war was far from over, the invasion marked "the beginning of the end." Or at least "the end of the beginning."

SO, NOW WHAT?

Soon there were around a million Allied troops on the Continent, slowly driving the Nazis back to Germany. But it wasn't going to be easy to finish the job.

Efforts on the part of the French Resistance to blow up the railways around

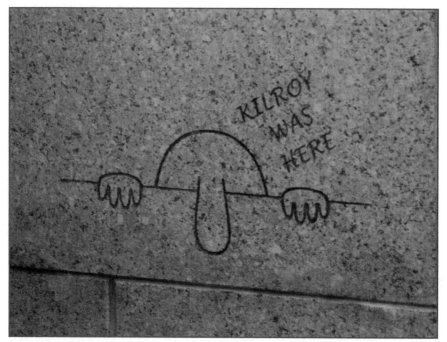

Some soldier starting writing "Kilroy was here" wherever he went. Who this was, or what it really meant, is one of those things that people argue about. In reality, several people were probably doing it; others seem to have copied whoever was doing it first, as the phrase soon showed up all over the world. If *you* write it on the wall at school, you can claim that you're paying tribute to American forces in World War II! As usual, don't come crying to us if you get in trouble.

France had been very successful in keeping the Germans from using them, but there was a drawback: once the Allies landed, they couldn't use them, either.

In August, the Allies regained control of Paris, but pushing farther through France was a difficult task. However, the German high command soon began to realize that defeat was inevitable.

Things were looking up in the Pacific, too. General MacArthur and his men finally returned, as promised, and dealt the Japanese navy a major defeat at the Battle of Leyte Gulf. There were still no plans for an actual ground invasion of Japan on the table, but the Japanese had to rely increasingly on kamikaze attacks—suicide missions in planes full of explosives. These attacks would eventually kill an estimated one hundred thousand American soldiers.

Back on the home front, Roosevelt was doing something no one else had

The Battle of the Bulge. Camouflage is pret-ty useless in the snow.

ever tried: running for a fourth term as president. In 1940, he had been so popular that when he decided to run for a third term (though no one had ever won one before), the Republicans decided that they might just as well run someone with a name like Wendell Willkie against him. Roosevelt defeated Willkie pretty handily.

In 1944, the Republicans ran Thomas Dewey, the governor of New York, against Roosevelt, and Roosevelt again won easily, despite the fact that he was deathly ill by then. He had always been a sick man, of course, but now doctors were pretty sure he was dying. We don't want to spoil the end of the chapter for you, but he would only live a few months into his fourth term.

THE BATTLE OF THE BULGE

In December of 1944, shortly after Roosevelt won his record-shattering fourth term, the Germans launched one last offensive. Because this surge looked like a bulge cutting into the

Allied lines, the fight became known as the Battle of the Bulge.

By this time, the Germans knew they were never going to win the war. Hitler's idea was that if he hit the Allies hard enough, they'd agree to just leave him alone rather than invading Germany. The Allies had no intention of letting Hitler remain in power under any circumstances, so the whole surge was a waste of time on Hitler's part.

The attack caught the Allies with their pants down and caused about nineteen thousand American deaths in the first few days. But in another way, the Nazis played right into the hands of the Allied forces. Running extremely low on fuel, the Allies were having a hard time pushing into France, and with the Battle of the Bulge, the German army kind of solved the problem for them. They couldn't get to the Germans, so the Germans came to them.

This isn't to say that it wasn't a rough battle, though. The Battle of the Bulge consisted of a couple of weeks of harsh fighting in the forest of Ardennes, which was freezing cold and covered in snow.

The Allies had figured that the Germans were planning an attack at some point, but the Ardennes Offensive, as the German operation was officially called, really took them by surprise; perhaps they thought Hitler had learned his lesson about fighting in cold weather when the winter ravaged his troops in Russia. But learning lessons just wasn't one of Hitler's strong points.

The element of surprise took its toll on the Allied defense, and the battle became the bloodiest that America fought in the war. Some twenty thousand Allied soldiers were killed, and another sixty thousand or so were wounded, captured or missing by the end of it. In the first three days, a couple of U.S. infantry divisions were even forced to surrender.

Midway through the battle, German forces encircled Allied forces near the town of Bastogne in Belgium, and the German commander sent a note to General Anthony McAuliffe, who was in charge of the Allies in the town, asking for him to surrender with honor to keep them from blowing up the entire town. McAuliffe responded by saying, "Nuts!"

The message was sent to German officers, reading, "Nuts—the American commander." Soon, German officers appeared at the camp to ask him exactly what the heck he meant. He explained that it meant that he wasn't about to surrender.

It took a couple of weeks for the Allies to halt the German offensive, but at the end of it, the German supply lines were heavily depleted. Since they were also unable to stop the Russians from advancing on their eastern border,

Germans found themselves under attack from both the east and the west without enough weapons left to defend either side. The war was coming to an end.

THE HOLOCAUST: JUST HOW BAD WAS HITLER?

Even as the Allies advanced ever closer to Germany and the defeat of the Nazis began to seem inevitable, few people had any idea just how bad Hitler really was. They knew he was a jerk who wanted to take over the world, but the horrors of his Final Solution had not yet been revealed.

Hitler had effectively brainwashed an entire nation. He had brought hope to the downtrodden Germans but had done so by giving them an enemy to blame all their problems on: the Jews. Jews had never been the most popular group in Europe; they'd been getting kicked out of one country after another for centuries. All through the late nineteenth and early twentieth centuries, there were occasional violent anti-Jewish riots and pogroms in which the Jews were forced to leave town (if they could even make it out alive, and the people kicking them out certainly tried to stop them from pulling that off). Countless thousands of Jews had already been kicked out of Russia during the twentieth century by the time World War II began.

Some have disputed whether "Nuts" was actually McAuliffe's response. About ten years later, when asked what his actual response to the request to surrender was, McAuliffe (above) apparently said he hadn't said "Nuts" at all. He claimed that he'd actually said an unpleasant synonym for poo that we can't print here if we want any schools to buy this book. Officers who were present, though, insist that he really did say "Nuts."

In Germany, many people were convinced that all of their economic problems existed not because there had just been a devasting war, but because there was some sort of massive Jewish conspiracy to control the world's banks.[54] Hitler had always been quite open about driving Jews out of Germany's political and cultural scene.

---

[54] Some idiots *still* go around saying that this is true, and that the Holocaust was just something the Jews invented to drum up some sympathy. See *The Smart Aleck's Guide to People Even Pacifists Can Enjoy Punching.*

When he took power, he slowly began to strip away Jews' rights. In 1933, they were barred from active involvement in politics and from practicing law and owning farms. They were kicked out of their jobs at newspapers, and the number of Jews allowed at universities became strictly limited.

In 1935, Hitler passed the Nuremberg Laws, which stripped Jews of their citizenship altogether. By 1939, Jews in any territory the Nazis were in charge of were being forced to live in ghettos and work for the German war effort. Many of these ghettos were set up near railroad tracks, partly because it would make people easier to transport when the time came. It was generally understood among Hitler's associates that there would eventually be a "Final Solution to the Jewish Problem": killing every last one of them.

As early as 1933, the Nazis began sending Jews to concentration camps, where they were tortured and forced into slave labor. Medical experiments were performed on some of them. Many were simply worked to death. Countless thousands were sent to gas chambers to be killed—thousands per day, in some camps.

In the end, around six million Jews were killed. Reports of what was going on in these camps had leaked out, but few people in the Allied countries

USING HITLER TO WIN AN ARGUMENT

Ever since the beginning of World War II, people have tried to score points on political opponents by comparing them to Hitler or the Nazis. Some people say that the first person to do this in any argument loses automatically; this is sometimes called Godwin's Law, though that law actually states, "As an online discussion grows longer, the probability of a comparison involving Nazis or Hitler approaches one." We think both versions are true.

Another form of using Hitler to win an argument is something called reductio ad Hitlerum, which is the practice of saying "Hitler liked X, so anyone who likes X must be like Hitler." For instance, "Hitler outlawed guns, so everyone who wants guns banned is a Nazi," or "Hitler was a vegetarian, so being a vegetarian must be evil." It's a classic debate trick for people who aren't very smart.

believed them. Even in Germany, where the rights of Jews had been stripped away so slowly that many barely even seemed to notice it was happening, many people had no idea what horrors were going on in the camps, even though some of them were right near the cities. News about the gas chambers was broadcast in 1943, but most people assumed it was just war propaganda on the grounds that it seemed too terrible to be true. Even now, some people *still* insist that the whole thing couldn't really have happened, despite overwhelming evidence that it did.

Of course, it wasn't just the Jews that

the Nazis were out to get. The Nazis were very much of the opinion that only "pure" Germans should be allowed any power in Germany, and that anyone who wasn't part of the "master race" was just getting in the way. In addition to Jews, they sent Poles, Roma (Gypsies), Slavs, and Soviet prisoners of war to extermination camps, as well as disabled, mentally ill, and homosexual people, and any others whom the Nazis deemed "inferior." In all, somewhere between nine and eleven million people were murdered.

It wasn't until the mortified Allies discovered the camps that many people truly realized just how bad things had been—and how big a mistake it had been for the United States not to get involved in the war sooner. Unfortunately, by the time the camps were liberated, it was practically too late. The Nazis had set out to murder every Jew in eastern Europe, and they were pretty much finished by the time the camps were liberated.

VICTORY IN EUROPE

In April of 1945, in what you could probably call a foreshadowing of the fact that the war was just about over, some of the major players in the whole affair died.

First, on April 12, President Roosevelt died of a brain hemorrhage at his

The official U.S. Army newspaper announcing the death of Hitler. Putting this in the book was considered a bit more tasteful than using the alleged pictures of his dead body (there are a couple of photos going around in which he sort of looks like a crash-test dummy with a mustache), though we wonder whether the words "tasteful" and "Hitler" have any business going together.

retreat in Warm Springs, Georgia, which he had often used as a quiet, out-of-the-way place to fool around with Lucy Mercer. Vice President Harry Truman was sworn in as president.

Meanwhile, in Germany, Hitler had retreated to a bunker (kind of like his own, less pleasant version of Warm Springs) where he continued to command his army, which was clearly falling apart. He had not made a public speech since fall of 1943. In April of 1945, as the Russian army invaded Berlin, he had something of a nervous breakdown and admitted to the people in the bunker with him that Germany was going to lose the war. He then announced his intention to commit suicide.

People reading more reputable history books might get to see the famous shot of the flag-raising at Iwo Jima. You, however, get stuck with this one.

* * * * * * * * * * * * * * * * * * * *

But first, he felt it would be wise to marry his longtime girlfriend, Eva Braun, who had been living at the bunker with him. They were married on April 29, 1945, in a small ceremony in the bunker. About forty hours later, with Soviet forces less than a quarter of a mile away, Hitler, Eva, and a couple of other bunker denizens had a light lunch, during which Hitler said his good-byes to everyone who had been holed up with him. He and Eva then went to his private study, where they drank some poison. Eva died from the poison, but Hitler survived long enough to shoot himself in the head.

German officers then dragged out the bodies, doused them with gas, and set them on fire. What remained of the bodies would be dug up and reburied several times over the years before finally being dumped into a river in 1970.

Of course, many people don't believe this story. Lots of people believe that Hitler actually faked his death and escaped, living the rest of his life in exile. Even Stalin insisted that Hitler was still alive. In the 1950s, rumors went around that he had escaped to the South Pole, of all places. Other people say he went to South America and became (get this) a priest.

Whether or not Hitler was dead, though, the Nazi regime was. About a week later, the Germans formally surrendered to General Eisenhower in France and to the Russians in Berlin. The war in Europe—and one of the grisliest episodes in human history—was over.

BUT DON'T FORGET JAPAN!

Around this time, things were starting to turn around for the Allies in the Pacific as well.

In March of 1945 came the Battle of Iwo Jima, a battle for an eight-square-mile volcanic island that served as Japan's last line of radar defense. If they

lost control of Iwo Jima, the Japanese would have no warning of American air attacks on the main islands of Japan.

The battle lasted more than a month, and the casualty rate was astronomical: the U.S. Marines suffered around a 50 percent casualty rate, the highest they'd ever suffered. About 6,800 were killed, and 28,000 were wounded. The Japanese fared even worse: approximately 21,000 Japanese troops fought in the battle, and around 20,000 were killed.

After the U.S. forces took control of Iwo Jima, they invaded Okinawa on Japan's main island on April 1. While the invasion was successful, it would be the bloodiest battle America fought in the Pacific, with some 80,000 casualties. By the time Okinawa finally fell, about 200,000 Japanese soldiers and civilians had been killed, along with more than 12,000 Americans.

A couple of weeks later, General MacArthur finally finished recapturing the Philippines. Having the Philippines, Okinawa and Iwo Jima under control, the United States was finally set up to launch a major ground invasion of Japan.

HIROSHIMA

You would not have wanted to be Harry Truman in the summer of 1945. The war in Europe was over, but the invasion of Japan was still to come—

A photo of what was left of Hiroshima, autographed by the guy who flew the plane that dropped the bomb, the *Enola Gay*. Captain Robert Lewis, copilot of the mission, wrote, "My God, what have we done?" in his journal the night after the bombing. On the other hand, Colonel Paul Tibbets, the pilot who signed the photo, later said, "Hell yeah, I'd do it again!" and even reenacted the bombing at air shows. ✱

and it wasn't going to be pretty. Truman's advisors told him that invading Japan would lead to as many as a million American casualties, and General MacArthur insisted that the Japanese would turn it into a guerilla war that

General MacArthur with Emperor Hirohito of Japan. We're guessing MacArthur is using every last bit of willpower he has to keep from challenging Hirohito to a wrestling match. ✱

would go on for at least ten years. Even though MacArthur was known to refer to the Japanese as "purple-pissing Japs," people were expected to listen to him.

Of course, the option was to employ a new weapon: the atomic bomb, a new bomb that was about as powerful as fifteen thousand tons of TNT and could wipe out an entire city. Development of the atomic bomb had been so secret that Truman hadn't even known about it when he was vice president. And no one knew exactly how destructive the thing was going to be; they knew it could destroy a city but didn't have any idea what else it might do. They had no way of knowing without actually using it.

It was a tough choice. People still argue today about whether Truman made the right decision when he decided to drop a bomb that was able to kill close to eighty thousand people instantly and wound another hundred thousand, not to mention leveling almost every building in the city of Hiroshima in the process. Some say that far more people would have been killed over the course of a long war following a ground invasion. Others say that MacArthur's claim that the Japanese would never surrender was just MacArthur being dramatic, as was his habit, and that, since the Russians had just joined the fight against Japan,

Japan was probably getting ready to surrender anyway. Some also suggest that dropping the bomb wasn't so much to scare the Japanese into surrendering as to show the Russians, who were already making Americans nervous, exactly what we were capable of if *they* ever started a war with us.

But whatever his reasons, Truman decided to drop the first atomic bomb on Hiroshima on August 6, 1945, annihilating the city. Three days later, another atomic bomb was dropped on Nagasaki. A few weeks later, the Japanese forces formally surrendered to General MacArthur, officially ending the war.

SOME OF THE STUFF WE MISSED

Anderson shelters: Cheap shelters installed in backyards in England (where they call backyards gardens). They didn't look like much, but they were surprisingly effective. The one above was eventually dug up and used as a shed.

Midway atoll: Small islands about a third of the way between Hawaii and Tokyo. Japan's defeat at the Battle of Midway in 1942 was the beginning of the end of their dominance in the Pacific.

Navajo code talkers: The Navajo language was the only code the Japanese were never able to break. Only about thirty non-Navajo people in the world spoke the language, and none of them was Japanese.

Nuremberg trials: Trials in Nuremberg, Germany, of many, many Nazi war criminals by the International Military Tribunal after the war.

The Great Purge: Stalin's prewar attempts to kill anyone he didn't like. We barely go into what a colossal jerk Stalin was in this book, but take our word for it—this guy was a jerk. Even Lenin, the guy who had been in charge of Russia before, thought so. Some say the only reason the Holocaust didn't happen in Russia was that the Jews had already been kicked out.

The Battle of Guadalcanal: A battle for one of the Solomon Islands that lasted six months. A turning point for the Allies.

The July 20 Plot: A plot hatched by several German military big shots to kill Hitler on July 20, 1944. The Nazis arrested about five thousand people for suspected involvement, and two hundred were executed.

Friedrich Fromm: A German commander who knew about the July 20 Plot but kept quiet until after it failed, at which point he started making arrests. He was later tried and sentenced to death by hanging. Hitler himself generously commuted the sentence—to death by firing squad.

Ludwig Beck: The guy who was probably going to become president of Germany if the July 20 Plot succeeded.

General George Patton: Another U.S. general serving on the European front.

The Marshall Plan: America's plan to rebuild Europe after the war, named for Secretary of State George C. Marshall.

END-OF-CHAPTER QUESTIONS

MULTIPLE CHOICE

1. What was the point of bombing Nagasaki?
   a. No one knows for sure—there were no orders *not* to, so the pilots went ahead with it.
   b. Symmetry.
   c. Just to drive the point home.
   d. Gotta nuke somethin'.

(ANSWER: PROBABLY A.)

2. What was Roosevelt's biggest mistake?
   a. Not integrating the army.
   b. The internment of the Japanese.
   c. Not acting on Pearl Harbor information.
   d. Dropping Welles as a running mate in favor of the more conservative Truman.
   e. Running in 1944 despite the fact that he was two-thirds dead.

(ANSWER: YOU DECIDE.)

3. Which animal did Winston Churchill look most like?
   a. A three-toed sloth.
   b. A toad.
   c. A turtle.
   d. None; show some respect! The guy was a hero!

(ANSWER: B AND D.)

4. Why did the Allies cross the English Channel at Normandy?
   a. Everyone prefers a lesser-known beach to the more crowded ones.
   b. Because just walking up to Hitler's bunker, leaving a burning bag of poo on the ground, ringing the bell, and running wouldn't have solved much.
   c. Don't ask me. Bob Hope might know. Write to his estate.
   d. To get to the other side!

(ANSWER: A, REALLY. IT WASN'T AS WELL KNOWN OR AS WELL GUARDED AS OTHER FRENCH BEACHES.)

ESSAY

1. What do you think would have happened to Hitler if he hadn't committed suicide? Trial by jury? Shot by Russian soldiers? New job as a used-car salesman?

2. Who was a bigger jerk, Hitler or Stalin?

VOCABULARY WORDS!

Write 'em down and make yourself some flash cards.

BABY'S HEAD: Meat pudding that was part of soldiers' food in England. Probably a step above firecake (or, say, gruel), but no match for a cool, crispy pickle.

BASE RAT: A soldier who didn't do much actual fighting. No one is known to have called Eisenhower one of these to his face (though MacArthur called him "the best . . . clerk I ever had." For his part, when asked about MacArthur, Eisenhower said, "I studied dramatics under him for seven years!").

DUGOUT DOUG: MacArthur.

HANGAR QUEEN: An aircraft that constantly needed repairs.

JARHEAD: A marine. No one knows where this one came from.

JUNGLE JUICE: Booze made from whatever was handy. Rarely tasty.

MAE WEST: A life jacket (named for an entertainer with a larger-than-average chest).

PUCKER FACTOR: How dangerous a mission was; the "pucker factor" did not refer to the pucker of the lips on one's face, if you get our drift.

SNAFU: An acronym for Situation Normal: All "Fouled" Up.

TARGET PASTE: A gravy that reminded soldiers of the glue used to patch bullet holes. Both were made from pretty much the same stuff.

TOKYO ROSE: A generic term for a group of female disc jockeys on English-language Japanese radio programs who broadcast anti-American propaganda but were often popular with soldiers anyway for their fine musical taste. For more information, look up information about Iva Toguri, a Tokyo Rose who was convicted of treason in a bout of postwar paranoia and was later pardoned.

WILCO: The contraction of "will" and "comply"; used in radio communications.

ASSIGNMENT!

Dig up the full lyrics of the song "Blood on the Risers" and make a diorama illustrating it. You'll need some ketchup. We here at the Smart Aleck Staff spent weeks ignoring our research so we could build our "Blood on the Risers" Action Play Set. Send us a picture of *yours* and we just might put it on our Web page! Be *somewhat* tasteful, please.

CHAPTER

10

1947–89:
THE "WE DIDN'T START THE FIRE" ERA

By the 1950s, the supply of public domain images (things we can print for free) starts to thin out, leaving cheapskate historians like us to resort to whatever they can find.

> "Haven't they heard we won
> the war? What do they keep on
> fighting for?"
> —Dr. Billy Joel,
> historian

INTRODUCTION

The economy got back on its feet after World War II, but it didn't happen right away. Millions of soldiers came back home and didn't have jobs waiting for them. The army had promised to teach them useful skills, but manning a machine gun or flying a fighter plane didn't really qualify you for very many postwar jobs. In the late 1940s, according to our source,[55] you couldn't *buy* a job.

Millions of soldiers celebrated the end of the war by comin' home, marryin' their best girl, and gettin' busy with her. Others took advantage of the free time unemployment afforded them and got even busier, if you get our drift (nudge nudge wink wink). All of this action, of course, led to the baby boom. About twenty-four million babies had been born in the United States in the 1930s. In the 1940s, the jump that occurred after 1946 pushed the number for that

Eisenhower was not named Ike, but having Ike for a nickname made it easy for supporters to come up with a slogan. For our money, no presidential candidate yet has come up with a catchier one.

decade to thirty-two million.[56] By the mid-1950s, four million babies were being born every year. By 1965, four out of ten Americans were under the age of thirty. The generation born just after the war grew up to be known as baby boomers.

Baby boomers grew up rolling their eyes as their parents talked about growing up during the Depression, but they grew up to be just about equally annoying themselves. Even now, you run into a lot of people who think 1956 was America's best year; to hear them talk, you'd think that in those days, all

---

55 Grandpa Carl.

56 The lesson here: Fool around, get pregnant. We have to throw in morals like this somewhere if we want to sell any copies of this book!

✱ 239 ✱

Billy Joel gets an honorary doctorate from Syracuse University, qualifying him to teach history to slackers like us (probably)! ✷

families got along, there was no crime, neighbors never fought,[57] everyone had plenty to eat, TV shows were better than they are now, no one used bad language, everyone went to church, and teenagers never had sex before marriage. They talk about it at great length, and listening to them is about as much fun as winning a gruel-eating contest.

These people have apparently mistaken the TV show *Leave It to Beaver* for a historical documentary. Sure, things were better for most people in the 1950s than they had been in the

previous couple of decades, and they finally had television to keep them entertained, but in many cities, black kids still went to different, invariably nastier, schools than the white kids. Interracial marriage was still illegal in many states. Animated cartoons still frequently relied on racist stereotypes for their humor. People could lose their job just by being *accused* of being or even knowing a Communist. And kids at school had to participate in air-raid drills so they'd know what to do when the Russians started bombing the United States back to the Stone Age.

Yes, this was the era when teachers told their students that they could duck

---

57 For the record, almost every single person who thinks this is white.

and cover under their desks and survive a nuclear assault. Make no mistake: people in the 1950s were awfully stupid. We had gotten a lot smarter by the time the Smart Aleck staff was in school; Adam's high school history teacher told him that the only thing to do in the event of a nuclear assault was bend over, put your head between your legs, and kiss your butt good-bye.

One of the millions of children who had to participate in air-raid drills was singer-songwriter Billy Joel, who, in the late 1980s, had a hit song called "We Didn't Start the Fire," which still gets plenty of radio play today. You've probably heard it. The song attempts to list every newsworthy event from 1947 up until the late eighties (or as many as Dr. Joel could cram into the rhyme scheme). Look up the lyrics online and you can get a pretty good idea of what's going to happen in the next section of this book.

In fact, we here at the Smart Aleck's Guide have a theory: you can learn all you need to know about U.S. history from 1947 to about 1990 just by looking up stuff from Billy Joel songs.

We tested our theory and found that "We Didn't Start the Fire" alone covers the time period reasonably thoroughly. Odds are fairly good that at some point in your education, a teacher (presumably one who's been using the same lesson plan since 1970) will make you

The Office of Civil Defense produced cartoons to convince kids that getting nuked could be safe— and fun! And yet people wonder why children raised in the fifties didn't trust the government by the 1960s.

look up everything from "We Didn't Start the Fire," a lesson concept that really caught on in the public education system in the 1990s and is still in use by many teachers today. Everyone here on the Smart Aleck staff who was still in school in the 1990s and 2000s had to do it. Adam had to do it in three different classes—only one of which was even a history class. If (or when) you get the assignment, you can use this chapter as a cheat sheet!

Oh, sure, we'll just gloss over some of the stuff, like the reference to Juan Perón, which have little or nothing to do with U.S. history (sorry, but this means we're also skipping "British politician sex," a line that turns up about two-thirds of the way into the song).

And we'll have to take plenty of side trips, because "We Didn't Start the

Fire" leaves a *lot* of stuff out. Luckily for us and our harebrained theories, most of these big gaps can be filled in with lines from *other* Billy Joel songs, most notably "Leningrad," "Goodnight Saigon," and his between-song patter at his famous Russia concert, which was recorded and released as a live album. We'll refer to these, too. There are still a handful of things Billy Joel missed, like Lyndon B. Johnson's presidency (for which he can hardly be blamed), but we'll throw those in as well, just to make sure we cover all the bases.

Still, after careful research, we're pretty confident that we were right:

Harry S. Truman, who probably always imagined that his first week as president would consist of picking out pretty new curtains for the Oval Office. Sorry, Harry. His middle name was simply the letter "S"—it didn't stand for anything.

you can learn just about all you need to know about the second half of the twentieth century from Billy Joel. Read on. "We Didn't Start the Fire" opens with a mention of . . .

. . . HARRY TRUMAN

No one really expected Truman to win reelection in 1948. As of that spring, when the election process got going, his approval rating stood at a paltry 36 percent.

One reason Truman was unpopular was probably his stance on civil rights. He was in favor of them, but many Democrats of the day were still truly members of the old, pre-FDR, more conservative version of the party. When Truman adopted a civil rights–heavy platform at the Democratic National Convention, representatives from several Southern states objected. Senator Strom Thurmond addressed the convention, echoing William Jennings Bryan by saying, "You shall not crucify the South on this cross of civil rights!" He then led all the delegates from Alabama, and several from Mississippi, out of the convention. They proceeded to form the States Rights Democratic Party, also known as the Dixiecrats, which adopted the slogan "Segregation Forever" and nominated Thurmond for president. The States Rights Democratic Party actually ended up winning a few of the Southern states in the general election.[58]

Without these states, which the Democratic party generally counted on in those days, nobody thought Truman had a chance at winning another term, and several Democrats tried to nominate other candidates, such as General Dwight D. Eisenhower, who was not even a member of the party (or any other party) at the time. But Truman won the nomination and vowed to press on, win the election, "and make these Republicans like it." He embarked on a whistle-stop tour in which he traveled by train from one small town to another, giving a speech from the back of the train at every stop.

Most political analysts thought Truman would be crushed by his Republican opponent, Thomas E. Dewey (the same guy who had lost to FDR before), but they turned out to be wrong. Maybe people just got freaked out by Dewey's mustache at the last minute.

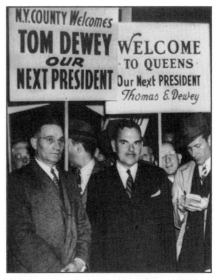

Thomas Dewey, Truman's Republican challenger, attempting to bring the mustache back to national politics. Theodore Roosevelt's daughter Alice (remember Alice? There was a whole sidebar about Alice) said that he looked like the little guy on top of a wedding cake.

Maybe the whistle-stop tour really made people see Truman in a different light. Or maybe all the postwar action that brought about the baby boom just put everyone in a good mood. Whatever the reason, Truman surprised everyone by narrowly defeating Dewey and winning a second term.

That term was no picnic for him, though. In 1949, the Soviet Union successfully tested an atomic bomb of their own, and everyone assumed that World War III was just around the corner. People started accusing their

---

[58] We often say that it's unfair to judge people from the past on things like race and religion according to today's standards, but it certainly seems like Thurmond should have known better by 1948. He did have a change of heart in his later years (and he had a lot of later years. He was still in the Senate on his hundredth birthday in 2002) and made many apologies for his earlier views.

It barely took half a century for the Korean War to be pretty well forgotten.

TRUMAN AND THE KOREAN WAR

In 1950, North Korean Communists invaded South Korea, quickly taking over the capital, Seoul. In those days, many Americans believed that if one country went Communist, others would soon follow, and if we weren't careful, the whole world could go Communist. Truman sent American troops into South Korea in an attempt to push the Communists back, and America was at war again—unofficially, at least. He didn't get formal approval from Congress, which would eventually make things tricky for him.

American forces weren't the only ones fighting. After World War II, many of the nations of the world had come together to form the United Nations, an organization based on Wilson's League of Nations. While American troops pretty much got their butts kicked across South Korea in the early days of the conflict, UN forces, led by America's favorite pain in the butt, General MacArthur, landed in Korea and started kicking North Korea's butt.

China, now led by Communist chairman Mao Zedong, stepped in with an army of its own and started pushing the UN forces back. In 1951, the war had basically become a draw,

244

with both sides stuck at a spot known as the thirty-eighth parallel (as Billy Joel reported in the song "Leningrad").

MacArthur wanted to start attacking supply bases in China and break out the nuclear weapons, but Truman told him not to. Casualties had already been high, and the president was afraid that if the fighting got any worse, the Soviet Union might join in on China and North Korea's side. But MacArthur, ever a pain in the neck, leaked his plan to the press, hoping to turn public opinion to his side.

In response, Truman fired MacArthur, which proved to be just about the least popular thing a president had ever done. Newspapers began to call for Truman to be impeached.

The war remained a draw, with neither side really gaining any ground while thousands of soldiers were being killed, for a good two years before a peace agreement was drawn up. By 1952, the Twenty-second Amendment, which limited presidents to two terms, had been added to the Constitution, so that no one could be elected to four terms, like Roosevelt had been (most other presidents had stuck to an unofficial tradition, started by Washington, of stepping down after two terms so no one started thinking they were kings or anything like that). The amendment

actually didn't apply to Truman, though, only to presidents that came after him, and he did plan to run for a third term. However, polls at the time put Truman's approval rating at 22 percent, the lowest ever recorded for a president up to that time. He ended up losing the first primary and pulling out of the race.

Truman left office an unpopular man, and a broke one. He hadn't been rich to start with, and didn't feel that it was ethical to take any of the high-paying positions that people offered him after his term just because he had been president. He said later that if he hadn't been able to sell some property that he and his siblings had inherited,

MacArthur on the front lines. We *think* he's the one on the right, but frankly it's hard to tell. This could practically be a MacArthur look-alike contest. Eventually, a park was named after MacArthur, and someone wrote a song about it. "MacArthur Park," made famous by Richard "Dumbledore" Harris, features some of the most overwrought and ridiculous metaphors ever.

245

JOE DI MAGGIO
Salutes His Bat

© 1941..The Sporting News Pub. Co.

Joltin' Joe before he met Marilyn Monroe (obviously).

he would have practically been on welfare.

Largely because Truman was broke, Congress began giving benefit packages to former presidents in 1958. At the time this law passed, only two former presidents were alive: Truman and Herbert Hoover, who had spent his postpresidential years writing books that slammed Franklin Roosevelt's administration, dodging rumors that he was trying to get nominated for president again, and, at Truman's request, helping to keep postwar Europe from starving to death. Keeping war-torn countries from starving had always been his real strength.

Though Truman was unpopular when he left office, after the dust of the Korean War and the civil rights upheavals started to clear, people started to look on Truman more favorably. His move to get rid of MacArthur had ruined his career, but it may also have stopped the Korean War from becoming World War III. Today when historians rank the presidents, he often ends up in the top ten.

JOE DIMAGGIO

So far, we've neglected a major part of American history: baseball. Long before modern steroid scandals, baseball dominated American culture. There were other sports, of course, but baseball was far and away the most popular for much of the twentieth century.

No one really knows how baseball got started; most likely, it was adapted from earlier British games. Credit is often given to Abner Doubleday, a Civil War big shot, for inventing the game, but this is complete nonsense. In 1905, the National League appointed a commission to figure out the origin of the game, and they came upon the story that Doubleday had invented it in a cow pasture in Cooperstown, New York. Most likely, they knew at the time that this was a myth; the whole point of the commission was really to make it look like baseball had been invented in America, not in England. The story of Doubleday came from a guy named Abner Graves, who almost certainly made the whole thing up. Graves went on to murder his wife.

But if baseball wasn't an American invention, it was certainly America's pastime. Players such as Mordecai "Three Finger" Brown, Ty Cobb, Lou Gehrig, and Babe Ruth became a part of America's mythology.

Joe DiMaggio of the New York Yankees (Billy Joel's favorite team) is widely believed to have been one of the greatest players of all time; he's the only player who ever made the All-Star team every year that he played. In 1941, he got a hit in fifty-six consecutive games, setting a major-league record that still stands today and will probably stand for years, as no amount of steroids can help batters connect bat with ball.

Once Babe Ruth was out of the picture, DiMaggio was widely believed to be the best player in the game throughout his career. His mention by Billy Joel probably commemorates his retirement in 1951, which was brought about by injuries, but his marriage to Marilyn Monroe (more on that later) made him even more of a national icon.

Babe Ruth. Part of what made baseball America's national pastime was that you could look like *this* and still be the greatest player in the world.

JOSEPH MCCARTHY

Perhaps no political figure symbolizes the 1950s better than Senator Joseph McCarthy of Wisconsin, who became one of the most popular men in America before being revealed as a national embarrassment.

McCarthy made a career for himself by being loudly outspoken about Communism. Politicians who build their careers on being anti anything generally end up looking like jerks, and McCarthy was no exception.

In the early 1950s, he began telling people that there was a big Communist conspiracy in the United States, and that many movie stars, writers, and even government officials were secretly

Here's a schoolyard ditty sung to the tune of "The Mickey Mouse Club March": "Who's the leader of the cult of personality? M-A-O, T-S-E-, dash T-U-N-G! Chairman Mao (Mao Tse-tung!) Chairman Mao (Mao Tse-tung!)." The fact that his name is now usually spelled "Mao Zedong" is probably the only reason you don't hear this one much anymore. ✗

✗ ✗ ✗ ✗ ✗ ✗ ✗ ✗ ✗ ✗ ✗

Communists. He famously gave a speech in which he held up a sheet of paper and said, "I have here in my hand a list of two hundred and five . . . names that were made known to the secretary of state as being members of the Communist Party and who nevertheless are still working and shaping policy in the State Department."

The list was a bunch of crap; he never made it public, and the number of names on it seemed to change every time he mentioned it. Still, many people believed him, and America was thrust into the era of McCarthyism ("McCarthy Time," as Billy Joel called it in the song "Leningrad"). It was an era in which just being accused of being a Communist could ruin your career, but naming *other* people as

Communists could *make* your career.

Congress had formed the House Un-American Activities Committee in 1938 to find out who was a Communist and who wasn't (this was, of course, a rather un-American thing to do, but the irony seems to have been lost on them). The committee's hearings in 1947 led to the creation of the Hollywood blacklist, an unofficial list of names of suspected Communists who were never able to work in Hollywood again. Some famous stars, such as Charlie Chaplin, had to leave the United States to find work after people accused them of being Communists. Meanwhile, people called before the committee who "named names" of those they knew to be Communists went on to careers that lasted decades,

MORE "WE DIDN'T START THE FIRE" LINES

DORIS DAY: A singer and actress known for her squeaky-clean image.
RED CHINA: In 1949, China became the People's Republic of China, a Communist nation led by Chairman Mao Zedong. People in the West often called it Red China, because Communists are known to be attracted to the color red.
JOHNNIE RAY: A popular singer who, though he wasn't a rocker, used to beat up his piano and roll around on the floor.
SOUTH PACIFIC: A musical.
WALTER WINCHELL: A journalist who pioneered the gossip column.

though many people thought that naming names was a really slimy thing to do. Even decades later, when director Elia Kazan won a Lifetime Achievement Award at the Oscars in 1999, some people refused to applaud—and comedian Chris Rock called him a rat onstage—because he had named names in the McCarthy era.

Though he wasn't actually involved in the committee, McCarthy continued to build his own career by accusing anyone who disagreed with him of being a Commie spy. In 1954, when the U.S. Army accused McCarthy and his chief aide, Roy Cohn (who would show up later in "We Didn't Start the Fire") of pressuring them to give preferential treatment to one of McCarthy's friends, the Senate began the famous Army-McCarthy hearings, during which McCarthy was exposed as a loudmouth bully.

During these hearings, whenever he found himself losing an argument, he'd just start accusing people of being Communists. Finally, in response to this, the army's attorney said, "Until this moment, Senator, I think I never really gauged your cruelty or your recklessness." McCarthy quickly spoke up to accuse someone who worked in that attorney's office of being a Commie, but the attorney interrupted and said, "You've done enough. Have you

McCarthy hated the Russians, but must have had a soft spot for Transylvanians. We like to imagine that one day Senator McCarthy went to the barber, showed him a picture of Dracula, and said, "Here! make me look like this!" The barber, not wanting to be accused of working for the Russians, did as he was told. ✷

✷ ✷ ✷ ✷ ✷ ✷ ✷ ✷ ✷ ✷

no sense of decency, sir, at long last? Have you left no sense of decency at all?" The Senate gallery, which was filled with people who were getting heartily sick of McCarthy's bullying, applauded.

At the end of 1954, the Senate voted to censure McCarthy. A censure doesn't really *do* anything to punish the censuree, but it had only happened to a couple of senators before. McCarthy finished out his term, but his remaining speeches were usually made to nearly empty rooms, as his fellow senators had started to avoid him. After the

"I hate war as only a soldier who has lived it can, only as one who has seen its brutality, its stupidity."—Dwight D. Eisenhower

censure, he descended into alcoholism, frequently showing up drunk in the Senate chambers, and when he died in 1957, it was generally agreed that he had drunk himself to death.

But the blacklist endured for years.

EISENHOWER[59]

Dwight D. Eisenhower wasn't a member of either political party during the war. This is fairly common for generals, though Eisenhower may not

---

[59] If you're following along with the Billy Joel song, you'll notice that the line about Eisenhower actually comes later than this. We're going a bit out of sequence, and are sooo sorry.

have been so extreme; many of them are actually sort of fanatical about not voting—or even having any political opinions of their own—since they have to work for whoever the commander in chief happens to be.

Everyone agreed that Eisenhower was a heck of a general—even though he never fought on the front lines himself—and after the war, both parties tried to recruit him to run for president in 1948. He turned both of them down.

But in 1952, Republicans launched a Draft Eisenhower movement. Over on the Democratic side, President Truman himself tried to get Eisenhower to run as a Democrat. Eisenhower continued to turn both of them down, even after the Draft Eisenhower guys started using the slogan "We Like Ike," which really caught on, helping him win the Republican New Hampshire primary despite the fact that he'd never spoken about his poitical views and wasn't even on the ballot—he's one of just a few modern candidates who have ever won primaries as write-ins. Figuring that he had better chances as a Republican, he announced his candidacy the next day as an official Republican.

He ended up in a campaign for the nomination against Robert Taft, the son of President William H. Taft, that lasted all the way to the convention. Voters at the convention might have been concerned that Eisenhower wasn't a "real" Republican, since he'd just joined the party a few months before, but they decided that Eisenhower was a safer bet than Taft to win the election, and he won the nomination on the first ballot. He went on to win the general election against Adlai Stevenson, the governor of Illinois.

As president, one of his most notable acts was to vastly improve the interstate highway system. Back in 1919, when he was in the army, he had been involved in the Transcontinental Motor Convoy, an experiment the army conducted to see if it was possible to drive automobiles all the way across the country. It was, but it took two months at an average speed of six miles per hour over lousy dirt roads and mud.

Eisenhower, who had been impressed by the Autobahn system in Germany while he was over there during the war, felt that America was going to need better interstates. The age of the automobile was clearly at hand. For another, he felt that American cities might be targets if there was a World War III, and a good interstate system was essential if they were to be evacuated.

Given Eisenhower's popularity, the Democrats hardly bothered with the 1956 election. They ran Adlai Stevenson again, despite the fact that he'd been pretty well crushed back in '52.

Adlai Stevenson tried to get nominated again in 1960, but the Democrats had learned their lesson by then.

He was crushed again in '56, but Stevenson still got an expressway named after him, which is more than a lot of people who *win* presidential elections get.

After winning his second term, Eisenhower was the first president to be constitutionally barred from seeking a third term under the new law limiting presidents to two terms. In his farewell address, Eisenhower spoke about what he called the military-industrial complex, warning that while a strong army was essential, people were going to have to watch out for big businesses,

Richard Nixon: A guy Billy Joel was just getting started with, showing a no-cavities smile that makes us suspect he must have just stolen something. The photographer's wallet, perhaps. ✴

which stood to make a whole pile of money manufacturing weapons, and which might push the country to go to war—and stay at war—just because it was profitable for them.

Apparently, few people paid attention.

RICHARD NIXON

Richard Nixon's real fame wouldn't come for another decade or so, but his loudly anti-Communist stance made him a good vice presidential candidate for Eisenhower, who some worried was soft on Commies. He was elected to the vice presidency in 1952.

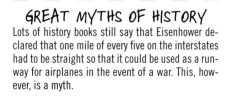

GREAT MYTHS OF HISTORY

Lots of history books still say that Eisenhower declared that one mile of every five on the interstates had to be straight so that it could be used as a runway for airplanes in the event of a war. This, however, is a myth.

He was best known at this time for his "Checkers Speech." In September of 1952, during the campaign, he was accused of keeping a chunk of campaign money as a slush fund for personal use. He became so unpopular that people began to pressure Eisenhower to replace him with another running mate.

Nixon took to the airwaves, making a televised speech in which he detailed his personal finances and claimed that he had, in fact, received only one contribution that was for personal use: a cocker spaniel that a donor had given to his daughters, who named the dog Checkers. "The kids," he said, ". . . love the dog . . . and regardless of what they say about it, we're gonna keep it." The Republican Party let him keep the dog, and decided to keep Nixon, too, though many thought that the Nixons got the better end of the deal.

Nixon went on to serve as vice president throughout the 1950s, taking the office at the young age of thirty-nine. He went on to narrowly lose the presidential election in 1960 to John F. Kennedy. After that, he tried to run for governor of California. When he lost that, too, he held a press conference in which he told reporters that he was retiring from politics, and that he felt bad for them, since "you won't have Nixon to kick around anymore."

In reality, the world was just getting its kicking shoes warmed up for Nixon's behind.

TELEVISION

Television, or TV, as the youngsters called it, had been around for a long time by the early 1950s, but it took a while for it to catch on. Early models cost a fortune, and during World War II, only about five cities even had television stations. Even people who lived in cities that *did* have stations didn't have many good programs to watch; one of the bigger shows of the day was something called *Missus Goes a-Shopping*.

OTHER STUFF IN THIS VERSE OF "WE DIDN'T START THE FIRE"

STUDEBAKER: A car that was about the size of a tank. Interstate highway systems improved remarkably in the 1950s, making cross-country road trips a whole lot easier.

NORTH KOREA, SOUTH KOREA: Here, Joel gives only a passing mention to the Korean War.

Does that sound awful or what?

In 1947, the year of TV's first hit (*The Howdy Doody Show,* a puppet show), there weren't quite two hundred thousand television sets in all of the United States. But by 1952, roughly the year Billy Joel has worked his way up to when he mentions television in the song, there were more than twenty million sets in the country. The number would keep growing until practically everyone had one and couldn't think of a single thing better to do than watch it, despite the fact that there was never anything good on. It was a running joke at the time that when you could get TVs to get a good picture in the first place (which practically required a degree in engineering), the only thing on was cowboy shows.

It's tempting to make wisecracks to the effect that most of the shows from back then couldn't have been any worse than they are right now, but the fact is that, despite what nostalgic baby boomers will tell you, practically everything on the air in those days really stank. Sure, there were some hits, like *I Love Lucy* and *The Honeymooners,* that are still watchable today, but most of the programs from the early days of TV have slinked off into obscurity by now because no one can possibly sit through them.

Among the biggest hits of the day

The quiz show *Twenty-one*. Why, just *looking* at it makes us want some Geritol! ✻

were quiz shows, which were sort of like modern game shows, only a lot less goofy. Most of the shows were simple question-and-answer shows, and right from the start, many of them were rigged. There was no grand conspiracy behind this or anything—producers figured out all on their own that supplying answers to popular candidates would help keep ratings up by keeping the popular people on the show longer. They were eventually caught, and people learned a valuable lesson about believing what they saw on TV.

MARILYN MONROE

Probably the biggest movie star of the 1950s was Marilyn Monroe, who became famous right around the time nude pictures of her began to spread around. Her ability to absolutely *own* every frame of a movie she appeared in made her a star, but it was the nude-photo scandal (which hadn't really happened to a movie star before), and her own casual reaction to it, that made her an icon. Few stars had ever been so risqué; when asked what she'd had on during the photo shoot, Monroe casually replied, "The radio."

But perhaps what truly made Monroe a legend in America was her 1954 marriage to Joe DiMaggio, even though the marriage didn't last a year. The era of short-lived celebrity marriages had begun decades ago—movie stars had been getting married and promptly divorced from day one—but the marriage of two such icons was huge. And unlike so many others who marry movie stars, DiMaggio was a class act. He never blabbed about the marriage in public, even though he lived for decades after Monroe's death.

Monroe then married Arthur Miller, a playwright whose 1953 hit, *The Crucible,* made several less-than-subtle comparisons between McCarthyism and the Salem witch trials.

As if that weren't enough to make her notorious, by the 1960s, rumors were going around that she was having an affair with none other than the president of the United States, John F. Kennedy. Her birthday serenade to Kennedy may be the sexiest song anyone ever sang to a president in public.

And if *that* didn't make her enough of an icon, she went on to do something that will make almost any star a legend: she died young under mysterious cir-

Cheapskate historians like us can't find free pictures of Marilyn Monroe to use, so here's one of James Monroe, our fifth president, whom we didn't show anywhere else in the book. His administration is best remembered for the Monroe Doctrine, the Missouri Compromise, and the Era of Good Feelings. He was not related to Marilyn, whose real name was Norma Jean Baker. Heck, in this shot, you don't even get to drool over his dynamite gams!

cumstances. She was found dead in her house in 1962, an apparent suicide, though many people believed, and many still believe, that it was murder.

THE ROSENBERGS

Being a Communist in America was never illegal, but it could get you into a whole lot of trouble. It may, in fact, have been all that Julius and Ethel Rosenberg were guilty of.

In 1951, the Rosenbergs were

accused of being employed by the KGB (the big Russian spy organization) and of passing secrets about the atomic bomb to the Soviet Union. At the time, McCarthyism was in full swing. The Rosenbergs were quickly convicted and were executed in the electric chair in 1953. The executions fueled people's fears that their neighbors might be working for the Russians.

Unlike many similar suspects, the Rosenbergs were widely believed to be guilty. However, as years passed, it became evident that they didn't really tell the Soviets anything of any consequence, and many began to believe they were convicted and executed for reasons more to do with McCarthyism than with anything they actually did (though we now know that they were indeed guilty).

VACCINE

Do you know anyone who has polio? You probably don't. And that's because of the Salk vaccine.

No disease was more feared by parents in the early 1950s than polio. It was a crippling disease that usually attacked children and could lead to paralysis and death, and no one really knew how it spread or how to keep their children from getting it.

In 1955 Jonas Salk introduced a vaccine that protected people from the disease. When it was announced in 1955 that polio could now be prevented, bells rang and drivers honked their horns for joy. Children everywhere rejoiced—until they found out they were going to have to get a shot, of course.

This began a huge push to get every kid in the country vaccinated against

OTHER STUFF IN THE SONG

H-BOMB: The hydrogen bomb, a newer, even deadlier version of the atomic bomb that the United States first tested in 1952. The Soviets had one soon after.

SUGAR RAY: A boxer, six-time world champion Sugar Ray Robinson.

PANMUNJOM: A village in Korea where peace accords were worked out.

BRANDO: Marlon Brando, an actor, a proponent of Method acting, the technique of "becoming" your character, which really caught on in the 1950s.

THE KING AND I: A musical by Rodgers and Hammerstein.

THE CATCHER IN THE RYE: A novel by J. D. Salinger that got banned a lot—and still does. Any book that's still getting banned six decades after publication is sure to be worth reading.

polio in an effort to eradicate the disease, which was pretty successful. Polio still exists around the world, but the last naturally occurring case in America was reported in 1979.

Salk, who famously refused to patent the vaccine (which would have made him ridiculously rich) on the grounds that it would be wrong to profit from a scientific discovery, went on to spend his later years trying to develop a vaccine for AIDS.

ROCK AROUND THE CLOCK (OR, WHY WE ALL WORSHIP SATAN NOW)

Popular music hadn't exactly sucked since about 1920; the Jazz Age ushered in an era when depressing parlor songs began to fall out of favor as the sound of the day. But it was rock 'n' roll that really began to shape the musical landscape of youth culture in the 1950s.

Rock 'n' roll music had been around for a long time; its origins go back at least as far as the blues music of the late nineteenth century, which combined European melodies and African rhythms. What we came to call rock 'n' roll mixed jazz, blues, country, gospel, and nearly every other kind of music into one big cultural mishmash. The wild (for its time) style began to catch on in America around the late 1940s.

The style was generally thought of as

COMMUNIST BLOC
A song to the tune of "Jingle Bell Rock," by the Smart Aleck Staff!

Communist, Communist, Communist bloc,
Spend all our time just waitin' in line.
All of the bourgeoisie[60] feared revolution—
Now the Commie regime's begun!
Communist, Communist, Communist bloc,
Seizin' the means to halt the machines,
Dancin' and prancin' around in Red Square
In the frosty air!
The proletariat will, this year, get
To rock the night away.
The Manifesto, from the get-go,
Seems to work in theory, anyway.
Hammer and sickle laid down at our feet,
Capitalists are stopped.
Lenin, Stalin, and old Chairman Mao,
That's the Communist, that's the Communist,
That's the Communist bloc!

exclusively "black music," but Alan Freed, a Cleveland disc jockey, began playing rock music for mixed-race audiences in 1951. He's usually credited with being the first to call the music "rock and roll," at least on the radio, but the term was a euphemism for sex and was used in rhythm and blues music frequently at the time. It was a "neutral" term race-wise, which helped it cross over to a mainstream audience that would have been afraid of "black music."

---

60 This is a term Communists love to throw around. Pronounced boor-zhwah-ZEE, it means, loosely, "middle-class people."

FROM ANOTHER BILLY JOEL SONG ("LENINGRAD"): THE COLD WAR AND "WHITE FLIGHT"

illy's song "Leningrad," from side two of *Storm Front* (if you're playing it on old-fashioned vinyl or cassette tape), mentions "Cold War kids . . . under their desks in an air-raid drill." He refers to himself as being "a Cold War kid in McCarthy time."

The Cold War was the name given to the time of tense relations between the United States and the USSR. It wasn't a regular war, in that no one was firing any missiles—it was fought with a lot of tough talk and a whole lot of spying. And, of course, with weapons stockpiles. Every time the United States got a new kind of weapon, the Soviet Union would have the same one a couple of years later. It may seem odd, but many people thought it was a good thing for the two countries to be just about even in the arms race, as the contest to build bigger and better weapons came to be known. The balance of power kept both countries from actually *using* any of the weapons. We never nuked Russia because we knew they'd nuke us right back. They never nuked *us* because they knew we'd nuke them back.

But people were still scared to death that the bombs would start dropping any minute. Some people dug underground bomb shelters in their backyards.[61] As useless as the bomb shelters would have been, nothing matches the air-raid drills that were held in schools in terms of pure futility. Public schools throughout the country installed air-raid sirens that would sound in the event of a nuclear attack (in case the huge explosions weren't enough of a signal). Every now and then, schools would have the students participate in drills: if the siren went off, they were to "duck and cover" under their desks.

Hahhaahahahahahahahahahahahahahaha!

You can't duck and cover and survive in the event of nuclear attack! "Duck and disintegrate" would be more like it.

Even though it's really about Russia, "Leningrad" is just bursting with U.S. history. Another line from "Leningrad" states that "children lived in Levittown," an American town Billy Joel contrasts with the Russian Leningrad. Levittown (above right) is a town that some say symbolized the whole Cold War era of American history.

---

61 There was a really cool *Twilight Zone* episode, later parodied on *The Simpsons*, where a guy builds a bomb shelter with enough room for his family, but not enough room for anyone else. The neighbors decide they want in, too, and bust their way in with a makeshift battering ram. Apparently, it didn't occur to these guys that a shelter that doesn't stand up to three guys with a battering ram is going to be useless against a nuclear bomb.

The 1950s marked a huge movement of citizens (especially white ones) from cities out to the suburbs. When World War II ended, there was an immediate need for a lot of affordable housing, and several planners hit on the idea of building whole planned communities—mass-produced suburbs that seemngly sprang up overnight.

There were actually four towns called Levittown, each of which was a prefab community planned by a company owned by Abraham Levitt. These towns were planned and built before anyone actually lived there. The company's method of building rows and rows of identical houses was so efficient that by mid-1948, they were building thirty new houses per day in the original Levittown, which was in New York. The houses generally came in five models (differing mainly in color and window placement) and were equipped with modern appliances such as refrigerators and later, notably, television sets.

By 1951, the company had built about seventeen thousand houses in Levittown, New York. Levittown became a symbol of the bland conformity of postwar suburbia—the American dream of home ownership was easier to achieve than ever (you could pick out a house and have the contract signed three minutes later), but these anonymous homes were mass-produced in towns that distinctly lacked character.

MORE STUFF IN THE SONG

ENGLAND'S GOT A NEW QUEEN: Queen Elizabeth II took the throne in 1952. Thanks to television, this was the first chance most people had to see a coronation.

MARCIANO: Rocky Marciano. Another boxer, who became heavyweight champ in 1952. Billy sure does like boxing!

LIBERACE: A really, really flamboyant piano player who was very popular and had his own TV show in the fifties.

SANTAYANA: George Santayana was a Spanish philosopher who died in 1952.

JOSEPH STALIN: The prime minister of the USSR and America's biggest enemy in the 1950s before his death in 1953. This guy was a serious jerk; many believe he was even worse than Hitler. But we never ended up fighting a real war against him.

MALENKOV: Georgy Malenkov was the guy who took over after Stalin died. He was kicked out of the Communist party.

NASSER: Gamal Nasser became president of Egypt in 1956.

PROKOFIEV: Sergey Prokofiev, a Russian composer who died in 1953. Because the line in the song is "Nasser and Prokofiev," the song makes it sound like he has something to do with Nasser, but he doesn't.

ROCKEFELLER: This is pretty vague, honestly, since there were a lot of really rich Rockefellers out there. The one in the song is probably Winthrop Rockefeller, who was the big Rockefeller in the fifties. We guess. They were *all* rich guys.

CAMPANELLA: Roy Campanella, catcher for the Brooklyn Dodgers, was one of the first black major leaguers. He was paralyzed in a car accident in 1958.

COMMUNIST BLOC: The name given to countries controlled by the Soviet Union, against whom the United States fought the Cold War.

ROY COHN: Joe McCarthy's attorney, and one of his best pals. A real jerk.

JUAN PERÓN: Off-and-on president of Argentina, best known now for having been married to Eva Perón, the subject of the musical *Evita*.

TOSCANINI: Arturo Toscanini, an Italian conductor.

DACRON: An artificial fiber. Artificial stuff, like Levittown, was very big in the fifties.[62]

DIEN BIEN PHU FALLS: The battle of Dien Bien Phu in 1954 led to the separation of Vietnam into North and South Vietnam, setting the stage for the Vietnam War, which is barely mentioned in "We Didn't Start the Fire," perhaps because Billy felt that he'd already covered it in "Goodnight Saigon," which he had recorded a few years earlier.

In 1954, Bill Haley and His Comets, a swing band, released "Rock Around the Clock," which, after being featured in the opening credits of *Blackboard Jungle,* a 1955 movie about juvenile delinquency, was the first rock 'n' roll song to become a major national hit.

[62] The official lyrics say "Dancron," not Dacron. However, as none of our interns could figure out what Dancron is, we assume it's a typo.

For most people—especially most white people—it was the first taste of the rock 'n' roll sound, and while many parents were horrified beyond all reason, teenagers were hooked.

Most people assumed—hoped, even—that it was all just a fad. They never would have believed that "Rock Around the Clock" was only the beginning.

JAMES DEAN

Teenagers emerged as a major cultural force in the 1950s. They'd always existed, of course, but teenage culture barely did. Lots of things changed for teens in the 1950s. One of the most important things was that, all of a sudden, teenagers everywhere had cars, which allowed them to be alone with their dates. This had previously been a whole lot harder for them to manage.

Somewhere along the line, drive-in movie theaters (where you would drive up and watch the movie through a windshield full of dead bugs while listening to the sound through a tinny speaker you hooked to your window) became popular. It was not a great way to experience a movie, exactly, but plenty of teenagers went to the drive-in regularly because all that time in the car made for a good opportunity for some serious making out, and movie studios began to make more and more movies that were marketed specifically to teenagers. And no teen

EINSTEIN: Albert Einstein (above), a physicist known for his Theory of Relativity and his work on the atomic bomb—which he really regretted in the end. Incidentally, he did *not* flunk math in school.[63]

PETER PAN: Disney released its film version in the mid-fifties. We assume that's what Billy Joel is talking about here. Either that or this was the year he actually *met* Peter Pan and got to go to Never Land and fight against pirates and native Never Landians. . . . Yeah, the first one.

DISNEYLAND: Opened for business in 1955.

BROOKLYN'S GOT A WINNING TEAM: The Brooklyn Dodgers finally won the World Series in 1955 after losing for several seasons. ✻

[63] See *The Smart Aleck's Guide to Urban Legends About Einstein,* one of our longest books!

✻ 261 ✻

STUPID HATS OF HISTORY:
THE COONSKIN. AGAIN.

No matter how bad the shows were, TV's popularity, and its impact on culture and trends, was impossible to ignore. After Disney showed a series of TV movies about Davy Crockett, Crockett became one of the most famous and popular figures in American history, particularly among kids. Coonskin caps, which were never worn by sensible people to begin with, made a huge comeback among otherwise rational children. That year, "The Ballad of Davy Crockett" was a huge hit record.

idol of the day became a bigger icon than James Dean.

In an era known for conformity, it was the "rebellious" movies, music, and people—the ones that scared their parents—that most excited teenagers. James Dean first caught national attention for his role in *East of Eden,* but he became an icon for his role in *Rebel Without a Cause,* a movie about a teenager who feels that no one can understand him. The movie was perhaps the most accurate portrayal of teen angst ever shown in movies, and Dean became the very personification of cool for a generation (some say he still is).

At the height of his fame, Dean was killed in a car accident, which, of course, made him even more of an icon. Some people say he never would have become a legend if he hadn't died young; he wasn't around long enough to make a bad movie, weather a scandal, or lose his looks, all of which he surely would have had to face eventually. Instead, he remained eternally youthful and rebellious. Of course, these people are forgetting that he was also a heck of an actor. He only starred in three movies, but he was nominated for an Academy Award for two of them.

There's a lesson here, kids: drive safely and buckle up.

ELVIS PRESLEY

Continuing Billy Joel's theme of teenage rebellion (after being interrupted, oddly, by the stuff about Davy Crockett and Peter Pan): if there was one star who really *owned* the 1950s and defined teenage musical taste, it was Elvis Presley. Teenagers in the 1950s had no idea that he'd go on to make a bunch of stupid movies, gain a bunch of weight, and appear in public wearing jumpsuits that were never, ever stylish.

Elvis Presley burst onto the musical scene in 1956. The way he shook his hips while singing "Hound Dog" on *The Milton Berle Show* so frightened adults that for a minute they forgot all about being scared of nuclear war and worried about Elvis instead. People began to circulate rumors that he was a Communist or a gay, drugged-up devil worshipper.

But this just made teenagers all the more fascinated with him. Though *Blackboard Jungle* had already shown

Historians tend to cringe when people talk about "the old days, when people got married so young." Through most of modern history, people actually married fairly late; Romeo and Juliet were teenagers, but most people in Shakespeare's day actually didn't marry until their late twenties. Getting married at seventeen or eighteen was common in the 1950s, though— far more so than it had been before and certainly more so than it is now.

parents that there was a link between rock music and teenage rebellion, Elvis was the first performer to combine the two really successfully. He became known as the King of Rock 'n' Roll, a title that stuck with him even after he'd stopped singing rock 'n' roll music.

In the fall of 1956, his performances on *The Ed Sullivan Show,* a popular variety show, were watched by upwards of sixty million people. Presley had become one of the biggest stars in the country, and had taken rock 'n' roll music to a whole new level of popularity and cultural relevance, even though, on one appearance, they only showed Elvis from the waist up, so as not to frighten parents with his Hips of Doom.

The government found an even better way to deal with Presley than simply censoring him: in 1957, he was drafted into the army (at the time, there was still a draft, even though there wasn't a war on). Though he hastily recorded several songs to be released while he was away, many of which were hits, he was never quite the same after he got out of the army—most of his postarmy music was a lot tamer than his early stuff. By 1960, rock music was in pretty bad shape; some even said it was actually dead— which it pretty much was. It wouldn't really come back to prominence or relevance until the Beatles hit America a few years later.

ELVIS
AARON
PRESLEY

JANUARY 8, 1935
AUGUST 16, 1977

VERNON ELVIS PRESLEY
and
GLADYS LOVE PRESLEY
father of
LISA MARIE PRESLEY

An important thing for historians—or anyone else—to learn is to call baloney on conspiracy theories, but if it turns out that Elvis is alive, we here at the Smart Aleck's Guide won't be all that surprised. After all, this is the sort of conspiracy that only needs to involve a handful of people to keep the secret, which is more plausible than those theories where everyone in the government has to keep their mouth shut. Though most Elvis sightings are certainly nonsense, the fact that his middle name is misspelled on his tombstone at Graceland is a little suspicious to some people, who say that since the tombstone reads *Elvis* Aaron *Presley,* it may indicate that Elvis *Aron* Presley (as his middle name was often, though not always, spelled) isn't buried under it (it's not like the staff couldn't afford to get the name right). Most of all, though, a phony death just seems like the kind of thing Elvis *would* have done. ✮

Rather than trying to stay ahead of the curve and inject new life into the genre, Elvis settled into the middle of the road. Many of the songs he recorded in 1960 were slow, conservative songs that didn't sound rebellious in the slightest. In fact, many were so dull that people wondered what the heck the army had done to Elvis. He went on to spend most of the 1960s making rather silly movies that featured a few good songs but also tended to feature songs like "Yoga Is As Yoga Does," "Ito Eats," "The Song of the Shrimp," and "He's Your Uncle, Not Your Dad."

By the time Elvis went back to performing live in the late 1960s, he had gotten some of his swagger back, but by then he was seen as old-fashioned and passé by many rockers. He died—or so they say—in 1977 in the bathroom at Graceland, his home in Memphis.

ALABAMA

The mention of Alabama at this point in "We Didn't Start the Fire" probably refers to the bus boycotts in Montgomery, Alabama, in 1956.

In those days, the way the bus worked in Montgomery and throughout the South was that black people sat in the back and white people sat in the front. If the bus filled up, black people were required to give up their seats so white people could sit. There were a few instances of black people refusing to give up their seats, but the best-publicized instance was that of Rosa Parks. This technically wasn't illegal, but she was arrested for failing to follow the seat assignment given to her by the bus driver. In Alabama in those days, when the driver on the bus said, "Move on back," his word was law. She was fined ten dollars, plus four dollars

One of very few public domain shots of Elvis: his "mug" shot, which was taken when he went to the White House in 1970. He looked a lot cooler than this in the 1950s. Of course, he'd practically have to.

Dr. Martin Luther King, Jr., who would go on to say that he had a dream that one day, people would "not be judged by the color of their skin but by the content of their character." We here at the Smart Aleck's Guide judge people by the content of their character freely, and occasionally harshly.

OTHER STUFF IN THE SONG

BARDOT: French actress Brigitte Bardot.

BUDAPEST: The city in which the Hungarian Revolution of 1956, a protest againt the local Stalinist government, took place.

KHRUSHCHEV: Nikita Khrushchev (pictured) made a speech denouncing Stalin and his cult of personality in 1956. Stalin was too dead to be upset, but the speech was seen as a sign of a major power struggle in Russia.

PRINCESS GRACE: Actress Grace Kelly, who in 1956 married a prince and went from being an American actress to being the princess of Monaco.

PEYTON PLACE: A bestselling novel that was considered awfully racy by 1950s standards. Keep in mind, this was an era when Elvis's hips were considered just as big a threat as missiles.

TROUBLE IN THE SUEZ: Britain, France, and Israel launched a military attack against Egypt in the Suez Canal in 1956 after Egypt tried to nationalize it. ✗

in court costs, but she appealed, and the case became national news, which helped publicize a boycott of the buses led by a group of civil rights leaders, including Dr. Martin Luther King, Jr.

The segregation laws were ruled to be unconstitutional, but the case remained in appeal, and the boycott remained in effect, throughout most of 1956 until the Supreme Court finally upheld the lower court's ruling. This certainly wasn't the end of racial segregation, but it was one of the first major victories of the modern civil rights movement.

LITTLE ROCK

In 1954, in the landmark case of *Brown v. the Board of Education of Topeka,* the Supreme Court ruled—finally—that racially segregated schools were unconstitutional. Eisenhower supported the ruling, and, in doing so, came about as close as any sitting president had come in decades to being a strong voice for civil rights.

But actually *getting* the schools integrated wasn't easy. In 1957, when nine black students tried to attend a previously all-white high school in Little Rock, the governor of Arkansas sent the Arkansas National Guard to block the door. Eisenhower had to send in the army to get the black students into the building; the students had federal protection for the entire school year to make sure they could get in every day. The city, intent on keeping schools segregated, actually went as far as canceling the next school year, forcing students to enroll elsewhere. Eisenhower's civil rights legislation was pretty weak compared to what came later, but you can see what the guy was up against.

KEROUAC

The 1950s became the first era in which it was really, really popular in mainstream culture to make fun of hipsters. The hipsters in those days were known as beatniks, a shorter version of the Beat Generation, a term coined by author Jack Kerouac.

The beatniks were a group, at least initially, of poets, writers, intellectuals, and assorted drug-takers who descended on San Francisco and New York in the 1950s. Soon, though, the term "beatnik" was applied to just about anyone who seemed unusual or unpleasant to "normal" people. Exactly what people meant by "beatniks" varied wildly—to some people, it meant bad artists who recited bad poetry while someone played bad jazz in a coffee shop, then went home to smoke marijuana and talk about Communism while having casual sex. To others, beatniks were no-good ruffians who rode around on motorcycles and hassled shopkeepers.

But at the center of the group were some fantastic writers who helped create

OTHER STUFF

PASTERNAK: Boris Pasternak, a Russian author, published *Doctor Zhivago* in 1957. It was quickly banned in Russia. Perhaps your teacher can make you find out why!

MICKEY MANTLE: A baseball player for the New York Yankees. Perhaps the biggest baseball star of the late fifties and early sixties.

ZHOU ENLAI: Zhou was the premier of China.

BRIDGE ON THE RIVER KWAI: A 1957 film that won seven Academy Awards despite its lack of teenage rebellion and a rock music score.

LEBANON: A Middle Eastern country that was engulfed in various forms of turmoil, such as a civil war, in 1958.

CHARLES DE GAULLE: A World War II general who became president of France in 1958.

CALIFORNIA BASEBALL: The Brooklyn Dodgers and the New York Giants moved to California, becoming the first baseball teams to have home fields west of Kansas City, Missouri. Some marked this as progress; others said it was the beginning of the end of baseball's golden era.

STARKWEATHER: Charles Starkweather, a murderer who killed eleven people before being captured. He was executed in 1959.

THALIDOMIDE: Thalidomide was a drug commonly prescribed to treat morning sickness in pregnant women. It also turned out to cause birth defects. In the song, the line about this comes right before a very short but rocking guitar solo.

Jack Kerouac, before he really got started drinking himself to death.

A stereotypical beatnik. ✳

✳ ✳ ✳ ✳ ✳ ✳ ✳ ✳ ✳ ✳ ✳ ✳

a whole new American style of literature. In 1956, Allen Ginsberg published "Howl," a long poem that opened with the famous line "I saw the best minds of my generation destroyed by madness." The poem, which also featured quite a few words that we still can't get away with printing very often, became the subject of a major trial after the publisher was accused of obscenity. "Howl" became a sort of manifesto for the Beat Generation, and one of the landmark poems of the twentieth century.

Because of the trial, many people heard about the poem, but very few people read it. Most people were first exposed to beat culture in 1957, when Jack Kerouac published *On the Road,* a wild account of traveling across the country with other beatniks. The sense of rebellion, freedom, and intellectualism in the book excited the imaginations of thousands of young people, who took to the road themselves and began hanging out in coffee shops writing free verse.

The popular image of beatniks as guys with goatees and berets who called everyone daddy-o came more from television than from actual beatniks; the style was popularized by characters like Kookie on *77 Sunset Strip* and Maynard G. Krebs on *The Many Lives of Dobie Gillis.* As with Elvis's hips, many people (squares,[64] in particular) thought beatniks would be the very end of society. J. Edgar Hoover, the head of the FBI, even said that the three greatest threats to America were Communists, eggheads, and beatniks. Communists and beatniks are now generally considered fairly harmless in America, but keep your eyes open for those eggheads. There may be one sitting next to you right now!

---

[64] "Squares" were uncool people. Like this one intern . . .

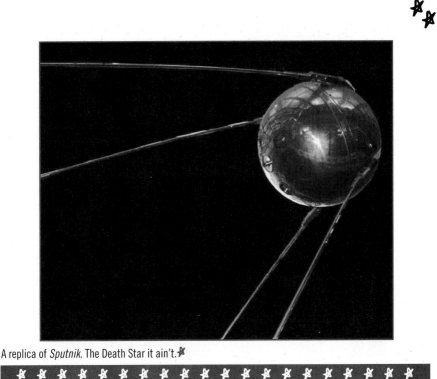

A replica of *Sputnik*. The Death Star it ain't.

SPUTNIK

Besides the arms race with the Soviet Union, America was also involved in a space race, as technology for blasting things, including people, into space was developing rapidly. People believed that whichever country got to the moon first would be able to launch missiles at the other country from the lunar surface and take over the globe. Actually, even if they *had* gotten missiles to the moon, they wouldn't have been able to fire them at anyone, but in an age when people believed that a particle-board desk could protect students from nuclear fallout, anything seemed possible.

The Soviet Union got a head start in the space race by successfully launching *Sputnik I,* the first man-made satellite, into space in 1957. It wasn't the most threatening device in the world–it was really just a ball of metal about the size of a basketball that had a flashing light on it–but it was a signal to the world that Russia was ahead of the United States in the space race. Anyone with a shortwave radio could tune in to the sound of the thing broadcasting a *beep beep* noise into space. A month later, the Russians launched another satellite, *Sputnik II*–and this one carried a live dog.

269

Prior to this, everyone in America assumed that they were ahead of the Russians in all fields. Though people tried to brush *Sputnik* off as no big deal, the little satellites' success felt like a smack in the face to many. The fact that the satellites the United States tried to launch had a tendency to fail (one was nicknamed Kaputnik) didn't help matters much.

The U.S. government quickly began several space initiatives, including the creation of NASA in 1958, but it would be years before people started to relax about the space race.

BUDDY HOLLY

Pinpointing when the first wave of rock 'n' roll died has always been a popular sport. Some say it died the day Elvis went into the army. Others point to the Day the Music Died, the day in early 1959 when popular rockers Buddy Holly, Ritchie Valens, and the Big Bopper (J. P. Richardson) were killed in an airplane crash in Iowa.

In fact, by this point in 1959, rock seemed to be on its way out. When asked by an interviewer if rock was dying, Holly cheerfully replied that it looked that way. "It might pick back up," he said, "but I doubt it." He went on to say that he'd really prefer to sing something quieter, anyway.

In winter of early 1959, Holly,

Valens, and the Big Bopper embarked on the Winter Dance Party tour, a tour of small, frozen Midwestern towns. To travel between towns, each band was crammed aboard a single crappy bus that tended to break down pretty regularly. After an Iowa show, the heater in the bus broke (not for the first time), and Holly, hoping to stay warm and save enough time to do some laundry (all of the members of the tour were starting to stink to high heaven), arranged for a small charter plane to take him and a few others ahead to the next stop in Minnesota. The plane crashed, killing everyone aboard. Rock 'n' roll had indeed fallen on hard times.

---

[65] Probably.

HULA HOOPS (AND WHILE WE'RE AT IT, OTHER FADS OF THE 1950S)

The age of television led to a golden age of fads—and the creation of new kinds of plastic led to the dawn of the Age of Cheap Plastic Crap. Never before had so much crap been on the market. Some of the fads of the 1950s actually lasted for decades and are still around today. Others, of course, just make our parents and grandparents look stupid in old photographs.

Hula hoops, plastic rings that you spin around your hips, were among the biggest fads of the day. Over a two-year

WINTER DANCE PARTY

One of the last shows of the Winter Dance Party tour was held at the Duluth Armory in Duluth, Minnesota. A young man named Robert Zimmerman was in the first row; after changing his name to Bob Dylan, he would become notable enough to get mentioned in "We Didn't Start the Fire," and to get a whole section devoted to him later in this chapter.

period, tens of millions of the things were sold.

Many people assumed that things like rock music and television would just be fads, but movie people worried that television would be the death of

This picture is actually from about fifty years after the first hula hoop craze, but the concept is pretty much the same.

STUPID HATS OF HISTORY:
THE BEANIE

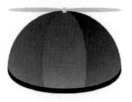

The 1950s was a golden age of stupid hats. The beanie was worn by thousands of the people who ended up running the country when they grew up. Scary, huh?

✗ ✗ ✗ ✗ ✗ ✗ ✗ ✗ ✗ ✗ ✗

every movie theater and began to work up gimmicks to keep people coming out to the movies. Some of these included 3-D movies, electric shockers in some of the seats (for a movie called *The Tingler*), wide-screen formatting, and Cinerama, which was sort of an early version of IMAX.

On college campuses, there was a rash of panty raids in the 1950s. Groups of male students would march into the female dormitories and demand that each of the residents give them a pair of underwear. Many of the female students actually claimed to get a real kick out of this, though others fought back at a couple of colleges by beating the raiders back with broomsticks and Coke bottles.

When we picture dances of the 1950s, we picture girls in poodle skirts dancing at sock hops with greasy-

haired guys in leather jackets, but some of the most popular dances of the day actually included the hokey-pokey and the bunny hop. People who think of the 1950s as a golden age of culture tend to forget that sort of thing.

EDSEL IS A NO-GO

By the end of the 1950s, the Ford Motor Company was no longer under the control of the Ford family. The new managers had plenty of cash to throw around due to the success of the Ford Thunderbird and decided to develop a spectacular new kind of midpriced car to unleash on the American public. The car they designed, the Edsel, was just about the biggest flop in history.

They spent months, and millions of

OTHER STUFF IN THE SONG
BEN HUR: A popular movie about the Ancient Romans.

SPACE MONKEY: The United States made its first serious headway in the space race in 1959 by sending two monkeys, Able and Baker, into space. Of course, the USSR just *had* to do us one better by sending a human up around the same time—which they did—but they wouldn't get a monkey into space until 1983. So there.

MAFIA: The Mafia does not exist. La la la.

CASTRO: Fidel Castro took over Cuba and made it a Communist country following a 1959 revolution there. He would be a thorn in America's side for decades, and Cuba would be one of the last Communist countries still in existence by the end of the twentieth century.

dollars, designing the car, and put considerable effort into naming the thing. They even invited the poet Marianne Moore to come up with a list of names, and she duly submitted names that ranged from the good (Thundercrest) to the odd (the Resilient Bullet) all the way to the just plain bad (the Intelligent Whale). The advertising firm Ford hired came up with thousands of possible names. For reasons that have never quite been determined, out of all of these, they ended up naming it Edsel, after Henry Ford's son.

Having designed and named the thing, the company set out to hype it as the car to end all cars. Early advertisements didn't even show the car, in an attempt to make it seem like a big mystery. They even had a television special, *The Edsel Show,* to introduce it to the public. The special starred popular actor and singer Bing Crosby and featured such notable guests as Frank Sinatra, Louis Armstrong, and Bob Hope singing songs, telling jokes, and talking about how great the Edsel was. Some of the music on the show was fantastic, but they wisely only showed the car for a couple of seconds.

The car looked odd (though we here on the Smart Aleck Staff think it's kinda stylish, honestly) and was set up in an unusual manner. The automatic transmission control was mounted on

Edsel Ford, who must have been bursting with pride from the grave.✖

✶ ✶ ✶ ✶ ✶ ✶ ✶ ✶ ✶ ✶

the front of the steering wheel, which probably seemed like an exciting and modern idea in the boardroom. On the road, however, people would try to honk their horns and end up switching gears.

After all the hype, the Edsel turned out to be a major flop. The Ford company lost a fortune and stopped producing Edsels after just a couple of years.

We *still* think they look better than Hummers.✖

JOHN F. KENNEDY

In 1960, Vice President Nixon ran for president against John Fitzgerald Kennedy, a young senator. One of Kennedy's most memorable official slogans was "We Can Do Better," but the Democrats' funniest move that year was circulating posters of a smarmy-looking Nixon with the caption WOULD YOU BY A USED CAR FROM THE MAN?[66]

Kennedy and Nixon participated in the first televised presidential debate. Many people who listened to the debate on the radio thought that Nixon did pretty well, but those who watched on television saw Kennedy looking like a dashing young go-getter and Nixon looking like a nervous, sweaty slob who needed a shave.

The election was a close one; some (Nixon included)[67] felt that Kennedy's people committed fraud in Illinois and Texas to put their guy over the top. People still argue about this today. Despite recounts and investigations in several states, Kennedy was declared the victor and became the youngest man ever elected president (Theodore Roosevelt was a younger president but wasn't *elected* to a full term until he was older) and also the first Roman Catholic president.

Kennedy had already captured the nation's imagination; he was a young guy who seemed to understand the changes that were coming to America and the world better than someone older, like Nixon, really did. One of Kennedy's first acts in office was to create the Peace Corps, a group that would help provide education and other forms of relief to third-world countries.

---

66 Neatly explaining our joke about Napoléon in Chapter 3.

67 Most investigations now say that there probably was some cheating, but not nearly enough to actually alter the results of the election. But in 1960, Nixon told friends, "We won, but they stole it from us." Some think he felt that since Kennedy cheated, he was entitled to cheat later in life, too. In any case, he certainly went on to fight dirty.

MORE STUFF FROM 1960 TO 1966 MENTIONED IN "WE DIDN'T START THE FIRE"

U-2: A kind of U.S. spy plane, one of which was shot down by the Soviet Union in 1960.

SYNGMAN RHEE: The first president of South Korea. The CIA had to rescue him from being killed after people began to suspect he'd rigged the election.

PAYOLA: A scandal came about when people found out that disc jockeys were given "payola," or compensated by record companies, to play songs on the air.

CHUBBY CHECKER: A singer who had a hit with "The Twist," which became the biggest dance craze of the early 1960s.

PSYCHO: A scary movie directed by Alfred Hitchcock.

BELGIANS AND THE CONGO: The Republic of the Congo declared independence from Belgium in 1960. Belgium was not amused.

HEMINGWAY: Ernest Hemingway, an American author who committed suicide in 1961.

EICHMANN: The most wanted Nazi war criminal of World War II, Adolf Eichmann was finally captured in 1961 and was eventually hanged.

STRANGER IN A STRANGE LAND: A science fiction novel by Robert A. Heinlein.

LAWRENCE OF ARABIA: A popular movie.

Everything we feel like saying about Kennedy's presidency actually comes up later in the song, so for the moment, we'll move on to a brief interlude about rock music.

DYLAN

Bob Dylan arrived in New York at the age of twenty in 1961. Less than three years later, he was already being hailed as the greatest songwriter in American history. A few of us here on the Smart Aleck staff (Adam in particular) are ready to punch anyone who says he isn't.

Dylan started out as a folksinger, patterning himself after Woody Guthrie and performing mostly old folk standards. He then hit on the idea of writing songs of his own, like Woody had a generation before, and had his first big success with "Blowin' in the Wind," which became a huge hit when it was recorded by Peter, Paul and Mary, a wildly popular folk trio.

By the time "Blowin' in the Wind" became a hit in 1963, rock music had fallen on hard times. For a while, there seemed to be only two kinds of dances: the twist, and variations on the twist. For a brief, strange period, the popular music of choice among many young people became folk music. Protest songs, in particular, seemed very relevant in the age of the civil rights movement and the nuclear bomb.

Most protest songs of the day, however, were really pretty awful. Most of them just tried to make a point by throwing the word "free" or "peace" into the lyrics as often as humanly possible, and more than a few ended with

Bob Dylan. If you say a word against him, Adam just might challenge you to a duel, Aaron Burr style.

an ironic reference to "the land of the free," which got old fast.

Dylan's protest songs were, by and large, much better. Songs such as "The Lonesome Death of Hattie Carroll," "The Times They Are A-Changin'" and "With God on Our Side" managed not to sound nearly as preachy as many other protest songs while making points about the world that people couldn't ignore. Furthermore, Dylan's combination of folk music with surreal, beatnik-inspired poetry redefined the way people thought of folk music. In 1965, when Dylan switched to playing rock music (which, by then, had been brought back to life by British bands such as the Beatles—see a later section), other rock bands followed his example and began to grow up a little. While

early rock songs were mostly just songs about teenage love designed to make people dance, Dylan's work made them realize that rock music could be artistic, too.

If you want to learn more about Bob Dylan, there are probably about five hundred books about him at your local bookstore, and he might very well be playing a concert in your town soon. As this book goes to press, Dylan is in his late sixties and still playing about a hundred shows a year. And he's still writing great songs.

BEATLEMANIA[68]

The Beatles formed in Liverpool and became famous in England in 1962, but wouldn't really take America by storm until February 1964. Their appearance on *The Ed Sullivan Show* was one of the most-watched television shows in history, and years later, practically everyone who was a kid in 1964 had memories of listening to their father complain about how long the Beatles' hair was.

The success of the Beatles was due to a mix of talent and timing. They were excellent musicians, and their

---

[68] Again, we're not totally following the order of history as dictated by Dr. Joel here—"British Beatlemania" is a couple of lines off. Again, we're so, so, sorry.

x

A public domain image of the Beatles as they appeared from the upper deck at their 1965 concert at Shea Stadium. It was our use of this shot that led the International Textbook Advisory Board to ask, "Have you no decency? Have you at long last no sense of decency at all?" We have plenty of decency, but not much shame!

songs, coming in the wake of the folk craze and endless variations on "The Twist," sounded almost unimaginably fresh by the standards of the day (and still do now, compared to most of what passes for popular music). Still, that alone doesn't account for just how big they became. Another factor was timing: they hit America only weeks after (spoiler alert) the assassination of John F. Kennedy. The nation was in need of cheering up.

Also, unlike many pop groups these days, the Beatles played their own instruments and wrote most of their own songs, which allowed them to grow artistically. Though Bob Dylan made it possible for rock music to be experimental, even artistically relevant, it was the Beatles who popularized this idea; their own music got more psychedelic and rock-influenced over the course of the 1960s.

 277

It's partly because of the Beatles that people—even, for once, people who weren't there—tend to regard the 1960s as a golden age of popular music. It's true that pop music was reaching new heights in those days, but remember, oldies and classic-rock radio stations nowadays only play the real cream of the crop. If you look at a list of the top ten songs from any given week in the 1960s, even the biggest rock fan on the block will probably only recognize a

✳ ✳

STUFF BILLY JOEL MISSED: MOTOWN

No discussion of music in the 1960s could possibly be complete without mentioning the influence of black music on the styles that became popular in the twentieth century. When rock 'n' roll became popular, many parents were terrified—partly because it was "black" music, at least in origin. Many of the songs that became hits were originally sung or written by black artists, and only became popular after being recorded by white performers.

But by the 1960s, things were beginning to change, and artists recording for Motown Records racked up a combined total of over a hundred top ten hits between 1961 and 1971. Unlike much of the popular music from the 1960s (or any other era), the music recorded by such artists as the Temptations, the Supremes, Stevie Wonder (then known as Little Stevie Wonder), the Four Tops, the Marvellettes, Marvin Gaye, and others is still very popular today, and the distinct Motown sound combining pop, soul, and blues is instantly recognizable.

Berry Gordy Jr., the head of Motown Records, was highly involved in his artists' images, dictating the way they would dress, perform, and behave in public. He instructed them to act like royalty to help combat the still-present stereotype that African Americans were, by nature, lower-class. This professionalism certainly helped many Motown performers gain white audiences around the world—though other labels had equal success (and have had similar success since) advertising their artists as uncivilized, violent, and ignorant (whether they actually *were* any of these things or not). Most Motown songs were (supposedly at Gordy's insistence) not political, but several with political messages, such as "War," recorded by Edwin Starr, and "What's Going On," by Marvin Gaye, became big hits.

couple of them. The rest of the list will be full of terrible pop songs that have long since been forgotten and swept away into history, leaving us with the small percentage of songs that stood the test of time.

We won't go into too much about the Beatles here. If you want to learn more, your local bookstore probably has almost as many books about them as it does about Bob Dylan, and odds are very good that some cable channel is showing a documentary about them right this very minute.

BERLIN

After World War II, many of the European countries that had been liberated from the Nazis had fallen under control of the Soviet bloc, effectively going from one totalitarian rule to another. Countries under Communist control were referred to as being behind what Churchill called the Iron Curtain that would divide Europe for decades.

After World War II, Germany had been divided into two separate countries: East Germany, which was Communist, and West Germany, which was not. Right in the middle of this was the city of Berlin. In 1961, a wall was constructed to separate the two countries and keep East Berliners from leaving the country. People trying to flee were often shot; about two hundred people were

Kennedy at the Berlin Wall. He's in there somewhere, anyway.

killed trying to escape over the years. Most West Germans were free to come and go, but they were always afraid that East Germany was going to invade them at some point, and many had friends and family members stuck in East Germany who were unable to leave.

In 1963, President Kennedy visited West Berlin, and thousands of people came to see him give a speech in the shadow of the Berlin Wall. The speech was one of Kennedy's best; it was a huge morale boost for West Berlin when he said, "Today, in the world of freedom, the proudest boast is 'Ich bin ein Berliner' [I am from Berlin] . . . and therefore, as a free man, I take pride in the words 'Ich bin ein Berliner!' "

According to a legend that many teachers repeat as fact, by saying "Ich

President Kennedy (showing us his good side) meeting with advisors, who, apparently quite calmk, are telling him to end the world. ✗

✗ ✗ ✗ ✗ ✗ ✗ ✗ ✗ ✗ ✗

bin ein Berliner," not simply "Ich bin Berliner," what Kennedy actually said was not "I am a Berliner" but "I am a jelly donut." This isn't exactly true; a Berliner *was* a type of jelly donut, but adding that "ein" was perfectly acceptable, and no one present thought that Kennedy was referring to himself as a pastry. The type of donut called a Berliner elsewhere was actually known as a *Pfannkuchen* in Berlin.

THE BAY OF PIGS INVASION (JUST WHEN YOU THOUGHT IT WAS SAFE TO THROW AWAY THOSE "LOOSE LIPS SINK SHIPS" POSTERS . . .)

Though his way of inspiring optimism in places as downtrodden as West Berlin made him a well-loved president, Kennedy had his share of screw-ups. Chief among these may

have been the Bay of Pigs invasion.

Before Kennedy was even president, the government had the idea to use anti-Communist agents in Cuba to overthrow Fidel Castro, the ruler of Cuba. In April of 1961, Kennedy authorized an invasion of Cuba to remove him from power.

However, due to a lot of talk about the invasion around Miami, the Cubans knew the invasion was coming, and were prepared for it. Many invaders were killed or wounded, and others were captured and sentenced by the Cuban government to terms in prison, though they were eventually released in exchange for fifty-three million dollars' worth of food and medicine.

The Bay of Pigs invasion not only failed to overthrow Castro, it made Castro begin to fear future U.S.–led invasions. Because of this, he made a deal to obtain nuclear warheads from the USSR, leading to the Cuban Missile Crisis, which may have been the closest the world ever came to starting World War III (see page 282).

OLE MISS

Early in his term as president, Kennedy tried to distance himself from the civil rights movement, fearing that he'd further alienate the many Southern Democrats in Congress who'd hated his guts from day one. These

George Wallace blocking the doors at the University of Alabama. He's the frowning, unpleasant-looking one in the doorway. He later had a change of heart about civil rights and spent the rest of his life apologizing.

same guys had been keeping the civil rights movement down for decades. But Kennedy ended up taking the strongest stance on civil rights of any president in decades. He felt that circumstances required him to do so.

Though racial segregation had been declared illegal years before, actually integrating schools, bus lines, and other public institutions took some time, and was still a major hot-button issue in the early 1960s. When a black student named James Meredith tried to enroll at the University of Mississippi in 1962, President Kennedy had to send in federal troops and U.S. marshals to help him get in the front door. Most of the students, according to firsthand accounts, were actually okay with Meredith's being there, but those who weren't gave him no end of trouble.

Certainly, the time for a president to

FROM BILLY JOEL'S "LENINGRAD": THE CUBAN MISSILE CRISIS

In October 1962, U.S. spy planes photographed missile silos being built in Cuba. This, of course, really freaked Americans out—all Americans had to comfort themselves about the fear of nuclear war was the knowledge that launching a missile from one continent to the other was no easy task, even for a rocket scientist. However, if the Soviets could launch nuclear missiles from a site provided by their friends in Cuba, they would have a much easier time hitting American cities.

Kennedy quickly set up a naval blockade to prevent any ships from carrying military equipment into Cuba. The joint chiefs of staff advising Kennedy, however, insisted that this would never be enough. They told the president that the only thing he could do was launch a full-scale invasion of Cuba—or at the very least drop a few big bombs on Cuba to show that we were serious.

Kennedy thought these were both bad ideas. He knew full well that the USSR would never let an invasion go unpunished. If they couldn't respond by launching missiles at Americans, they would probably attack West Berlin instead, and then America would have to get involved by fighting on West Berlin's side. One way or another, he knew, an attack on Cuba would lead to World War III.

But the Soviets showed no sign of backing down, and Kennedy secretly began to prepare for war. The military prepared not only an invasion of Cuba but also a plan for a nuclear assault on the USSR, in the event that they invaded West Berlin. Nuclear war seemed to be hours away. Kennedy, however, urged the joint chiefs to wait as long as possible before launching the invasion, giving him more time to negotiate.

After some very, very tense dealing, Kennedy sent a secret message to the Soviets, offering a deal. If the missiles were torn down, he said, the United States would assure the USSR that they wouldn't invade Cuba. No one really expected it to work, and the joint chiefs continued to assume that nuclear war would start within hours—possibly by the next morning.

Eventually, a secret deal was reached: if the United States would tear down the missiles they had set up in Turkey, which gave them a shot at hitting Moscow if they felt like it, the Soviets would tear down their missiles in Cuba and turn their ships around. The crisis was averted.

At the time, no one knew that the United States had agreed to take its missiles out of Turkey, so it looked as though Kennedy had emerged the victor in a big embarrassment for the Soviets.

U.S. military commanders, though, were still ticked off. One even called it the greatest defeat in American history, and insisted that the invasion of Cuba should still begin at once.

Nearly thirty years later, it became clear that the Soviets hadn't just been building missiles in Cuba; they'd already *had* a handful over there that were operational. It seems pretty likely that if Kennedy had authorized the invasion, as the joint chiefs angrily begged him to, those missiles would have been fired right at the United States, leading to a full-scale nuclear war and all the devastation that would come with it. It was only Kennedy's sneaky negotiating that kept it from happening.

JOHN GLENN (ABOVE): An astronaut who became the first American to orbit the Earth in 1962. He later became a senator and an unsuccessful presidential candidate. He returned to space in 1998 at age seventy-seven, becoming the oldest person ever to go there.

LISTON BEATS PATTERSON: More boxing.

POPE PAUL: Pope Paul VI became Pope in 1963.

MALCOLM X: A guy so controversial we're afraid to say much about him even now, though we recommend that you read his autobiography and make up your own mind.

BRITISH POLITICIAN SEX: The British secretary of war was caught having an affair with a showgirl and tried to lie about it before admitting the truth and resigning in 1963.

BIRTH CONTROL: Birth control pills became available in the mid-1960s. ✵

step up on the issue was long overdue. In 1963, when two black students tried to enroll in the University of Alabama, Governor George Wallace himself blocked the door to keep them from getting in, only stepping down when federal troops forced him to. That

evening, Kennedy gave an address supporting civil rights that was broadcast on television and the radio, even though his advisors told him that the address was political suicide. The speech led to the Civil Rights Act of 1964, which Kennedy, alas, would not live to sign.

JFK, BLOWN AWAY (WAY TO PUT IT DELICATELY, MR. JOEL!)

Here's another one that'll probably get us more than a few letters. . . .

In November of 1963, while gearing up for his reelection, President John F. Kennedy, who had been the target of a number of assassination attempts and had, like any self-respecting president, more enemies than Batman, took a trip to Dallas. While riding in a car in a motorcade, he was shot and killed. His vice president, Lyndon B. Johnson, was immediately sworn in as president.

The Dallas police quickly arrested Lee Harvey Oswald, who, they said, had shot Kennedy from an upper window of a book depository. Oswald wouldn't live to see his trial, though, as he was shot to death two days later by a nightclub owner named Jack Ruby.

Numerous conspiracy theories about Kennedy's assassination have been going around ever since. Some people argue that there must have

One of the "backyard pictures" of Lee Harvey Oswald that *Life* magazine retouched for publication. All the work they did to make it clear enough to publish made it look rather fake, fueling the fire of conspiracy theories for decades to come. ✯

been a second shooter hiding in the bushes. Some say that the Mafia was behind it. Others say it was the CIA. Very few groups *haven't* been accused of being behind the assassination at one time or another.

The Warren Commission, appointed by President Johnson and led by Chief

LBJ—with his clothes on, thank goodness.

Justice Earl Warren, conducted a ten-month investigation of the assassination beginning a week later. The commission concluded that Oswald had been guilty, and that he had acted alone. In the 1970s, though, the House Select Committee on Assassinations determined that he might have been working for some bigger organization.

There are, of course, plenty of questions: for one thing, what was Kennedy thinking riding around in a convertible with the top down? And, for another, on the day he was shot, Oswald had a whole crew of bodyguards behind him—but why didn't he have any in *front* of him?

We don't know. We're too busy trying to figure out that thing about Elvis's tombstone.

So, Billy Joel asks at this point in the song, "What else do I have to say?"

Plenty, of course. There's a whole long verse left to go, but he didn't have anything at all to say about . . .

. . . LYNDON B. JOHNSON: OUR *REALLY* FORGOTTEN PRESIDENT

We've had our fair share of forgotten presidents over the years, as you've seen, but no one, it seems, has been forgotten quite so quickly and thoroughly as ol' LBJ. Ask your parents or grandparents who was president between Kennedy and Nixon, and odds are pretty good that they'll have to think about it for a minute.

EXPERIMENTS TO TRY AT HOME!

Go up to someone on the street and ask them who was president after Kennedy. You'll be surprised by just how many people, including people who were alive and voting in 1964, will have to think long and hard about it, even if you give them a bunch of clues. The main thing people seem to remember about him is that his wife was called Lady Bird. They might remember that *some* president used to hold meetings while he dropped anchor in the White House bathroom, but may or may not remember which president it was. We've tried this experiment all over the country, and only about one in ten could answer the question without at least a few hints.

So now that you've read this chapter, you're better informed that nine out of ten people on the street. Feel free to start acting like an elitist.

LBJ, a grouchy conservative, was taken on as the more liberal Kennedy's running mate, despite the fact that it seemed like no one could really stand him. He balanced the ticket out and made Kennedy more attractive to Southern voters; the Texan Johnson's presence on the ticket probably won Kennedy the election.

Johnson, a Texas millionaire, was sworn in as president after the Kennedy assassination. Johnson had some good moments, such as signing the Civil Rights Act of 1964, but today he's remembered mainly for being crude and unpleasant. When Johnson had to take a dump in the middle of a conversation with his cabinet, he'd just move the

Walter Cronkite, who was probably the most respected news anchor of the day, announced on television that he thought the Vietnam war was unwinnable and that the most anyone could hope for was a stalemate. President Johnson is said to have stated that if he'd lost Walter Cronkite, he'd lost the American people. Ever since then, news footage of military operations has been pretty well restricted so that people don't have to see that there's more to war than waving flags and being proud.

The Civil Rights Act of 1964 was the most sweeping civil rights legislation of its day, and included women's rights as part of its reforms. Ironically, the section on women's rights was added by a senator from Virginia who opposed the whole thing and was said to be sure that if he stuck something about womens' rights into it, it would never pass. The bill passed anyway, though, much to the chagrin of a certain wiener from Virginia.

meeting into the bathroom and keep on chattering while he did his business. He also used to skinny-dip in the White House pool—and make fun of anyone who didn't join him.

While he did a lot of good work as president, such as his War on Poverty, much of it is overshadowed nowadays by his connection to the Vietnam War.

LBJ showing how nice he is. ✶

✶ ✶ ✶ ✶ ✶ ✶ ✶ ✶ ✶ ✶ ✶ ✶ ✶ ✶ ✶ ✶ ✶ ✶ ✶ ✶

This made him so unpopular that even though he could have run for a second full term in 1968, he didn't bother, fearing that he would lose the primaries to Eugene McCarthy, an antiwar senator who had decided to challenge him for the nomination. Johnson had initially planned to run, but McCarthy enlisted

The other *public domain picture of Elvis, taken during his meeting with Richard Nixon. For the meeting, in which Elvis offered to be a special agent in charge of sniffing out drug use, Nixon wore a suit, and Elvis wore what appears to be a professional wrestling championship belt.*

thousands of young volunteers who shaved, cut their long hair, and even put on clean pants to be "Clean for Gene" as they went door to door to promote his candidacy. Johnson won the first primary against McCarthy 49 percent to 42 percent, a margin *much* smaller than anyone had predicted. This made Johnson look vulnerable, and when several other candidates, including Senator Robert F. Kennedy, brother of JFK, jumped into the race as well, Johnson decided to give up. The nomination would eventually go to his vice president, Hubert Humphrey, but only after a bitter, chaotic primary season and convention.

RICHARD NIXON: BACK AGAIN

Despite telling reporters that they wouldn't have him to kick around anymore a few years earlier, Nixon ended up running for president again in 1968. At the start of the campaign, he was terribly unpopular, and few felt that he really had a chance of winning.

However, 1968 was a pretty bad year

Nixon's most famous pose.

all around. In April, Dr. Martin Luther King, Jr., was assassinated. In June, Robert Kennedy was assassinated in the middle of his attempt to win the Democratic nomination for president. After a season of bitter primaries, the Democratic Convention in Chicago to nominate someone was a disaster, with protestors engaging in riots and fights with the police all over the city.

People in America were in such a bad

AS MENTIONED IN BILLY JOEL'S "GOODNIGHT SAIGON": THE VIETNAM WAR

Right around this point in "We Didn't Start the Fire" comes a mention of Ho Chi Minh, which is the closest Billy really gets to mentioning the Vietnam War. Ho was president of North Vietnam from 1954 to 1969.

The conflict between the United States and the North Vietnamese Communist forces was already getting under way when Kennedy was president, but it was Johnson who started drafting more and more people who didn't want to fight in the war into the army. The peacetime draft had been going on for more than a decade, but not *too* many people were being drafted, and anyway, there wasn't a war on, so not too many people complained.

But once the fighting started, things changed. The draft to build the army for Vietnam wasn't much more popular than most other wartime drafts, and thousands of young people either fled to Canada or enrolled in college, as college students could usually get around being drafted. The draft became especially unpopular because of this—people who could afford to go to college or to hire a draft lawyer could usually get out of having to go to war, but poor people couldn't, leading many to state (all together now), "This is a rich man's war, and a poor man's fight."

Though there was never a formal declaration of war, U.S. efforts to stop the

Communist North Vietnamese (the Viet Cong) from taking over South Vietnam dragged on for ten years, leaving more than fifty thousand American soldiers dead. The Viet Cong suffered even greater losses—more than a million deaths were reported—but the United States never won. This wasn't an old-fashioned "beat the other army and it's all over" sort of war. The Viet Cong knew that they could actually lose just about every battle, and, as long as more people kept fighting (or being forced to fight) them, they could drag the conflict on and on until the Americans gave up. If this sounds familiar, go back to Chapter 2 and see how the colonists won the Revolutionary War. One North Vietnamese leader said that if the Americans wanted war for twenty years, they would *have* war for twenty years.

It's worth noting that this was the first war that was really televised. People at home were able to see firsthand just what a messy business war really was, and every time dead bodies were shown on television, support for the war dropped.

Violence in Vietnam continued to escalate for years, even after Johnson left office and was replaced by Richard Nixon. Nixon promised "peace with honor," but Henry Kissinger, one of his top advisors, told him (at least at first) that victory was the only way to exit with honor. Nixon was prepared to do whatever it took to win the war, even if it meant escalation of violence.

Meanwhile, the antiwar movement was gaining strength in America. As actually "winning" the war seemed more and more like a remote possibility, there began to be more and more pressure on Nixon to pull everyone out. But an equally loud voice, which included the voices of the military-industrial complex Eisenhower had warned about, pushed for U.S. troops to stay in Vietnam for as long as humanly possible and stated that people who opposed the war were traitors.

It wasn't until early in 1973, shortly after winning his second term, that Nixon declared a halt to American offensive operations, but the war wasn't officially over until President Gerald Ford announced the end in 1975. The North Vietnamese took over Saigon days later.

Protestors put flowers into guns. Note: This does not stop guns from working. It only works symbolically.

In theory, going to the moon sounds awesome. In practice, there's so little to do there that you might as well go to Omaha, which at least had a really wicked arcade last time the Smart Aleck staff was there.

mood that they actually elected Richard Nixon, who managed to squeak into office despite having won only 43.4 percent of the popular vote. His main competitor, Hubert Humphrey, received 42.7 percent. Thirteen percent went to George Wallace, the guy who'd stood in the doorway to keep black students out of the University of Alabama a few years earlier. Wallace ran for president in 1968 as an independent candidate and won most of the Southern states.

Nixon is generally thought of as an ultraconservative president, though his policies were actually fairly well to the left. He supported civil rights and opened relations with China, which had been cut off ever since they'd become a Communist country in 1949. It was his tough talking that made him seem conservative—well, that and his private comments about Jews, blacks, Italians, Mexicans, homosexuals, and any other group he felt like taking a shot at, many of which were captured on tape recorders that he left running in the White House at all times.

Yes, there was always something about Nixon that made people want to throw things at him. In fact, when he was vice president and visiting South America, people threw vegetables at his car. In a rare moment of humor, he noted that people weren't throwing things at *him,* they were throwing things at the *car.* He was riding in an Edsel.

But say what you will about the guy (and we here at the Smart Aleck's Guide say a *lot* about him), at least he never expected his cabinet to watch him take a dump.

THE MOON SHOT

It was President Kennedy who suggested in 1961 that America could put a man on the moon by the end of the decade. When he said it, wheels were put in motion to develop the technology that would actually put a living person, not just a monkey, on the moon and bring him back safely.

By this time, the United States was finally pulling ahead of Russia in the space race, though by 1969, it was fairly obvious that there wasn't much of a military advantage to going to the moon. The space race was really just about bragging rights.

Still, having developed the technology, NASA launched the Apollo 11 spacecraft in July of 1969, and a few days later, Neil Armstrong became the first human being to set foot on the moon. He was followed shortly therafter by his shipmate Edwin "Buzz" Aldrin, Jr. Armstrong promptly said, "That's one small step for man, one giant leap for mankind." He meant to say "for *a* man," which would have made more sense, but people knew what he meant.

WOODSTOCK

Just when you thought we were done talking about people who smelled bad . . .

Hippies were sort of the 1960s equivalent of beatniks, only they wore much brighter clothes and usually favored rock and folk music over jazz. Many beatniks, such as Allen Ginsberg, actually ended up becoming hippies themselves.

In many ways, hippies are the cowboys of the twentieth century, in

YES, THE MOON LANDING HAPPENED.

Nowadays, more and more people seem to believe that the whole moon landing thing was a hoax. You'll probably meet a few of them over the course of your life. All we *really* have to say to them is that faking the moon landing and getting that past the Russians would have been twice as hard as getting to the moon in the first place, but arguing with conspiracy theorists is usually a fool's errand. No amount of proof will persuade some of them to change their minds.

The Russians never doubted that Americans had been on the moon. They just pointed out that we could have sent robots to the moon instead and gotten the same scientific results for a *whole* lot less money, without risking any lives.

But the race to the moon was never about scientific results. It was about getting there before the Soviets.

Mission accomplished.

Conspiracy theorists say that the flag shouldn't be blowing in the wind, since there's no wind on the moon. And it's not. It's held up by a horizontal bar, as you can see just by looking at the picture.

that they've become incredibly roman-ticized over the years. We generally think of them as gentle, happy people who stood up for peace, for social and political change, and for individuality and idealism, while making some pretty awesome music along the way. Some of them really were like this. However, there were also a lot of them who were just, to quote Beatle George Harrison, "horrible, spotty[69] drop-out kids on drugs."

Woodstock, a three-day concert in up-state New York, was one of the biggest hippie gatherings, and certainly the most publicized. It's also one of the reasons the romanticized image of hippies has endured. The festival shows that there was at least a kernel of truth behind the image. Featuring such acts as Jefferson Airplane, the Grateful Dead, Jimi Hen-drix, and Janis Joplin, the concert was a veritable Who's Who of rock music in the sixties (except for the Beatles, who weren't touring at the time; Bob Dylan, who lived right nearby but didn't per-form; and the Rolling Stones, who tried to stage their own festival a few months later in California, which ended badly). Though about 150,000 concertgoers were expected, almost half a million showed up.

---

69 A British term meaning "pimply." They also call French fries chips!

Nixon leaves the White House for the last time after resigning—and pauses to strike his trademark pose again. Gotta give him credit for going out with style. Ford issued a full pardon to Nixon, figuring that he'd suffered enough.✺

As cool as this was, there wasn't enough food for half a million people—which was a relief, in a way, because there also weren't enough toilets. The rain made the whole place a mud pit, the conditions were awful, but the mu-sic was great, and the fact that it didn't become a huge riot scene made it one of the most famous events of the day.

Rose Mary Woods does her freestyle floor routine and shows off her taste in bland office art.

WATERGATE

When Nixon took office, his approval ratings really had nowhere to go but up. He easily won a second term in 1972. But for Nixon, things sort of went downhill from there.

In the middle of the campaign, Nixon operatives, led by future radio talk-show host G. Gordon Liddy, broke into a Democratic Party office in the Watergate Hotel in Washington, D.C., to snoop around. After they were caught, no one really believed that Nixon had been involved in the crime or the subsequent cover-up. After all, he'd been way ahead in the polls—why would he have risked getting involved in a stupid break-in? But as time went on, some people began to suspect that Nixon *had* been involved, including Bob Woodward and Carl Bernstein, a couple of *Washington Post* reporters who were getting information from a secret source who called himself Deep Throat.

What got Nixon in real trouble was that it turned out that he was *also* (get this) snooping on himself. He had been taping everything that went on in the White House. When one tape revealed Nixon telling people to cover up the break-in, Congress ordered him to turn over all the other tapes so they could see what else he was up to. He turned most of them in, but he'd erased eighteen and a half minutes from one of them. To this day, no one knows what was erased.[70] His secretary, Rose Mary Woods, claimed that she'd accidentally hit the foot pedal that erased the tapes while talking on the phone, but the kind of stretch she would have had to do in order to pull this off would

For years, trying to figure out who Deep Throat really was was a popular game among political buffs and historians. In 2005, it was revealed that it was an FBI guy named W. Mark Felt.

---

[70] Another theory: Arlo Guthrie, the son of Woody Guthrie, says that a copy of his humorous antidraft song "Alice's Restaurant" was found in the Nixon Library, and points out that the song is, amazingly enough, almost exactly the length of the "missing minutes." Few believe that Nixon actually erased those minutes to cover up the fact that he liked Arlo Guthrie, but, hey, who knows?

THE WATERGATE TAPES

In addition to connecting Nixon to the break-in, the Watergate tapes, as all tapes turned over during the investigation are known, revealed a side of Nixon that he probably never wanted people to see. Among the questionable things he said on the tapes:

"I have the greatest affection for them [blacks] but I know they're not going to make it for five hundred years. They aren't. You know it, too. . . . The Mexicans are a different cup of tea. They have a heritage. At the present time they steal, they're dishonest. They do have some concept of family life, they don't live like a bunch of dogs, which the Negroes do live like."

This is a good example of the kind of quote (like that one about Grant resigning his commission) you shouldn't believe until you see the source. For the record, it was transcribed straight from White House tapes from 1971 that were released to the public in 1999.

have been a remarkable feat of acrobatics. Rose Mary was no slob, but she *was* in her mid-fifties, far past her prime years for gymnastics.

Nixon went on TV and said, "I am not a crook," but by that time, most people had already decided that he *was,* in fact, a crook, and his approval ratings plummeted. Congress began drawing up the paperwork to impeach him. Before they could finish the paperwork, Nixon resigned, leaving Gerald Ford, a guy Billy Joel didn't see fit to mention in *any* of his songs, in charge of the country.

PUNK ROCK (OR, HOW THE NATION DEALT WITH DISCO)

In the mid-1970s, as the nation finally saw the end of Richard Nixon's political career, the country settled into a generally happy mood—at least, the people who ignored the fact that the economy was in the tank did.

Television got better. More and more people had color TV sets, and the general quality of the shows was improving. Shows like *All in the Family* dealt with tough issues like racism, sexuality, religion, and politics but managed to be seriously funny at the same time. The age of *Leave It to Beaver* was over. Of course, there was also plenty of crap on the air—especially in the form of corny comedy variety shows—but those could be ignored.

As television started to get better, music took a turn for the worse. Most of the best groups of the 1960s were broken up or, in some cases, dead. Only a few of the biggest bands of 1967 were still doing anything notable by the mid-1970s: the beginning of the disco era.

The real problem was that rock music was over, for all practical purposes. There was still good—even great—rock coming out; it just wasn't viewed as quite so rebellious anymore. Men with long hair had gone mainstream. Presidential candidates were quoting Bob

Punk Rockers plotting to destroy everything. Scared? You should be!

taining lines like "God save the Queen / she ain't no human being," which, apparently, was about the worst thing a British person could possibly say in public. If that's true, then the British were in desperate need of punk rock.

As a band, the Sex Pistols had several disadvantages: for one thing, they didn't have a whole lot of raw musical talent (they made up for it with attitude). For another, they had to perform under fake names, such as S.P.O.T.S (Sex Pistols On Tour Secretly), Acne Ramble, and the Hamsters, because the "Sex Pistols" were banned from pretty much every town in England. When they appeared on television and swore like sailors, they spent the next several days on the cover of every tabloid. Rumors went around that they spent their afternoons roaming the streets puking on old ladies. Members of the government spoke out, saying that the band would be the end of society.[71] Lead singer Johnny Rotten said, "I don't understand it. All we're trying to do is destroy everything."

There was only one real problem with it: the whole thing was basically an act. A couple of members of the band were, in fact, completely out of

Dylan in campaign speeches. Elvis was still alive but was buried under a whole lot of rhinestones as Vegas-y glitz. Few people were trying to ban rock or saying that it would be the end of society anymore, which probably took some of the fun out of it.

And so along came punk rock, a hard, fast-paced music that people associated with nihilism and apathy. Punk fans spiked their hair, put safety pins through their face, and generally scared the crap out of most older people.

The blueprint for punk was more or less set by the Ramones, an American act, but most of the horrified public were introduced to the punk scene through media coverage of the Sex Pistols, an English band whose message was "no future for me" and who sang songs con-

---

[71] If you're keeping track, this is the 9,876,587,236th time someone has said something would be the end of society so far.

their minds, but the group's manager, Malcolm McLaren, went out of his way to get the band into fights and get them in the news in any way possible. He even hired film critic Roger Ebert to write a movie about them. At their final concert (until the 1990s), in San Francisco, Johnny Rotten finished the set by saying, "Ever get the feeling you've been cheated?" and walking off the stage.

This was probably the first time punk died. It would die and be reborn several times over the next few decades.

REAGAN:
FINALLY, A PRESIDENT WHO CAN HOLD HIS OWN ON-SCREEN AGAINST A CHIMP!

Ronald Reagan, a former actor known for such movies as *Bedtime for Bonzo,* which co-starred a chimpanzee, became governor of California in 1966. The idea of "President Reagan" instantly became a joke made by every comedian on television. Reagan *did* run for president in 1968 and 1976 but couldn't make it past the primaries. Then, in 1980, he won the Republican nomination and the election.

Right from the beginning, people *loved* Reagan. There was just something really likable about the guy. When he was shot in a failed assassination attempt early in his term, he fa-

mously told his wife, Nancy, "Honey, I forgot to duck." It may not be as inspiring a thing to say as "It takes more than that to kill a bull moose," but really—how charming can you get?

Reagan was known by the press as the Teflon president, because no bit of bad news seemed to stick to the guy. His administration was plagued by all sorts of scandals, but he remained popular. When it turned out that his administration had been illegally selling arms to Iran in the mid-1980s, he came up with an excuse that would become very popular with politicians: he claimed not to have known about the deals. Later he tried to suggest that he simply didn't remember making them. The excuse that he hadn't broken the law himself, he was just incapable of managing his staff, didn't work that well even for him. It began to look like he was going to be impeached; his approval rating dropped twenty points in

The Reagans, Ronald and Nancy. Nancy promoted the bold idea that people could "just say no" to drugs, which, apparently, she didn't think would occur to them otherwise. For reasons not entirely clear, Reagan often called his wife Mommy.

the course of about a month. But, being the Teflon president, he soon bounced right back. By the time of his death in 2004, he was one of the most beloved figures in America again.

The economy did improve a bit under Reagan. It had been in very bad shape under Ford and Carter (the presidents who came after Johnson), but things started to pick up somewhat in the 1980s, though many felt that Reagan's policies helped the rich a lot more than they helped anyone else. All over the country, factories were closing down (as chronicled in Billy Joel's song "Allentown").

One reason for Reagan's enduring popularity, of course, is that it was during his administration that the Cold War finally came to an end. Early in his term, he had called the USSR an

evil empire, but during a visit to Russia in 1988, he said that he was referring to "another time, another era." In 1987, on a trip to Berlin, which was still divided into East and West Berlin by the infamous Berlin Wall, Reagan sensed how unpopular the wall was with citizens on both sides and made a particularly famous speech in which he addressed the president of the USSR, saying, "Mr. Gorbachev, tear down this wall."

That same year, the Russians let Billy Joel into the country to play a series of concerts. He closed his set by singing Bob Dylan's "The Times They Are A-Changin'," an act that probably would have gotten him arrested by secret police just a few years earlier. Clearly, things *were* changing.

Two years later, the Berlin Wall was torn down. People from the two sides got together for a party that lasted for days, and America and the Soviet Union began to get friendly just in time for the Soviet Union to fall apart, which it officially did in 1991. The Soviet bloc countries began the long, long process of reinventing themselves as capitalist countries.

Some credit Ronald Reagan with finally bringing about the end of the Soviet Union, but others say its decline was inevitable. Still others say that it would have lasted much longer, but the

The Berlin Wall is torn down. Thank you, Billy Joel! ✵

✵ ✵ ✵ ✵ ✵ ✵ ✵ ✵ ✵ ✵ ✵ ✵ ✵ ✵ ✵ ✵ ✵ ✵ ✵

Communists turned out to be quitters who did not give 110 percent.

A small minority, believe it or not, credit rock 'n' roll with tearing down the Iron Curtain. Soviet youth's affection for the Western culture that their government had banned made them into doubters. Czech film director Milos Forman, who grew up behind the Iron Curtain, has always been quite open about saying that it was the Beatles (at least partly) who brought Communism down. "Suddenly the (Communist) ideologues are telling you these four (the Beatles) [are] apes escaping from the jungle," he said in 2001. "And I thought, 'I'm not such an idiot, and I love this music.' All of a sudden, the ideologues were strangers." By the late 1960s, Soviet youth were stealing parts from pay phones to turn acoustic guitars into electric ones and making copies of records using an ingenious method involving discarded X-ray plates. The thrill of rebellion that came with rock music had worn off in the States, but to be a rock fan in the Soviet Union was truly subversive.

Months after the Berlin Wall fell, Communism also fell in Czechoslovakia after what came to be called the Velvet Revolution. Václav Havel, who became the new Czech president, has been known to claim that it was named after the band the Velvet Underground. Even the U.S. Congress knew that music could be a weapon for freedom; it broadcast rock music over the Soviet airwaves through its Radio Free Europe program. Keith Richards of the band the Rolling Stones[72] summed up the whole idea by saying, "After those billions of dollars and living under the threat of doom, what brought it down? Blue jeans and rock 'n' roll."

In reality, music probably wasn't the only thing that brought the Soviet Union down—but it was certainly one of the first, and most obvious, cracks in the wall.

A WHOLE SERIES OF DOWNERS

The final verse of the song, the one that mentions Reagan, seems to indicate that Billy Joel, too, thought that the end of civilization was at hand. The last verse is mostly bad news; get your hankies ready.

Begin (sounds like he's singing "bacon," but it's "Begin"): Menachem Begin became prime minister of Israel in 1977. Not exactly bad news, but things start to go downhill in the song soon.

Palestine: The Palestine Liberation Organization, a group dedicated to

destroying Israel, was in the news.

Terror on the airline: There were numerous aircraft hijackings.

Ayatollah's in Iran: In 1979, the Ayatollah Ruhollah Khomeini led a revolution that took over Iran. Until then, the country had been led by the shah as a constitutional monarchy, but the revolution turned it into an Islamic republic. The shah's regime was pretty brutal, but, as sometimes happens with revolutions, the new regime turned out to be just about as oppressive as the old one.

Russians in Afghanistan: In the late seventies, the Soviets launched a ten-year war with Afghanistan that sort of became their Vietnam—a long, unwinnable war.

Wheel of Fortune: Why Billy Joel thought mentioning a game show was important here in the middle of all this gloom and despair is anyone's guess. Maybe he really hates Pat Sajak, the host.

Sally Ride: The first American woman in space, another bit of good news amid the gloom of the last verse.

Foreign debts: In the 1980s, the amount of money the United States owed to foreign countries skyrocketed.

Homeless vets: Many Vietnam veterans were unable to get the care they needed for mental and physical ailments suffered in the war. A great many ended up homeless on the streets by the 1980s.

---

[72] Okay, so Keith Richards isn't a properly licensed historian, but the quote is too good for us to ignore, and it *does* sum up what many people felt had happened: culture, not politics, won the Cold War.

AIDS (Acquired Immunodeficiency Syndrome): The AIDS virus first became known to researchers in the early 1980s and became one of the greatest health problems of the twentieth century.

Crack: Cocaine was a very popular drug among the rich. Crack cocaine, a cheaper, deadlier version of it, became popular, particularly in poor areas, in the mid-1980s.

Bernie (Bernard) Goetz: A New Yorker who shot four people on the subway when he thought they were attacking him. The young men approached him to ask for five bucks, and he shot three of them, then shot the fourth in the spine while the boy lay on the ground. Whether Goetz had acted in self-defense became a big subject of controversy.

Hypodermics on the shore: For years, loose environmental laws had allowed pretty much anyone to dump pretty much anything into the ocean. This began to change when dangerous medical waste started washing up on the shore in New Jersey. Dumping it in the ocean was already illegal, but stuff like this helped wake people up to the idea that environmentalism was a real issue. The same guys Eisenhower called the military-industrial complex went right to work convincing people it wasn't, and that the environment was just fine, so they could keep dumping garbage wherever they pleased.

HEAVY-METAL SUICIDE

In the mid-eighties, several heavy-metal bands were taken to court over charges that their music caused kids to worship Satan and commit suicide. Would you have let a guy in spandex and a whole lot of mascara convince you to switch religions? Legions of parents were convinced that their children were, in fact, just about that stupid.[73] Never mind the fact that it didn't make much sense for singers to want their fans to kill themselves—if their fans were dead, who would buy their records, T-shirts, and other products? Maybe we should go ask the tobacco companies, who seem to have figured that one out.✱

China's under martial law: In 1989, students rallied for democracy in China's Tiananmen Square. China declared martial law so that it could send in tanks to remove them by force.

---

[73] Others didn't think their kids were dumb but thought the heavy-metal bands were hiding subliminal messages in the music. Back in the 1950s, a guy named James Vicary said he had run tests showing that if you flashed messages about popcorn in movies so quickly that people didn't notice them, it could raise sales of popcorn by 58 percent, because viewers' brains would pick the messages up "subliminally." Some people believe that music, movies, →

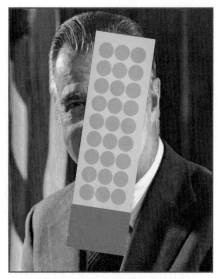

Spiro Agnew, Nixon's vice president, who had to resign after it turned out he'd been cheating on his taxes.

Rock 'n' roller cola wars: Throughout the eighties, Coca-Cola and Pepsi tried to outdo each other by hiring musicians to endorse their products. Coke had been the number-one soft drink in the country for decades, but Pepsi began to really cut into their market share. Coke initially tried to shake things up by changing their formula to New Coke, which tasted more like Pepsi. This is widely seen as the biggest flop since the Edsel, and they quickly scrapped New Coke and went back to

commercials, and even Ritz crackers have been full of subliminal messages ever since. Actually, though, Vicary's results were falsified, and no other tests have ever shown that subliminal messages are actually effective. See *The Smart Aleck's Guide to Getting All Freaked Out over Nothing.*

the original formula. They began to recruit celebrities like Paula Abdul and Elton John to endorse Coke, while Pepsi hired Michael Jackson.

Given just how grim the last verse of "We Didn't Start the Fire" is, it seems odd that it was the rock 'n' roller cola wars that prompted Billy Joel to declare "I can't take it anymore!" but, well, there you are. Other people saw the end coming due to the end of slavery, women voting, or jazz. We all have our breaking points!

THE STUFF WE—ER . . . BILLY JOEL MISSED

MTV: The music-themed TV channel premiered August 1, 1981. Brian Eddlebeck of the Smart Aleck Staff became the first person ever to say, "MTV used to be cool, but now it sucks," on August 2.

The Daisy Ad: A commercial for Lyndon B. Johnson's 1964 presidential campaign that showed a little girl plucking the petals from a daisy, followed by a mushroom cloud from an atomic bomb. It only aired once, but the message was clear: Vote for Johnson or the little girl gets it.

Live Aid: A giant rock concert for charity in 1985 that did not feature Billy Joel.

Kent State shootings: The Ohio National Guard shot thirteen students at

Kent State University in Ohio, killing four of them, when they protested Nixon's invasion of Cambodia in 1970. People still argue about exactly why the Guard fired on the students.

The Exxon Valdez *oil spill:* A 1989 oil tanker spill that became a huge environmental disaster. The effects from it are still seen today—and as of this writing, the *Exxon Valdez* is still sailing.

M.A.S.H.: A TV show about the Korean War that lasted *way* longer than the actual Korean War. The last episode was the highest-rated TV show ever, and will probably remain so, now that network TV shows have so many other cable channels to compete with.

The Iran Hostage Crisis: Fifty-two U.S. citizens were held hostage for 444 days from 1979 to 1981 after Iranian students took over the U.S. embassy during the Iranian Revolution.

PRESIDENTS BILLY JOEL MISSED!

There were two presidents besides LBJ whom Billy Joel didn't mention in "We Didn't Start the Fire":

No one ever voted for Gerald Ford. He became vice president after Spiro Agnew resigned and took over the presidency when Nixon resigned. One of his first acts was to grant Nixon a full pardon, saving Nixon from going on trial and saving the public from having to deal with Nixon anymore. Com-

Gerald Ford.

ing from an athletic background, Ford is the only president ever to have tackled a Heisman trophy winner. He also became the only president to survive an assassination attempt by anyone known by the name Squeaky, after Lynnette "Squeaky" Fromme, a disciple of murderer Charles Manson, pointed a gun at him in 1975. The economy went down the toilet (as it tends to do from time to time) during Ford's term, though, and his attempt to win a full term failed.

Ford was the first president to be parodied on *Saturday Night Live,* which was a brand-new show at the time. Chevy Chase, who looked nothing like Ford, played him as a buffoon who tended to fall down a lot, which is how many people ended up remembering Ford in the years that followed.

Jimmy Carter.

In 1976, people were, quite understandably, sick of political "insiders," and ended up electing Jimmy Carter, a former peanut farmer from Georgia. As president, he urged the nation to make sacrifices for the economy (he was even said to have ordered his staff to drive their own cars) and to work to save energy. At the time, the country was in the middle of an energy crisis as people realized that the supply of fossil fuels wasn't going to last forever. Carter himself wore sweaters around the White House to stay warm and had solar heating panels installed in the White House roof. However, the economy didn't seem to be getting any better, and Ronald Reagan beat him in a landslide in the 1980 election. Carter went on to work for human rights around the world, and spent time building houses for the Habitat for Humanity charity. He won the Nobel Peace Prize in 2002. As for the energy crisis . . . well, thank goodness *that's* over, huh?

Jimmy Carter claimed to have been attacked by a mysterious swimming rabbit once while he was fishing. No one believed him until this picture turned up.

END-OF-CHAPTER QUESTIONS

MULTIPLE CHOICE

1. The story of Richard Nixon was
- **a.** A tragedy.
- **b.** A farce.
- **c.** A romantic comedy.
- **d.** Both a and b.

(ANSWER: WE'RE GOING WITH D.)

2. Air-raid drills in school:
- **a.** Represented time that could

have been spent on long division.

b. At least made people feel like they were doing *something* to keep kids safe.

c. Were excellent chances to check out the butt of the person sitting in front of you.

d. All of the above.

(ANSWER: D.)

3. **Who killed President Kennedy?**

a. Lee Harvey Oswald.

b. The Mafia.

c. The CIA.

d. The KKK.

e. You and me.

(ANSWER: WE'RE GONNA GO WITH E, BECAUSE MICK JAGGER SAID SO IN "SYMPATHY FOR THE DEVIL," AND WHEN MICK TALKS, WE LISTEN. ALSO, THIS ANSWER PROBABLY WON'T GET US ANY HATE MAIL.)

4. **Why was Ronald Reagan called the Teflon president?**

a. Because nothing could stick to him.

b. Because he loved to cook.

c. Because he was made from three kinds of fluorine-containing polymers and was a copyrighted brand name of the DuPont company.

d. Because he was so inspirational that he was even able to inspire a nickname for Prime Minister Tony Blair of England, who was known as Teflon Tony, years before Blair even took office.

(ANSWER: A.)

ESSAY

1. Would Robert Kennedy have won the nomination in 1968 if he had lived? Why or why not?

2. Was the moon landing a good use of money or a big waste? Should we go back to the moon? How about a trip to Mars?

3. How did we get past the energy crisis?

RESEARCH

Still another Billy Joel song, "Miami 2017 (Seen the Lights Go Out on Broadway)," is a sort of science fiction song about the banks foreclosing on the bankrupt city of New York, shipping all the residents down to Florida, and blowing up Manhattan. One line is "They burned the churches up in Harlem, like in that Spanish Civil War." Were churches in the section of New York known as Spanish Harlem burned during the Spanish Civil War, or is Billy just referring to how churches in *Spain* were burned?

CHAPTER

AND ON INTO THE FUTURE

As Barack Obama posed with then-president George W. Bush and three former presidents shortly before his own inauguration, people around the country took bets on how long it would be before he, too, had gray hair.

Dan Quayle: one of history's easier targets.

"Contrary to the rumors that you've heard, I was not born in a manger. I was actually born on Krypton and sent here by my father, Jor-el, to save the planet Earth."—Barack Obama, smart aleck, during his 2008 campaign

INTRODUCTION

We were going to end the guide right here. We really were. History books almost never go right up to the present day. After all, the dust hasn't settled from more recent events enough for us to judge them and make fun of them properly. And it's not like your teacher will get past about 1950 in history by the end of the school year, anyway, because you'll be too busy getting ready for standardized tests to learn anything historical.

But then we realized something: if we stopped history with the moment Billy Joel decided that he couldn't take it anymore, not only would we be leaving out the 2008 election (making us instantly out-of-date; even more so than *most* history books, which are all at least a *little* out of date), we wouldn't have a chance to make fun of Dan Quayle. Clearly, one last, short chapter is necessary.

In case you hadn't noticed, the Smart Aleck staff is really a bunch of comedians who snuck into being historians

through the back door. And no comedian can resist the urge to make fun of Dan Quayle. Or anyone else whose real first and middle names are James and Danforth, for that matter. James Danforth Quayle is a name that just screams "Give me a wedgie," isn't it?

After Reagan left office, his vice president, George Bush, ran for president against Michael Dukakis, the Democratic governor of Massachusetts, and brought a handsome young senator named Dan Quayle along as his running mate to inject some excitement into the ticket. It must have worked, too, because he managed to win the election and become our forty-first president.

If Bush's son hadn't become

George H. W. Bush emits an eerie glow, possibly due to the aftereffects of an alien probe. ✴

✴ ✴ ✴ ✴ ✴ ✴ ✴ ✴ ✴ ✴

president twelve years later, Bush himself would have been on the fast track to becoming just another forgettable one-term president. About the most memorable thing he did (besides, you know, the Gulf War) was puking at a really hoity-toity dinner in Japan.

But his vice president, Quayle, became God's own gift to comedians. It wasn't that Quayle was actually stupid—he just had a real tendency to say things that made him *sound* stupid. One of his more memorable blunders came when he was serving as the judge at a spelling bee. A contestant spelled the word "potato" correctly, and Quayle said it was wrong and that it should have been "potatoe." He later

said that that seemed wrong to him, but that was what it said on the sheet, so he went with it. It's true that being vice president doesn't give you a whole lot of real power, but we're pretty sure he could have overruled an obvious typo on a spelling sheet.

And that was just the start of a long list of misstatements Quayle made. Something about being on TV just seemed to make the guy uncomfortable. When asked if the United States should send someone to Mars, Quayle said, "Mars is essentially in the same orbit (as Earth). . . . Mars is somewhat the same distance from the sun, which is very important. We have seen pictures where there are canals, we believe, and water. If there is water, that means there is oxygen. If (there is) oxygen, that means we can breathe." Scientists honestly didn't know where to begin saying what was wrong with that.

When the 1992 elections rolled around, many people believed that keeping Quayle was a bad idea, but Bush was determined to keep him on the ticket. Bush might have won reelection, too, except for a short, wrinkly guy with big ears—not unlike Yoda—named Ross Perot, who ran as a third-party candidate and split the Republican vote. Democratic candidate William Jefferson "Bill" Clinton won the most votes and ended up president.

THE 1990S:
WILL WE EVER FORGET BILL CLINTON?

Bill Clinton was the third-youngest president ever, after Kennedy and Teddy Roosevelt. His two terms could have been a lot worse; he presided over eight years of relative peace and prosperity. However, his second term, in particular, was marred by one scandal after another, and he became only the second president in history to be impeached. (The first, if you remember, was Andrew Johnson, who was impeached for breaking a law Congress wrote specifically to get him to break it.) Clinton was impeached for lying about cheating on his wife. Eventually, he admitted that he had had an affair with an intern. When the sordid details of the affair were made public, many wished he had just kept on lying about it. Congress acquitted him, and though many felt he should resign, he stayed in office for the remainder of his second term.

The world changed greatly during the Clinton years. People stopped buying vinyl records altogether, and CDs overtook the sales of tapes. The number of TV channels available skyrocketed (though it seemed like there was *still* never anything good on). Mobile phones, which were once the size of shoe boxes and cost a fortune, became increasingly common. And per-

Bill Clinton: the face that launched a thousand radio talk-show hosts' careers. He was a popular president, but many people who disliked him made lucrative careers out of it. His well-known love of Big Macs made him a pretty easy target, as did the fact that, as a teenager, he had lined the bed of his pickup truck with Astroturf. Yeeee-haw!

haps most importantly, the middle of the 1990s saw the rise of the Internet.

The Internet had existed for years, of course. But at the beginning of the Clinton era, it was mostly used by the truly geeky. Throughout the 1992 campaign, Clinton's running mate, Senator Al Gore, spoke about building up the "information superhighway," which still sounded like science fiction to most people at the time. But during the 1990s, computers and Internet access grew cheaper and easier to use (ask anyone who was online in 1992 what a pain in the neck it was to get connected back then).

Before the end of Clinton's term, the Internet would revolutionize the way people communicated, as well as the way people found information, were entertained, and browsed for pornography. When the Clinton era began, teenagers who wanted to see naked people had to rely on begging their parents to let them rent *Revenge of the Nerds* for the ninth time, or on sneakily browsing through artistic photography books at the bookstore. The Internet changed everything.

But the 1990s weren't all about peace, prosperity, and nudity. There was a downside as well. Saddam Hussein, the president of Iraq, had been defeated by American forces in the brief Gulf War in 1991, which began after he took over nearby Kuwait, but throughout the nineties, it seemed like Clinton would have to consider sending troops back to Iraq every six months or so. The way we here at the Smart Aleck staff recall it, Iraqi planes would be seen in the no-fly zone every now and then, and Clinton would have to start threatening to send in the troops. Saddam would say, "No-fly zone? Oh! I thought it was the no *pie* zone! No pies here!" or something to that effect. And then things would quiet

down for another few months before starting all over again.

In 1999, after years of anticipation, the first new Star Wars movie since 1983 came out, and *wasn't* the greatest film of all time. That was a crushing disappointment. Spider-Man comic books were stuck in the seemingly endless "clone" saga that no one really liked. Most of the popular "grunge" music of the day was really pretty awful when we look back on it. And though New Year's Eve 1999 had plenty of good parties, it wasn't nearly as big a deal as people had imagined it would be, partly because we had to listen to people pointing out that "year 2000 is *not* the millennium, year 2001 is" (as if anyone really cared), and partly because we were thrust into a decade whose name no one could ever agree on (The zeroes? The aughts?).

Still, it was eight years without any big wars, and the economy was in pretty good shape. Looking back, it's hard to

Clinton is only the second president to have changed his last name (the first was Gerald Ford, who was named Leslie King at birth).

George "Dubya" Bush, in a flight suit worn, we think, to make voters think he just blew up the Death Star.

complain too much; despite all the scandals, Clinton finished out his term as one of the most popular presidents of all time. Of course, how popular a president is in his lifetime doesn't have much of an effect on how historians will view him. So, will Clinton be yet another forgotten president? Only time will tell.

AND ON TO THE TWENTY-FIRST CENTURY . . .

The 2000 election was quite a circus. George Bush's son, George W. Bush, ran against Al Gore, Clinton's vice president, in what turned out to be the closest election in decades. Gore got about half a million more votes than Bush, but on the day after the election, no one was exactly sure who had won more electoral votes. The ballots in Florida had to be recounted, and the election dragged on

for days before the Supreme Court ordered the recount to be stopped, handing the presidency to Bush.

Bush's first few months in office were fairly calm, but on September 11, 2001, terrorists hijacked commercial airplanes and crashed them into the Pentagon and the World Trade Center in the most devastating attack on American soil in the modern era. Though it was clearly an act of war, no one could quite say which country we should declare war on, since we had been attacked by terrorists, not a foreign government.

Bush launched a war against Afghanistan, which had been taken over by the Taliban, a radical religious group that had been allowing terrorists to set up camp within the country. Before that war was even over, Bush launched another war on Iraq, a country his father had waged a war against twelve years earlier when Iraqi president Saddam Hussein had taken over Kuwait. That had been a short, successful war, but Saddam Hussein remained in power.

When the second Iraq war started, George W. Bush's approval rating was higher than 80 percent. Most assumed that the war would be another quick one—indeed, Saddam Hussein's forces were overtaken very quickly, and Hussein himself was eventually captured and put to trial. However, defeating Saddam didn't end the war, as other groups within Iraq began fighting for power. And many of the reasons Bush had given to justify the war (most notably that Iraq was hiding "weapons of mass destruction") turned out not to be true, which didn't do much for Bush's approval ratings.

His popularity had already taken a real nosedive following his administration's response to Hurricane Katrina, which devastated New Orleans in 2005. Most thought the response was badly botched, and Bush spent most of his second term with an approval rating in the twenties and thirties. As the economy fell into worse shape than it had been in since the days of the Great Depression, the unpopular war in Iraq dragged into its sixth year, America's national debt soared, and things began to look bleaker and bleaker, environmentally speaking,

Bush's approval rating only got worse.

Bush was so unpopular by 2008 that even his own party's candidate for president used the word "change" in its slogan—something the incumbent party (i.e., the party currently in office) generally doesn't do. The Democratic primaries that year dragged on for months as Hillary Clinton (former president Bill Clinton's wife, who had become a senator in New York a few years earlier) battled for the nomination against Barack Obama, a junior senator from Illinois. Obama won the nomination in what some said was the biggest primary upset in decades, and though the 2000 and 2004 elections had been very, very close ones, Obama's soaring speeches, bold ideas, and ability not to be George W. Bush helped him defeat Republican nominee John McCain handily in the general election.

The election of Obama would have been unimaginable a century or so before; after all, Obama had no facial

Crowds in Chicago gather to hear Barack Obama's victory speech on election night 2008. Even the buildings got into the spirit.

hair. In fact, he told reporters he couldn't grow facial hair at all! Somewhere on election night, the ghost of Chester A. Arthur was shaking his head, tearing at his ghostly muttonchops, and wondering if the election of a man who couldn't grow a beard would be the end of society.

Obama had only a couple of years' experience as a politician on the national stage when he announced that he was running for president, but he succeeded at something that most of the more memorable presidents had succeeded at before him: he captured the imagination of, and inspired optimism in, the American people.

The number of people who came to see Obama's inauguration on January 20, 2009, was estimated to be upward of two *million*. One member of the Smart Aleck Staff who attended sent a text message back to headquarters saying, "Astounding. I'm in awe . . . but I'm still an engineer, so I'm worrying about infrastructure. Two million people? That's a lot of pee."

A FEW QUESTIONS ABOUT THE 1990S AND 2000S

MULTIPLE CHOICE

1. Why does *The Smart Aleck's*

President Barack Obama. Some people said that a man with such an unusual name could never win the election. These people had apparently forgotten that we'd had presidents named Rutherford, Ulysses, Millard, Grover, and Lyndon. They *were* all part of our "forgotten presidents" sections. ✱

✱ ✱ ✱ ✱ ✱ ✱ ✱ ✱ ✱ ✱ ✱ ✱

Adam of the Smart Aleck staff in Chicago on election night 2008, experiencing history instead of just making fun of it (for once). ✱

Guide to American History **stop when it does?**

a: Because we don't have a time machine (yet).

b: Because we are quitters who don't give 110 percent.

c: Because we always leave 'em wanting more.

d: Because January 20, 2009, is the end of history and the beginning of the future.

(ANSWER: AS OF THIS WRITING, D.)

2. Would Clinton have been impeached if he had lied about his personal high score on Pac-Man instead of lying about having an affair?

a. Yes.

b. No.

c. Maybe.

(ANSWER: PROBABLY B, BUT C IS ACCEPTABLE, WE SUPPOSE. ESPECIALLY IF YOU'RE AN ASPIRING LAWYER.)

3. True or False: Obama was the first Irish president.

a. True.

b. False.

(ANSWER: B.)

ESSAY

1. Briefly outline the causes of the recession that struck America around the end of Bush's second term and suggest punishments for the people you blame.

2. Find out if Richard Nixon would be eligible to run for president again if he were still alive, and briefly outline a strategy for how *you* would run his campaign.

ONE LAST MNEMONIC!

Here's an easy way to remember all of the presidents in order! Look at this list of presidents, and the word (starting with the same letter as the corresponding president's last name) at the right. Memorize the (somewhat coherent) paragraph formed by the list of new words, and you just *might* have an easier time remembering your presidents. But as usual, we aren't taking responsibility if you don't.

Obama takes the oath of office on January 20, 2009. He actually took it twice; Chief Justice John Roberts flubbed it the first time, so it was redone privately later. Oops! ✷

✷ ✷ ✷ ✷ ✷ ✷ ✷ ✷ ✷ ✷ ✷

BUCHANAN
LINCOLN
JOHNSON
GRANT
HAYES
GARFIELD
ARTHUR
CLEVELAND
HARRISON
CLEVELAND
MCKINLEY
ROOSEVELT
TAFT
WILSON
HARDING
COOLIDGE
HOOVER
ROOSEVELT
TRUMAN
EISENHOWER
KENNEDY
JOHNSON

WASHINGTON
ADAMS
JEFFERSON
MADISON
MONROE
QUINCY ADAMS
JACKSON
VAN BUREN
HARRISON
TYLER
POLK
TAYLOR
FILLMORE
PIERCE

NIXON
FORD
CARTER
REAGAN
BUSH
CLINTON
BUSH
OBAMA

WELL
ACTUALLY
JUST
MY
MAIN
QUIRKY ACTIVITY:
JUGGLING
VICIOUS BROWN
HYENAS
THEN
PORTRAYING
THE
FIRST
PICNIC
BASKET
LOOTER.
JUGGLING
GORILLAS
HURTS.
GET
ANOTHER
COUPLE
HUNDRED
CHILDREN,
MAN.

REALLY.
THEY
WORK
HARD.
COULDN'T
HAVE
REHEARSED
THE
ELEPHANTS
KIDLESSLY.
JUGGLING'S
NOT
FUN.
CAN'T
REALLY
BEAT
CANADIAN
BULLFIGHTING.
OLÉ!

ASSIGNMENT

Come up with a *better* mnemonic for remembering all the presidents; some A+ entries may end up on www.smartalecksguide.com!

FINAL EXAM

Note: Under the No Reader Left Behind Act, we have to give you one of these. If you fail, you'll have to repeat a grade, your teachers will look incompetent, and the Smart Aleck staff will be classified as a failing group of historians and be forced to allow you to transfer to more reputable history books. And to top it all off, everyone will laugh at you.

We will, however, be lenient about the whole #2 pencils thing. Use whatever the heck you want—heck, use a crayon if you feel like it. It's also an open-book test, and you can use any notes you may have taken. And chew yourself some gum.

ESSAY

1. What *is* freedom, exactly?
2. What was the Civil War about?
3. Who was the best president and why?
4. Of all the people who never became president, who would have made the best one? Why?
5. Compare and contrast William Henry Harrison to a bug.
6. What would Abraham Lincoln have thought of Star Wars—both the movie series *and* the missile defense program Ronald Reagan was always trying to fund (see other history books).
7. Who invented the Franklin stove?
8. Would America have been better off with a parliamentary system like most other democratic countries have? Why or why not?
9. Find something we completely left out from each of the following decades and write an essay about it:

1750s (good luck with this one)
1880s
1940s
2000s

10. Okay. Just give me the pickle and nobody gets hurt.

TRUE OR FALSE

1. George Washington had wooden teeth.
2. General MacArthur was a pain in the butt.
3. The Great Gatsby really *was* a great guy.
4. Benjamin Franklin invented the stove.
5. Thomas Jefferson is on the quarter.
6. Theodore Roosevelt was only four feet tall.
7. Andrew Jackson had six fingers on one hand.
8. LBJ got a real kick out of showing off his privates.
9. Gouverneur Morris kicked butt.
10. Franklin Pierce could win in a fight with Millard Fillmore.

RESEARCH

Find out about:
• The Hollywood Ten
• The New York Nine
• The Chicago Seven
• The Watergate Seven
• The Secret Six

PICTURE QUESTIONS!

Where are these guys going, and what's that one guy doing on his back?

What year is THIS flag from?

Look at the (ridiculously unrealistic) picture (above right) of the Battle of Fort McHenry from the War of 1812, then answer me these questions three:

1. Who's the guy patriotically ignoring the rules of boat safety?

2. What's in the bucket?

3. Is that a capotain or a stovepipe that that one guy is wearing?

BONUS QUESTION FOR EXTRA CREDIT

Do you suppose that when the guy in the picture's descendant wrote about the Great Gatsby staring at the green light on Daisy's pier and comparing it to "those Dutch sailors" staring at the "fresh green breast of the new world . . . face to face for the last time in history with something commensurate to his capacity for wonder," he might have wanted people to draw comparisons to this picture? Why or why not? And while you're at it, compare and contrast something, just to prove to us once and for all that you can do it.

THE END

So there you have it. History. Now you know it, which puts you head and shoulders above most of the idiots on the street.

Now go out and make more of it.

Maybe someday you, too, can be mentioned in a song like "We Didn't Start the Fire."

But first, just pull Uncle Sam's finger, okay?

"He's your uncle, not your dad."
—Elvis Presley

INDEX